*The Other Carl Sandburg*

# the *Other*
# Carl Sandburg

*Philip R. Yannella*

UNIVERSITY PRESS OF MISSISSIPPI 🍃 *Jackson*

99   98   97   96      4   3   2   1

The paper in this book meets the guidelines for permanence and dura-
bility of the Committee on Production Guidelines for Book Longevity
of the Council on Library resources.

Library of Congress Cataloging-in-Publication Data

Yannella, Philip.
    The other Carl Sandburg / Philip R. Yannella.
       p.   cm.
    Includes bibliographical references (p.    ) and index.
      ISBN 0-87805-941-5 (alk. paper).—ISBN 0-87805-942-3
(pbk. : alk. paper)
       1. Sandburg, Carl, 1878–1967—Political and social views.   2. Com-
munism and literature—United States—History—20th century.
3. Politics and literature—United States—History—20th century.
4. Radicalism—United States—History—20th century.   5. Poets,
American—20th century—Biography.   6. Journalists—United
States—Biography.   I. Title.
PS3537.A618Z885   1996
811'.52—dc20
[B]                                                        96-17019
                                                              CIP

British Library Cataloging-in-Publication data available

# CONTENTS

# ACKNOWLEDGMENTS

Many people supported and encouraged my work on this book. My colleagues at Temple University provided me with a study leave. Mort Levitt, Tom Patterson, Phil Evanson, Carolyn Katcher, Patricia Bradley, and my brother Donnie read parts or all of the manuscript, gave me their good advice, heard me out, and otherwise moved me forward. John Hoffman helped me immensely when I worked in the invaluable Carl Sandburg Collection, Rare Book and Special Collections Library, at the University of Illinois at Champaign-Urbana. My wife, Terri, and my children, Phil, Amy, Casey, Richie, and even little Ben, helped in many ways, sometimes just by being there. My thanks go to all.

# INTRODUCTION

At mid-century, Carl Sandburg was one of America's most popular and honored writers. He won two Pulitzer Prizes, one in 1940 for his *Abraham Lincoln: The War Years,* the second in 1951 for his *Complete Poems.* High schools and elementary schools were named after him, and a number of colleges and universities awarded him honorary degrees. Groups as different as the Chamber of Commerce and the National Association for the Advancement of Colored People gave him awards. He was a popular lecturer and entertainer, giving performances in which he read his poems, sang folk ballads, and talked about Lincoln. His poems were taught to schoolchildren and were widely read by the general public. He was a personality on early television, making appearances on the Ed Sullivan, Milton Berle, Dave Garroway, Ernie Kovacs, and Edward R. Murrow shows. He went to Hollywood as creative consultant for *The Greatest Story Ever Told,* George Stevens's life of Jesus. Mass magazines wrote adoringly about him. On December 4, 1939, he was pictured on the cover of *Time* magazine. He was on the first transcontinental jet flight and reported it for *Life* magazine. A stage show starring Bette Davis, *The World of Carl Sandburg,* was made up from his life and words. In 1959, he became one of the very few private citizens ever to address a joint session of Congress. Presidents Franklin Roosevelt, Harry Truman, and John F. Kennedy, as well as Adlai Stevenson, were among the many political friends to whom he lent his name and fame.

A banner year for Sandburg was 1940, when he received the Pulitzer Prize for *Abraham Lincoln: The War Years* and, shortly afterward, honorary degrees from Harvard and Yale (on consecutive days), Wesleyan, New York University, Lafayette, Rollins College, and Lincoln Memorial University. A while later, according to Harry Golden, one of his biographers, he was asked by some Republican party stalwarts to stand as their candidate for president in the upcoming election. Sandburg declined—as he would do again in 1942, when Democrats in Michigan wanted him to run for Congress—but the invitation was itself an honor that, so far as I know, was never given to any other American writer or intellectual (140–43). He played a significant role in the 1940 presidential election, however. On election eve, the Democrats put on a two-hour national radio show plugging Roosevelt for a third term, and at the end of it,

Sandburg spoke for five minutes, saying that Roosevelt was Lincoln's twentieth-century heir (*Home Front Memo* 29–30).

Over the years, Sandburg gave his Lincoln benediction to other politicians, among them Governor Frank Murphy of Michigan because of his handling of the auto industry sit-down strikes of 1936 and 1937, Adlai Stevenson, and Kennedy. In 1962, he wrote the foreword for Kennedy's *To Turn the Tide,* a collection outlining the early accomplishments of the New Frontier, praised the president's style and substance, and put him in the grand tradition of Jefferson, Lincoln, Wilson, and the two Roosevelts. On occasion, he also served his political favorites by attacking their opponents. During the Kennedy years, for example, *Newsweek* carried a story about Sandburg meeting with the president and then holding a press conference at the Library of Congress. At the beginning, he attacked Henry Miller's *Tropic of Cancer,* then a highly controversial book. "Christamighty! That fellow was sick with something when he wrote that book," he was quoted as saying. Then he got to his real subject, Dwight Eisenhower's recent comment that the Kennedy administration's Peace Corps plan was a "juvenile experiment." He banged away at Eisenhower, focusing on the former president's fear of the welfare state and socialism. Eisenhower, he said, was a hypocrite. He had been living off the government since he was a boy, first as a soldier, then as a politician: "Ever since he left the creamery in Abilene, Kans., he's never been out of work, never bought a suit, never paid a doctor's bill . . . all the anxieties that go with a man in a free-enterprise system. He has not known them. He has lived in a welfare state ever since he left the creamery in Abilene and went to West Point." So much for Eisenhower's meddling in the new administration's business. Like Henry Miller—the *Newsweek* caption yoked it together with "Carl Sandburg offered some harsh words for Henry Miller and Dwight Eisenhower"—he was not to be taken seriously ("Politics").

Of the public celebrations of Sandburg that occurred at mid-century, none was more impressive or telling than the huge birthday party that was given for him in 1953, when he turned seventy-five. Held at Chicago's Blackstone Hotel, the party was attended by five hundred guests, among them major politicians, foreign dignitaries, and famous scholars. *Publishers Weekly,* alert to the event because the release of Sandburg's autobiography of his childhood and young manhood, *Always the Young Strangers,* had been timed to correspond to the birthday, said the media coverage for the occasion was "perhaps never equalled for one author."

In a piece published on the eve of the celebration, Fanny Butcher, the syndicated columnist, called Sandburg "America's cultural sweetheart," which summarized the feelings expressed in the testimonials given at the party. Some of those testimonials were broadcast across the country on radio, and CBS television's Eric Sevareid paid his tribute on the 11 o'clock news ("Sandburg's 75th"). In a taped message played at the dinner and later quoted in the press, Governor Adlai Stevenson of Illinois, like Sevareid and Butcher a good friend of Sandburg's, measured the writer's full significance in sweeping continental metaphors of the sort usually reserved for political convention nominating speeches. "Carl Sandburg," Stevenson said, "is the one living man whose work and whose life epitomize the American dream. He has the earthiness of the prairies, the majesty of mountains, the anger of deep inland seas. In him is the restlessness of the seeker, the questioner, the explorer of far horizons, the hunger that is never satisfied. In him also is the tough strength that has never been fully measured, never unleashed, the resiliency of youthfulness which wells from within, and which no aging can destroy" (Calkins).

As Stevenson's remarks indicated, like no other writer before or since (Robert Frost probably came closest) Sandburg was treated as a great national leader. He was often referred to as a living national monument and, in fact, two of the houses he lived in became monuments. The simple worker's house in Galesburg, Illinois, in which he had been born was preserved as a state historic site. Connemara, the imposing twenty-two-room North Carolina house and its 245 acres of rolling land to which he and his family moved in 1945, became a National Park and Historic Site and is still a popular tourist attraction. Chicago, his adopted city, could obviously not be renamed for him. But when after World War II the first high-rise complex was built on Lakeshore Drive, this symbol of the new Chicago was called Sandburg Towers. Befitting a great national leader, too, when he died in 1967 at the grand age of eighty-nine, there was national mourning. A majestic service—chaired by Chief Justice Earl Warren, attended by President Lyndon Johnson—was held at the Lincoln Memorial in Washington.

Why was Carl Sandburg so celebrated at mid-century? Partly it was because he was an extraordinary writer who, at his best, could eloquently express the concerns of ordinary Americans. He could say what they wanted to say but could not, and he could say it in a way that sounded, sometimes, almost biblical; he could write and talk history with sensitivity and conviction, but in plain English; he could write poems average people could understand and remember; and he behaved like a regular fellow rather than like the hypersensitive, effete snob-poet of popular legend. Partly it was because he was a charismatic, spellbinding public performer with a full and rich voice, a broad, happy smile, a boyish charm even as an old man, and a healthy bearing that seemed to exude self-confidence, happiness, and, most of all, genuine enjoyment of all the things he had done and continued to do.

Those gifts and talents help to explain Sandburg's popularity and importance in his time. But there were two larger causes. One had to do with the central message of his work, especially his poetry and his monumental Lincoln biography. The other had to do with his own life story.

Judging by the attention it received, his *Lincoln*, a huge work made up of the two-volume *Prairie Years* (1926) and the four-volume *War Years* (1939), was a landmark achievement not just because of its scholarship or its command of dramatic narrative, as some said, but also because it was perfectly timed. With its vintage story of Lincoln's log cabin beginnings, *The Prairie Years* fit the widespread interest of the 1920s in rediscovering (or inventing) the pioneer national roots, the native genius. *The War Years* fit the public mood of the late 1930s by seeming to answer pressing questions about national destiny. Those volumes told how ordinary and extraordinary men and women had behaved in an earlier crisis, how the Civil War era was analogous to the Depression, how the choices to be made in troubled times were never clear or pure, how the nation had survived and prevailed in the 1860s, and finally how, because *The War Years* pulsed with faith in democracy, it would again. Beyond those vital messages, *The War Years*, like nearly all of Sandburg's writing, also said what Americans of that era never tired of hearing from politicians as well as writers and moviemakers (in 1940, when Sandburg received it for his *Lincoln*, John Steinbeck won a Pulitzer for *The Grapes of Wrath* and Frank Capra an Oscar for *Mr. Smith Goes to Washington*): that it was the ordinary people who were the heart and soul of democracy, that it was the much-abused but enduring and sacrificing people who were the salt, and sugar, of the earth.

The timeliness of this glorification of ordinary men and women was closely related to the second large cause of Sandburg's popularity and importance, his own life story. Sketched by hundreds of interviewers, repeated in studies of his work, it was a variant on the country's favorite life story and, as well, on the story of Lincoln which Sandburg narrated in his biography, that of the spectacular rise of a person raised in poverty.

Born in 1878, Carl Sandburg was the child of Swedish immigrant parents. His father was a lowly blacksmith's helper in a railroad shop. The family struggled in Galesburg, Illinois, on the endless prairies of the heartland. He went to school through the eighth grade, then left to help support the family. He worked at menial jobs, enlisted in the army at the beginning of the Spanish-American War, then, admitted as a special student, worked his way through college (though he never graduated) with more menial jobs. Then there was more hard work and more education in the college of hard knocks, then work and more work. And ultimately—magically, almost—there was huge, worldly success. But success did not change him. He was still, the storytellers always said, the same Carl Sandburg, one of the plain-talking, simple-dressing, hard-working folk. He knew and loved his roots. He was without pretensions.

The Sandburg legend, in short, was as inspirational as the most pristine of Horatio Alger novels, as finely pointed as a well-planned civics lesson. America, it said, was a place where hard work was rewarded. Humble beginnings did not prevent an individual from rising.

Sandburg and his commentators always acknowledged that for about a decade after his turn-of-the-century college years he was a practicing socialist, hardly a recommendation for popular heroism in mid-century America. But unlike more radical kinds of socialism, it was said, Sandburg's had been idealistic, moderate, and unthreatening, akin to an acceptable form of liberalism. He had stressed that change should come through the American political process, not through violent class conflict. He had wanted the country to adopt reforms such as unemployment insurance and social security. He had wanted people to work less and have the time to enjoy some of the good things of life. And in any case, Sandburg and his commentators said, his socialism had ended in his early career, a few years before he became a famous writer. Penelope Niven, for instance, his most recent and most authoritative biographer, summarized his early political maturation by quoting from a 1915 autobiographical sketch Sandburg provided to Henry Holt and Company, his first trade publisher. Sandburg there said that he had "quit the Socialist Party as a party" in 1912. Then, Niven writes, he began to articulate his political concerns "from the wider, more objective angle of the journalist and commentator rather than the immediate involvement of the activist and partisan" (285).

As we shall see, there was another Carl Sandburg unknown to the mid-century or later public and unacknowledged by his commentators. During the crucial, watershed years surrounding World War I, when the future of American domestic and foreign policy was being shaped and the circumstances of the common people were as much a subject of fierce public debate and confrontation as they were at any moment in American history before or after, this other Sandburg was a profoundly different writer from the Sandburg lionized at mid-century. This other Sandburg believed that America was a faithless monster of a country. From his writing could be drawn no pieties about success through hard work, no civics lessons about the American way of life. He saw no possibility that the conditions in which most Americans then lived could be bettered by liberal reforms such as he would later champion as a New Dealer and Stevenson and Kennedy Democrat. He held out only one hope for the country and its ordinary people. If the United States collapsed, the other Sandburg believed at that time, then there would be hope. Massive direct action by workers, class conflict in the form of strikes and crippling general strikes, and, finally, revolution to overthrow capitalism was the way to change the lot of the ordinary people. Rather than renouncing his socialist beliefs and moving on to become a more objective writer, in short, Sandburg became deeply radicalized, was absolutely partisan, moved startlingly leftward.

Sandburg's newfound political beliefs were expressed most clearly and directly within forty-one remarkable articles he published in the Chicago-based *International Socialist Review* between 1915 and 1918. Its title could mislead a modern reader into believing that the *Review* was a staid academic quarterly. But at least during the period Sandburg wrote for it, after it had given up on electoral socialism and become fully supportive of the direct-action revolutionary tactics of the Industrial Workers of the World (IWW), the *Review* was no such thing. Sandburg's contributions were as down and dirty, as far removed from politeness as they could be. Written in what he called "workingman's language," they were rough and tough and, most of all, "manly," a word he, like other radicals, women as well as men, used regularly. They were usually scurrilous, often brilliantly so, especially about politicians, businessmen, and "respectable" union leaders. Eleven of Sandburg's forty-one articles were lead pieces and editorial summaries of the *Review*'s ultra-left positions. Eight were printed under the byline of Carl Sandburg. Most of these were his earliest contributions. Then Sandburg began cloaking his identity. Fourteen articles were unsigned, and the rest were printed under pseudonyms. But Sandburg acknowledged his authorship of the pseudonymous articles near the end of his life (Golden 122), and the anonymous ones are easily identifiable on the basis of internal evidence.

Sandburg's *Review* articles were only one aspect of his radicalism. During this crucial phase of his career, which I believe was his most complex and interesting phase, a considerable number of the poems he published were strongly informed by radical theories and events. In addition, many of the articles he wrote as a reporter for two Chicago newspapers, though not radical in the same way as his poetry or his *Review* articles, were about left events and trends. Aside from writing from a radical perspective and writing about radicalism in more mainstream newspapers, Sandburg also took part in the dynamic, fractious internal politics of American radicalism, at one point became involved with Russian Bolsheviks intent on exporting their revolution to the United States, and, perhaps inevitably, was investigated by the Military Intelligence Division of the United States Army, one of the government agencies trying to contain American radicalism and Bolshevism.

The radical Sandburg developed in a particular context that needs to be understood by readers of this book. From the 1870s to 1920, the United States was rocked by ideological conflicts, broad public discussion of the failures of capitalism, widespread exposures of political and corporate corruption, periodic financial panics and depressions, and, most important for Sandburg's work, titanic strikes and bloody confrontations between corporations and workers. Class conflict in the form of labor-management disputes broke out sporadically in the last few decades of the nineteenth century. Major events in the development of the American labor movement—for example, the great railroad strikes of 1877, the eight-hour-day movement that was behind the Haymarket tragedy of 1886 and the ensuing hysteria about anarchism, the strike at Carnegie Steel in Homestead, Pennsylvania, in 1892, the Pullman strike of 1894—made it clear, at the least, that whatever harmony may have existed in the American workplace in earlier years had gone a long way toward eroding. Shortly after the turn of the twentieth century, class conflict accelerated and deepened, when strikes in the Pennsylvania coal fields and steel mills, the Paterson, New Jersey, silk mills, the textile mills of Massachusetts, and the Colorado mines, to name just the most famous among hundreds, made it seem, even to cool observers, as if a working-class revolution was just around the corner.

During the first decade of the new century, when Sandburg was emerging as a writer, a wide range of political perspectives was represented in public discussion of root causes and prospective cures. Pragmatic reformers proposed an array of piecemeal solutions, incremental adjustments, and regulatory laws aimed at modifying the country's way of doing business and caring for its citizens. Socialists of various kinds agreed, though most usually added that a final adjustment, a socialist revolution, would replace the capitalist system. Trade unionists of the recently formed American Federation of Labor (AFL) sought better wages and working conditions. Anarchists and radical industrial unionists of the Industrial Workers of the World, the group Sandburg would support during the crucial 1915–20 phase of his career, agitated for immediate cataclysmic change. There were, as well, responses of an altogether different tone and temper. Social Darwinists took the position that no change was necessary because selective evolution of the "race" was in process: those people who deserved to survive the brutalities of living would survive. Nativists urged getting rid of the problems by getting rid of non-Americans. Some well-to-do citizens settled the issues, at least for themselves, by moving to exclusive new suburbs. Food cranks recommended a healthier diet and plenty of exercise, while temperance proponents promised a new beginning when Demon Rum was outlawed. This is not by any means a full accounting of the range of public responses to the core issues of the period, nor does it indicate the startling ways in which individuals changed their affiliations and how groups could fracture, conflate, and overlap. It does, though, provide some fundamental sense of the debaters and their positions.

Despite their differences, most serious commentators of the period shared an understanding of how the complex of contemporary problems was to be described and a conventional wisdom about causes and effects. First, there was the belief that the root of all troubles was "trustification," the formation of business monopolies such as Standard Oil, Anaconda Copper, various coal and railroad empires, and United States Steel. These huge conglomerations were typically seen as cruel, rapacious beasts (the trust as octopus was a commonplace image) that were destroying American ideals of independent enterprise and individual opportunity. Their owners and managers were commonly depicted as un-American "robber barons," "feudal overlords," or "plutocrats" who ran hellacious "plutocracies" bent on subjugating a free people. Because of the trusts, it was said, the United States was now, as it had never been before, a land of contrasts, a place of haves and have-nots, a Promised Land that was devolving toward Old World social conditions.

Most contemporary observers also associated vast impoverishment with the dependence of the new industrial order on mass production processes and the consequent undermining of the traditional meaning of work and the traditional role of the worker. This belief usually involved the idea of a golden age, a glorious past in which poverty, exploitation, slavery, and class conflict were unknown. In those great and good days, believers said, individuals had been free to shape their own destinies. Work had been a profoundly moral activity, a matter of character development and self-fulfillment as well as a contribution to community well-being. Hard work had been its own reward, but hard work had also been a way of getting ahead in the world, securing a better life for one's children, and so forth. These principles had in large part, it was said, defined the American contribution to civilization. And that was what was being undermined by the trustifiers and the new order. The promise of a chance for everyman was being replaced by consignment to a place as a dependent employee of an octopus, an underpaid, overworked "wage slave" in a "plutocracy," in the words of less moderate commentators.

The rosy sense of history aside, there was considerable truth in these perceptions. The new industrial order of the post-Civil War period had in fact necessitated major changes in the way Americans did business and worked. It demanded the massing of enormous numbers of workers who, far from being independent, owed their living, literally, to employers. It demanded that work processes be subdivided into tasks that could be accomplished rapidly and in a standardized manner so as to make production absolutely predictable. It demanded minimal competency of workers, stressing an entirely new concept of the interchangeability of all workers while "deskilling" those who brought traditional skills into their new mass production jobs. It demanded that managers exercise tight control over every aspect of the workplace (and sometimes over the private lives of their employees) through an array of disciplinary measures, rationalizing and regularizing a worker's every move. Taken together, these demands amounted to nothing less than a comprehensive assault on traditional work arrangements and values.

To make matters worse, these changes were accompanied by profound changes in the very nature of the American work force. Earlier American philosophers and moralists about work had at least been confident about who workers were. With the prominent exceptions of African Americans and Irish Catholics, they were, of course, Americans or soon-to-be Americans from countries whose histories and cultures were part of the same historical stream; most spoke English; the vast majority were Protestant. That confidence slipped away between 1880 and 1910 as unprecedented numbers of eastern, central, and southern Europeans entered the country. From this time forward, any effort to reform the American workplace, or to restore work to its rightful position in the order of the republic, or to mass enough workers to commit a revolution had first to address a series of difficult and explosive questions having to do with who workers were and what they wanted. Deceptively simple in their phrasing, such questions quickly became pivotal in all descriptions of early twentieth-century social conditions, all efforts to define and understand work, all efforts to restore workers to their past glory or to launch them toward new glory, all theories of political and social change.

Public interest in questions concerning who workers were, how they lived, and what they wanted led to the production of an enormous body of writing. Practitioners of the newly formed discipline of sociology contributed some major studies. Journalists, sometimes disguising themselves to work lowly jobs, reported on their investigations in hundreds of newspaper and magazine articles. Novels focusing on particular occupations were published with stunning regularity. Following the success of Edward Bellamy's *Looking Backward* in the late 1880s, there was a spate of other utopian novels, many focusing on fantastic transformations of work, including, most prominently, Ignatius Donnelly's *Caesar's Column* and William Dean Howells's *A Traveller from Altruria*. Socialist romances and novels, the most famous American examples written by Jack London and Upton Sinclair, documented the plight of the working class and, more often than not, announced the good news of the coming cooperative commonwealth. Much "naturalistic" fiction was also focused on themes of work. Stephen Crane's *Maggie: A Girl of the Streets* was a careful study of life on New York's Lower East Side and the making of a prostitute. Frank Norris took on the issue of trustification in his "Wheat Trilogy," providing readers with detailed accounts of the lives and work of farmers, brokers, railroad barons, and managers; in *McTeague,* Norris attempted an analysis of an untrained dentist who, in the terms of contemporary sociologists, was being displaced by the recent professionalization of dentistry. Theodore Dreiser's *Sister Carrie* documented the careers of a small-town migrant and a selection of middle-class arrivistes, and Dreiser's later novels *The Titan, The Genius,* and *The Financier* minutely mapped the careers of powerful men. Against the backdrop of the times, even one of the pillars of "disengaged" literary modernism, Gertrude Stein's *Three Lives,* could be read as an attempt to write the psychologically "real" interior lives of limited, inarticulate women who worked as domestic servants.

Many American poets of the period pursued the complex of inter-related ideas surrounding work and the worker with at least as much energy and passion as had novelists. Perhaps the most famous liter-ary account of the subject appeared on the eve of the new century, when Edwin Markham achieved spectacular success with the publication of "The Man with the Hoe" in the *San Francisco Examiner* and its rapid reprintings in newspapers across the country. In many respects, Markham's poem summarized popular images of what had become of the ordinary worker. It began by picturing unrelieved hardship:

> Bowed by the weight of centuries he leans
> Upon his hoe and gazes on the ground,
> The emptiness of ages in his face,
> And on his back the burden of the world.
> Who made him dead to rapture and despair,
> A thing that grieves not and that never hopes,
> Stolid and stunned, a brother to the ox?

It ended with a cry and a warning for a future "when whirlwinds of re-bellion shake all shores" (15–18). Markham was followed in the first two decades of the twentieth century by poets such as Arturo Giovannitti, John Reed, James Oppenheim, Vachel Lindsay, and Charles Ashleigh. The large socialist and anarchist press of the period often published poems that inspired and instructed. The Industrial Workers of the World especially depended on poems and songs for organizing purposes, as forms of expression capable of overcoming language barriers (a poem or song could be learned "by heart" even if English reading and speak-ing abilities were severely limited), and as a form that could provide quick, sharp analyses of the situation of the working class.

Unlike the novelistic work of writers like Dreiser, Norris, Crane, Bellamy, London, and Sinclair, much if not all of this poetry has been forgotten, primarily as a result of changing poetic tastes after the Great

War and the emergence of literary theories that deemphasized the social role of poets and the public nature of poetry. Sandburg himself was caught up in this shift. Beginning in 1918, his poetry, shaped by the earlier aesthetic, was subjected to sometimes withering critiques by literary professionals who thought of involvement in the mainstream politics of the day, popularity, and nonalienation as prima facie evidence of fatal smarminess.

Sandburg's work in the first two decades of the century, his prose, his poetry, and his other activities, arose directly and precisely from the public policy debates, ideological disputes, and especially the apocalyptic labor-management struggles that characterized the era. As he correctly said in his later years, he was at the start of his career a moderate socialist. Around 1912, he made an abrupt shift leftward, became the "other" Sandburg of my title. Beginning in 1915 and continuing until the government closed it down in early 1918, he wrote monthly reports and editorial roundups for the *International Socialist Review.* Simultaneously, he published poetry, including the all-time favorite "Chicago," that attempted to meld art, including elements of early literary modernism, and revolutionary politics; two volumes, *Chicago and Other Poems* (1916) and *Smoke and Steel* (1920), represented major achievements in that regard, while a third, *Cornhuskers* (1918), was interesting and distinguished in other ways. He reported on labor and related events for Chicago newspapers, first for the small *Chicago Day Book,* then for the mass-distribution tabloid *Daily News.* He was deeply involved in the fierce political disputes within the American left which followed the country's entrance into World War I in 1917. Near the end of the war he went to Stockholm to report on events in northern Europe, tried, he claimed, to report fairly what he saw and heard, and ran up against the omnipresent government censors and spies. He played a role in the efforts of Russian Bolsheviks to export their revolution to northern Europe and the United States and, once again, came under the scrutiny of American spy agencies, one of which now referred to him as a "Bolshevik courier." In the summer of 1919, when the country was rocked by race riots, he wrote a series for the *Daily News* that was among the wisest contemporary discussions of the conditions that African Americans faced when they came north in the Great Migration.

*The Other Carl Sandburg* begins with an overview of Sandburg's involvement in two of the more moderate social change movements of the first decade of the century. This chapter serves as backdrop. The following chapters focus on the superheated, contradictory, murderous years around the Great War, when, like many of his contemporaries, Sandburg lived a virtual lifetime. In writing it, I have of course drawn on my knowledge of the political, labor, and literary history of the period. In the opening chapter, I have used, for example, the seventy-seven signed pieces Sandburg published in the *Milwaukee Social-Democratic Herald* and the *Milwaukee Leader* during his "right-wing" socialist phase as well as some writing he did in the business magazine *System*. In subsequent chapters, I have especially relied on the forty-one articles he published in the *International Socialist Review* and the three volumes of poetry he published between 1916 and 1920. On a few occasions, I have drawn on his reporting for the *Chicago Day Book,* the small tabloid newspaper he worked for for several years, as well as on his writing for such news organs as *Reedy's Mirror* of Saint Louis and the *Cleveland Press;* more frequently, I have used his uncollected reporting for the *Chicago Daily News.* In one chapter, I have used his collection drawn from that newspaper, *The Chicago Race Riots.* In two chapters, I have used files developed by the U.S. Army's Military Intelligence Division on Sandburg's activities in 1918 and 1919. These files, fragmentary, biased, and full of animus, still provide considerable insight into how government agents helped to change Sandburg's political behavior. Because so much of this book is based on material that has never been republished or discussed since the originals appeared—I have used almost two hundred uncollected magazine and newspaper pieces by Sandburg—and some is archival, I have consistently tried to provide readers a reasonably detailed sense of both content and tone through quotation and paraphrase. Because I expect that many readers will not be expert in the radical politics of the period, I have also tried to provide a reasonably detailed if not exhaustive discussion of those politics.

It is important that readers of this book bear in mind throughout that although Sandburg was deeply engaged in American radicalism, he was not a single-minded zealot. As is made abundantly clear in Penelope Niven's biography, during these years, as during much of his career, he was usually a virtual dynamo of activity. The other Sandburg, so to speak, existed side by side with the Sandburg who was a husband, a father, and an emerging poet trying to make his way in the world of the literary avant-garde. He was developing relationships with Amy Lowell and Ezra Pound, for example, at the same times that he was involved with Eugene Debs, the leader of the Socialist Party of America (SPA), and Big Bill Haywood, the leader of the Industrial Workers of the World. He composed good poems about his wife and children and his backyard garden in the same weeks and months, apparently, that he composed good poems about radical heroes and martyrs, the horrible behavior of the ruling class, and portents of revolution. There were times when he was being surveilled as a dangerous radical by Military Intelligence and, simultaneously, giving recitals to groups of polite people who were distinctly unradical. I do not know what readers will make of this multidimensionality, though I expect that some would prefer that Sandburg had been more pure, more a driven zealot. My own sense, which I briefly discuss in the epilogue, is that, given the necessities of his private life and the shape of American radicalism in 1920, he went as far as he could.

Perhaps predictably in a study of a quicksilver personality living through an explosive period, the underlying theme of *The Other Carl Sandburg* is transformation. It is about Sandburg's involvement in efforts at social transformation. It is also about how Sandburg went through several interesting and dynamic changes during his early career. Transformation is also one of my goals. I hope this book serves to provide readers with a detailed account of the other Carl Sandburg, who lived and wrote before he became a popular culture icon and legend, America's "cultural sweetheart," Lincoln's modern spokesman, or, as Adlai Stevenson put it, the "epitome" of the American Dream.

*The Other Carl Sandburg*

# I

## *Journeyman*

Carl Sandburg began his working life with low expectations. When he left school at thirteen, his main goal seems to have been to find a steady job at something he did not hate, and, as he wrote in *Always the Young Strangers,* he had a long series of menial jobs in his hometown of Galesburg as well as a period when he worked his way across the Midwest. In 1898, when the Spanish-American War broke out, he joined the army, shipping out to Puerto Rico, where he spent his time marching and fighting the mosquitoes and heat. He apparently distinguished himself in some way, however, for after he was mustered out, he was given an appointment to West Point. But a career as an army officer was not in the cards—he failed the academy's entrance exam in mathematics and so never attended. He then returned to Galesburg and enrolled as a special student at Lombard College, a local school.

College, American educators of the period claimed, had extraordinary powers to shape character, and in some ways, beyond the classroom and library, that was its main purpose. The idea that four years on a campus could strengthen the moral fiber of the children of the well-to-do had earlier roots, of course, but in the later nineteenth century, under the pressure of social events, two variations on the tradition emerged. One was that college would serve to develop a new middle class. The other, revolutionary for the time, now commonplace, was that some working-class children, even if underprepared, would be admitted, either at specifically designed "workingmen's colleges" such as Temple in Philadelphia and City College in New York or at institutions like Lombard. The social theory involved was simple, clear, and seemingly comprehensive. Talented working-class children were to be given the opportunity to rise above their circumstances; exposure to great ideas and culture and the examples set by their professors would

3

transform their language, taste, manners, and aspirations. Presumably, they would then serve as models for other children of the working class and, more important, as living proof that there was indeed social mobility in America.

Sandburg could have served as a textbook illustration for these claims. When he entered Lombard in 1899, he was a working-class boy who looked to be a "proletariate" youngster, a "rough featured, healthy boy," to the man who became his favorite professor (*In Reckless Ecstasy* [3]). When he left in 1902, he was a cultivated gentleman, as fine an example of a well-behaved, well-spoken, proper-thinking, socially concerned young person as higher education could produce. As a boy, he had changed his name from Carl to Charles for reasons that apparently had to do with a wish to assimilate and not seem so obviously Old World. Now he had the manners, tastes, and bearing to go along with the name.

Looking back from the perspective of the 1950s in *Ever the Winds of Chance,* the unfinished sequel to his autobiography, which ended in 1908, Sandburg remembered his collegiate transformation, especially the airs he took on, with wry amusement. During college, he decided he wanted to be a writer (or a bum, as he told his brother). Adopting the dress conventions of the unconventional, "for a year or two I took to wearing a black tie known as an Ascot, with long drooping ends." He also learned to imitate what he identified as high writing style, a style he was to cultivate for years afterward. One of the editorials he wrote in the college magazine, for example, was remembered as a collection of ready-made phrases: "I believed 'impugning' was a dignified verb and I had seen the phrase 'detracting one iota' in the Chicago papers for years and couldn't help using it for once. I had seen 'unduly prejudiced' and 'nevertheless attributed' so often that I had to use them like a bush league pitcher imitating a major league thrower" (110). As his letters from this period indicate, his memory was not faulty. Usually, he sounded like an aristocratic gentleman—ironically, just the sort of person he would deride in later years, after he had discovered the beauties and practicalities of working-class English. Before college, he had written from army camp to his family in homespun English: "There is many a young fellow here learning to appreciate home. . . . As far as my health is concerned, don't you worry. I can pick out lots of boys here whose only ailment is homesickness." Now he sounded positively British, writing in a letter to his sister during a vacation, for example, that "I have a most congruous boarding place here; a private house, cultured people, two clever daughters, books and music" (*Letters* 3–4).

A couple of years after college, he summarized his new understanding of life in a letter to Philip Green Wright, his favorite Lombard professor, saying that he agreed with Ralph Waldo Emerson that "expression is half the man" (*Letters* 16). But it was clear that an extremely important part of the other half—important both to his life at that moment and to his immediate future as a young writer and intellectual—had to do with vocation. A few years earlier the prairie-town boy had looked hard for a decent, steady job. Now, reflecting one of his preoccupations, he spoke not of a job but of joyful work, work infused with high spiritual meaning. In one letter he lectured his sister about her career, advising her to read Elbert Hubbard, then, in some circles, considered to be a sage: "I believe you are strong enough to read Hubbard, that you are able to throw yourself into work with such spirit that early phantoms can not mock you. There is talk of love and art and beauty, but there is no joy compared to that of doing a work however small and doing it well" (*Letters* 5–6).

During and just after college, Sandburg was obviously conscious of fashion, and sometimes he sounded as if he were simply a set of inauthentic postures. But as he made clear in *Ever the Winds of Chance,* he was also a good student, making up for his eighth grade education with hard work and intelligence. Most important, at college he developed his first interest in writers and intellectuals who, in many cases, were to continue to influence his work. Little American literature was then taught at Lombard or, for that matter, at any other American college, but, in a moment of lasting significance, he managed to discover Walt Whitman on his own. From Professor Philip Green Wright, he learned about John Ruskin and William Morris, the English social critics and artists. Wright, who later went on to an important career as a Harvard economist, also taught him traditional economics, including Marxist theory, and probably also introduced him to Thorstein Veblen's *Theory of the Leisure Class.* While he was at Lombard, he also heard speeches by some of the most prominent social commentators of the period: Jacob Riis, the author of the famous *How the Other Half Lives;* Samuel Gompers of the American Federation of Labor; Eugene Debs, who was soon to become the perennial socialist candidate for president; and Elbert Hubbard, the artist-philosopher he quoted at his sister. Together, his reading and his listening gave him a serviceable outline of turn-of-the-century social change ideology from Riis's antislum reformism and Gompers's "pure and simple" trade unionism, to Veblen's ironic analysis of economic culture, to the socialisms represented by Marx, Debs, Morris, and Hubbard.

At the time, there were a number of definitions of the word *socialism,* ranging from the loose meaning of having a concern for society (as opposed to purely individualistic concerns) through the precise meaning given to the term by Marxists. As there had been earlier when Owenite and Fourierist socialisms as well as "biblical communist" experimental communities such as the Shakers, Oneida, and Amana had flourished, there were in turn-of-the-century America a variety of socialisms vying for public attention, some of them regional in nature, some emphasizing change through class conflict, some emphasizing change through an evolutionary or electoral process, some looking to rely on a strong, centralized state apparatus, some looking toward decentralization, some secular, some religious, based on the idea of Christ as the first "true socialist." In a broad sense, of course, the various socialisms were related. They were tied together by the basic idea that capitalism had devolved into a new form of feudalism; they all looked forward to a new era of a "cooperative commonwealth," a fruition of the democracy promised by the American Revolution; they all had messianic, evangelical convictions. But those broad similarities more often than not cloaked enormous fundamental differences in approach, method, intellectual content, and political culture.

One of the immediate results of Sandburg's collegiate metamorphosis was that for a time he became a follower of the Arts and Crafts Movement, in many respects the most elitist of these socialisms, a believer in social salvation through, as its leaders put it, the transformation of work into art. The intellectual roots of the Arts and Crafts Movement were in William Morris, the British poet, architectural preservationist, master of several of the decorative arts, and socialist intellectual. Morris, like many social change theorists of those ideologically energized years, saw industrial mass production as the snake in the garden, the root cause of all the problems festering in modern society and especially the central problem as he identified it, the dehumanization of work and the worker. The social transformation he called for in the last years of his life, following a long intellectual development, was seemingly crystal clear: work needed to be restored to its preindustrial conditions and the worker needed to be restored to his proper central position. In a series of writings pointing toward utopia, the late Morris thus proposed a new (or, if one believed his theory of history, an old) system of democratized, loving hand production in decentralized, federated cottages and small shops, where people would work not to avoid starvation but—and this was the central point—for pleasure because society would be founded on the idea that the only "true incentive to useful and happy labor is, and must be, pleasure in the work itself." Work, then, would be art, which he defined, in an oft-repeated slogan, as "the expression by man of his pleasure in labor," and the ordinary worker would be—willy-nilly!—an artist. In the future, there would be fully developed democracy, because art/work would be the "outcome of the aspirations of the people toward the beauty and true pleasure of life."

If theorizing about this comprehensive, rational, humane utopia was easy, saying precisely or even approximately how it would come about was somewhat more difficult. Thus, at various times in his last twenty years, Morris was a Social Democrat, a state socialist, a bitter opponent of state socialism, and a parliamentary socialist. According to the contemporary biography popular among his American followers, near the end of his life in 1897 he announced for "passive" socialism, a method, he said, which consisted of "the making of Socialists, i.e., convincing people that Socialism is good for them and is possible." The choice of method, he added, perhaps with a sigh of relief, could be deferred to the judgment of future generations: "When we have enough people of that way of thinking, *they* will find out what action is necessary for putting their principles into practice." As his contemporary biographer put it, Morris's final word was that living and thinking socialism would suffice for the present (Mackail 2: 248–51).

It was perhaps inevitable that these ideas—centered on a belief in the creative imagination of the artist as an instrument of social change, giving artists and art tremendous social utility, expressing a strong commitment to "democratic" art—would be attractive to artists and would-be artists like Sandburg. The call to "passive" socialism, to do no more than to live and think socialism, was also powerful, for it was, in fact, an invitation to believers in socialism to demonstrate political commitments not in the usual ways, by agitating or ministering to the exploited, but by living and thinking with sensitivity and good taste and, with Morris's own activities as a model, by joining like-minded people in cooperative ventures aimed at demonstrating that, most of all, socialism meant sanity, sweetness, gentility, and beauty. Taking their cues from Morris's famous Merton Abbey workshops, his center for the design and production of hand-crafted wallpaper, tapestries, and stained glass, and his Kelmscott Press, where he pursued his passionate interest in printing painstakingly crafted books, the leaders of the movement from its beginning in 1897 were always deeply concerned with establishing arts and crafts cooperatives—that was their most practical step toward the "cooperative commonwealth"—and, paradoxically but predictably, for there was a solid spirit of entrepreneurship among them, selling their wares to people of taste (or just selling them).

There were several strains of the movement, so many that even the idea that there was in fact a movement at all is debatable. Some followers were hostile to Morris's social ideas. The aristocratic Boston Society of Arts and Crafts thought Morris's social theories were claptrap and consequently depoliticized the master so that they could address the "proper" concerns of designers and artists, that is, aesthetic concerns. At the opposite extreme from the Bostonians, some few, most notably Oscar Lovell Triggs of the Chicago center and Horace Traubel, famous mostly for having been Walt Whitman's secretary in his last years but also noteworthy as the editor-publisher of the *Conservator*, a long-lived socialist monthly, who was then associated with a Bucks County, Pennsylvania, group, were militant social critics in the spirit of Morris. In the hands of others such as Gustav Stickley, the furniture entrepreneur and publisher of the *Craftsman* magazine, and Elbert Hubbard, the leader of the Roycrofter Crafts Village in East Aurora, New York, Morris's social thought was sometimes adopted by allusion but more often violated in practice.

In these early years, Sandburg came under the influence of Hubbard, seeming to have been totally taken in by his peculiar melding of social uplift and self-promotion, visiting with Hubbard at East Aurora, writing adoringly about his spirited, healthful, wise bearing, even pronouncing him "one of the greatest men the world ever saw" (*Letters* 7). Hubbard, a successful small businessman and a gifted salesman before the 1890s, when he took up his new career as a master of the arts and crafts and his new identity as the "Fra," was then one of the most quoted of the movement's Joy-in-Work-Well-Done sermonizers. Sandburg often repeated Hubbard's wisdom on this subject, as when he advised his sister about her career or when he proclaimed that his own work—he was then earning his living as a door-to-door salesman of stereopticon photos—was far more important than it might seem at first glance, for he was really changing men's minds (*Letters* 20). On one occasion, Sandburg sounded as if he had also taken on Hubbard's obsession with printing. Philip Green Wright, his college professor, had a small press in his house in Galesburg and published a few early Sandburg items. The first of these—*In Reckless Ecstasy,* a title that summarizes the liberated, romantic pose of much of his writing during this period—led Sandburg to offer Hubbardesque advice about bookbinding: "Now if I were to offer a suggestion—unasked—as to improvement in any further work the Asgard Press may essay, I would say that maroon cord might be better—might harmonize more—with cream paper than blue ribbon. Blue, I think, is well with white. This may be only a personal liking." A short while later, he proposed to Wright that they should think about doing what Morris's Kelmscott and Hubbard's Roycrofters did, that is, begin an institution engaged in craft production and a publication "which should be bold, reckless, joyous, gleeful, yet sometimes sad and austere and mocking, in dealing with socialism, 'New Thought', sexology, and themes on which I have decided convictions" (*Letters* 23–24). For a few years, he imitated the high aphoristic style with which Hubbard delivered his own derivative preachings about the meaning of life, human happiness, friendship, love, and so forth. His own contributions to the wisdom genre sounded just as literary and just as vacuous as most of Hubbard's, as when he wrote in balanced cadences, "Culture, like madness, can run off of a steep place and be drowned in the sea. Let us pray that books may always be a light on life that makes us wonder and be children in beautiful mystery, rather than we should think learning (not wisdom) is life" (*Letters* 14).

This first period in Sandburg's career crested in 1905 and 1906, when he was a regular contributor to *To-Morrow* magazine in Chicago, a small journal of "freethinking" opinion that had been founded by Oscar Lovell Triggs. At about the same time, he began to try seriously to become a stage performer on the country's Chautauqua and Lyceum circuits, developing lectures and a stage manner. But his stint with *To-Morrow* ended, his lecture proposals attracted little attention or dates, and he struggled to find work. At one point he returned to selling stereopticon plates, at other points he did hack writing in Chicago.

Then, in late 1907, according to Sandburg, he was approached by Winfield Gaylord of the Milwaukee branch of the Socialist Party of

America. Gaylord had a reputation as a no-nonsense, pragmatic opera-tive. But, implausibly, without much ado and with apparently no regard for the fact that Sandburg had no connection with Milwaukee, had no experience whatever in day-to-day political affairs, and had no sense of the administrative detail necessary, Gaylord asked him to work as an organizer in rural Wisconsin. After getting an explanation of what an organizer did—he did not know at the time, he said, a detail that nicely summarizes the otherworldliness of his early idealism—he gladly signed on. The story of this remarkable recruitment came solely from Sandburg himself, who when he wrote about it was some forty-five years removed from the event (*Ever* 162–63), and one documentary source indicates that Sandburg actually applied for the job and was hired on a trial basis (CS Coll: E. H. Thomas to CS, November 29, 1907). But in any case, he was about to begin the second phase of his career.

Shortly after beginning his new job in the Fox River district of Wisconsin, Sandburg met Lilian Steichen, a devout young socialist who was closely connected to Milwaukee's party leaders. Within a few weeks, the two young people were in love, and over the next several months they conducted their courtship by mail, meeting only twice. For several reasons, their letters, which were preserved and recently edited into a book, are very relevant documents. They provide a good deal of insight into the assumptions, thoughts, and feelings of Sandburg and Steichen, who were educated, cultivated young socialists. More important, they provide a sharp picture of Sandburg's development at this stage.

The most obvious feature of their correspondence was that it indicated on page after page that politics and culture and romantic love, at least for them, were intertwined. Both Sandburg and Steichen were as rapturous about their future as socialist co-workers as they were about each other. Steichen, for example, wrote breathlessly about how the couple, working together for socialism, was sure to do good, "all the good we have strength to do!!" by working "hard and joyously and well." Five days later, Sandburg remarked, "We'll always keep up this fight for better living conditions and a greater civilization," and a few days later said that the two lovers would be held together by their passion "to work for socialism and help usher in the New Civilization" (*Poet and Dream Girl* 74, 97, 112).

Even allowing for the hyperbole involved in all courtship pledges, their letters recorded some of the central beliefs of young socialists living through an era that in many respects marked the height of the movement in the United States. Steichen occasionally described the insufferable dullness of the small-town bourgeoisie of Princeton, Illinois, where she was teaching after her graduation from the University of Chicago (she had taken courses with Oscar Lovell Triggs of the Arts and Crafts Movement), at one point remarking on the repressive tolerance of the good citizens of that town. She had taken to going hatless on the street, she talked socialism whenever she could, she didn't go to church on Sundays, and still, to her chagrin, she was accepted. "I am regarded as harmless," she wrote, "they do not see that my non-conformity is part and parcel of a large, really formidable movement—a movement that threatens to overturn their institutions. If they scented the danger, they would cease to be tolerant." Later, Sandburg told a story about the priggish bourgeois who had turned out in one Wisconsin town to hear him give his oration on Walt Whitman. Perhaps the speech was not as dangerous as going hatless, talking socialism, and not attending Sunday service, but Sandburg had still faced a tough audience. He wrote Steichen about his triumphant evening: "The gigglers are everywhere! The world is Princetonian!—They started when I opened at Hartford. I played them along, softened them into real laughter, & then took them off in a lonely place & hung shot corpses of their dead selves for them. Then I gloried life without giggling—and they gave me an encore—they applauded until Tyner led me up for a final bow.—I made friends for us when we go there for socialism" (*Poet and Dream Girl* 192).

A similar belief in the power of oratory and the innate power of socialism as an idea coursed through their letters. It was common for less Marxian American socialists of the time to believe that education was all that was necessary to bring about the dawning of the great cooperative commonwealth—even John D. Rockefeller would convert if he just heard a socialist speech or read a pamphlet, according to "millionaire socialist" Gaylord Wilshire—and the circumstances of one's birth were no barrier whatever: class, culture, prior experience, all would wither away before the truth. If this was so for captains of industry, it was more so for the "people." Their culture was barely acknowledged by young evangelicals like Steichen and Sandburg; in fact, despite all the senti-mental glorifications, it sometimes sounded as if working-class culture existed only so that it could be changed easily by the socialist missionary.

The end of Upton Sinclair's *The Jungle*, in some ways the classic statement of early twentieth-century American socialism, had the central character, Jurgis, by then a woebegone drifter beaten down by the capitalist system, enter a socialist meeting hall to get out of the cold, sit down next to a "lady," who, unperturbed by his looks, smiles at him, and listen to a speech by a socialist firebrand. In an instant, Jurgis was transformed, overcoming the hundreds of blows he had received from the corrupt capitalist system. Sinclair put his character's metamorphosis in stark poetic terms: "There was a falling in of all the pillars of his soul, the sky seemed to split above him—he stood there, with his clenched hands upraised, his eyes bloodshot, and the veins standing out purple in his face, roaring in the voice of a wild beast, frantic, incoherent, maniacal. And when he could shout no more he still stood there, gasping and whispering hoarsely to himself: 'By God! By God! By God!' "

The Steichen-Sandburg courtship letters recorded similar startling conversions. In one especially evocative passage, Steichen wrote of attending a socialist meeting in the Polish quarter of Milwaukee, "the priest-ridden Polish Catholic quarter," she said, and witnessing the transformation of 120 men through a speech made by Emil Seidel, one of Milwaukee's socialist leaders. This was impressive but no match for her vision of a man she saw later that night:

> After the meeting—a young fellow begrimed of face—stunted of growth—but with fiery Isaiah-eyes—distributed literature. One of the silent heroes. He was a worker. Showed us his button—said he had been a worker in the party for eight years—and his eyes gleamed! Isaiah, without the prophet's tongue! Distributing literature! He was quiet—repressed—but the eyes! the eyes! Another incarnation of the old man in my Chicago local—A worker losing himself in the Cause. God bless him!
>
> How a meeting like this stirs me! Such exaltation! Such hope—Such faith in man!—I *see* the dynamics of the movement! I *see* the yeast that will leaven the bread! And there is plenty of yeast! Plenty! (*Poet and Dream Girl* 55).

On another occasion she was again stunned by the potential of the people when she went to see a good political play. What struck her most was that the people liked it so she concluded that "this is the day of the People's Awakening—the wheels are beginning to go 'round in our heads! Erotic stories—erotic plays—must make room for graft exposures and problem plays" (*Poet and Dream Girl* 157).

The Sandburg-Steichen courtship letters recorded several other aspects of early twentieth-century socialist culture. There were entirely conventional remarks on democratic art, there were occasional apostrophes by both to the great Walt Whitman, there were remarks on unconventional marriage, or at least on marriage without wedding rings, there were occasional comments on healthful bearing and diet (Steichen favored meals of olive oil and shredded wheat). The two usually seemed deeply and fashionably forward-looking, culturally avant-garde, except when on one occasion Steichen, pressed by Sandburg to write for publication and to join him on the platform, wrote a defense of women as essentially different from men, women as childbearers, moral leaders, and so forth, but not workers (*Poet and Dream Girl* 166–70, 224–25).

As he courted Lilian Steichen, Sandburg appeared to be rising rapidly in the Milwaukee party bureaucracy. Even though he was a newcomer, he was selected as a Wisconsin delegate to the 1908 national Socialist party convention in Chicago. There he served on the Ways and Means Committee considering the crucial question of the strategy the national party would counsel to bring socialism to the United States (the committee came out in favor of local option, that is, the choice would be left to state and local entities) (*Work* 308–10). Later that year he campaigned vigorously for Eugene Debs, the party's presidential candidate, and even joined Debs on the famous "Red Special" train near the end of the campaign (*Letters* 78–79), thereby beginning a relationship with Debs that lasted into the 1920s. After the election, he apparently wrote to Debs, asking him for a testimonial to be included in a circular advertising his talents as an orator. Debs graciously complied (*Debs* 1: 290–91).

But his evangelical enthusiasm for socialism was sometimes tempered by the mundane necessities of making enough of a living to support himself and Lilian Steichen, whom he married in the summer of 1908. His job in the Fox River district lasted only until the autumn 1908 elections were over. At that point, Sandburg began paying more attention to his career as a platform performer on the Chautauqua and Lyceum circuit, but because, like earlier efforts, that did not work out, he was once again forced to turn to hack work. First, he wrote advertisements for a Milwaukee department store, then he worked as a reporter for a number of nonsocialist newspapers. By September 1909 he was lecturing for the Wisconsin Anti-Tuberculosis Association.

Then, once again, he went to work for the Wisconsin socialists, writing for the movement's weekly Milwaukee newspaper, the *Social-Democratic Herald*. In early 1910, beginning another period of party activism, he campaigned for Emil Seidel, the socialist candidate for mayor, and, suggesting that he was finally finished with the pretense of being "Charles," he began to sign himself "Carl," a name which, whatever his reasons for the change, probably made him seem somewhat more an insider within the heavily Germanic culture of the Milwaukee movement. Seidel won the election, and Sandburg was rewarded by being made his private secretary, a post he held for several months. In 1911, he was back writing regularly at the *Herald*. Late that year he joined the staff of Victor Berger's *Milwaukee Leader*, which published its first issue in December.

Sandburg published seventy-seven signed articles in the *Social-Democratic Herald* and the *Leader* between December 1909 and August 1912, seventeen in the *Herald* and sixty in the *Leader*. Uniformly, these were party-line pieces written on behalf of a movement that, in contrast to most socialist movements of the period, was tightly controlled, hierarchical, and intolerant of deviation. Five party themes dominated the vast majority of the articles. First, there were reports on municipal corruption and other forms of chicanery by Republicans and Democrats alike. These, predictably, were written fast and furiously during the election of the spring of 1912, when Democrats and Republicans fused into a "Non-Partisan" movement to defeat Seidel in his mayoralty reelection bid as well as other socialist candidates. Second, there were comments on the excesses of local capitalists and the deprivations workers endured at their hands. Third, there were a great number of comments extolling socialist wholesomeness and efficiency. Fourth, there were comments on socialist legislation and other reform efforts, shop-floor safety regulation, saloon regulation, wages and hours legislation, and so forth. Fifth, in a series under the heading of "Work and Workers" (most were compilations, not original material), there were news items having to do with local trade unions, union meetings, public events, and the like and news clips reporting on labor events in other parts of the country. Beyond such articles, there were a few occasions when Sandburg did investigative reporting of local labor conditions and commented on important national events such as the confessions of the McNamara brothers, the dynamiters of Harrison Gray Otis's *Los Angeles Times* during a labor dispute, confessions that came after the Socialist party had vociferously claimed a capitalist frame-up, and the great textile strike in Lawrence, Massachusetts.

Most obviously, Sandburg's *Herald and Leader* articles, like those he contributed to periodicals such as *La Follette's Weekly Magazine* during this period (*LA* 1–7), in which he educated readers about the basics of socialism while sometimes claiming that the movement stood for moral uplift, suggest that he was a reliable party man. But they also indicate that while he was in Milwaukee he began to write journalism that was solidly specific, hard in the sense of being well-grounded in facts, direct and clear. Gone, for the most part at least, were the dreaminess, softness, and gentlemanly gestures that so often characterized his earlier prose. Furthermore, while his *Herald* and *Leader* articles were ideologically moderate, reflecting the Milwaukee movement's position within American socialism—those on the left always referred to Milwaukee socialism as right wing and indistinguishable from other forms of bourgeois reformism—there were some indications of preoccupations and stylistic changes which were to dominate his radical journalism in his later *International Socialist Review* phase.

On a few occasions, there were angry comments such as he would later make characteristically when he was most deeply involved in the rhetoric of class warfare. In one article he pilloried those who expressed their horror at the bombing of the *Los Angeles Times* and the recent confessions of the perpetrators: "Yes, good gentlemen, while you are shrieking horror at the bloody hands of the McNamaras, please shriek a few shrieks at the bloody hands of the business interests, who have also used dynamite, and filled long rows of graves, but whose crimes are protected by a cunning and vicious class government" (*Lead* 5). Another, apparently the text of a Labor Day speech he made, sounded as revolutionary as his later comments: "So we are done with asking. We do not go to our masters now and beg for favors. We have learned that our masters are BLIND to the things we need. We have learned there is only one thing on God's earth that our masters will respect and listen to. That thing is POWER. The masters respect power and fear power and listen to power" (*SDH* 7). An attack he launched on Charles Post of Grape-Nuts fame, who recently had been taken to court for false advertising of the health benefits of his cereal, anticipated a number of his later bare-fisted attacks on the mighty. He began:

> Crazy with hate and uttering wild words that outreach the farthest vituperation and foulest mouthed speech that ever came from any paid agitator, Charles Gripe-Nuts Post is again out with big advertisements costing many thousands of dollars, appearing in the metropolitan newspapers.
> Poor Charlie.
> Poor Gripe-Nuts.

He is a proper object for much pity because his own class calls him a fool of the kind that squirts a filth that spatters over on his own capitalist class and spoils their clothes and peace of mind (*Lead* 19, reprinted *SDH* 16).

An article on a local company pointed to his later interest in the exploitation of women workers: "You will find, if you inquire, that among the girls who work here are none of the daughters of the stockholders of the Milwaukee Bag company. Some of the stockholders are members of churches and believe in the Golden Rule, they say. Yet they are willing to do unto other men's daughters as they would not do to their own." He then provided the names and addresses of two such stockholders (*Lead* 29). One 1912 local election postmortem went so far as to yoke the Non-Partisan victors with the pimps and prostitutes of Milwaukee's infamous River Street: "THEREFORE, LET IT BE REPEATED HERE THAT THE PROCURERS, THE VICE TRAFFICKERS, THE PIMPED AND DRUNKEN CREW THAT LIVE ON THE SHAME-EARNINGS AND THE DEATH-DOLLARS OF SCARLET WOMEN, WERE SUPPORTERS OF THE NON-PARTISAN POLITICAL MOVEMENT, TUESDAY, APRIL 2" (*Lead* 32).

In addition, two articles in the *Leader* anticipated the postradical phase of his career. An article on a 106-year-old black woman living in Milwaukee, full of admiration for her dignity and wisdom, suggested themes he would later develop with regard to African Americans. Sandburg moved well beyond the human interest subgenre of newspaper prose, capturing something of what the woman meant historically: " 'Yes, God's been good to me,' she says again, huskily. And crouches by the stove—a blind, gray, bent form that was once a singing toiler in the cotton fields—owned, written down and taxed as the cows and dogs of her day—when you go away from her presence, she haunts you as a shadow and a reminiscence rather than a living person mumbling her last, long day in the heart of Milwaukee" (*Lead* 2). Similarly, his later interest in Lincoln found expression in an article celebrating the president's birthday. Here, using the orthodox left understanding of Lincoln, an understanding that the Milwaukee movement specifically shared ("Lincoln and Socialist Principles"; Hunter, "Lincoln the Emancipator"; Spargo), he commented that though he was now honored by "grafters, crooks, political pretenders, and two-faced patriots who dine and wine and fatten on the toil of workingmen," Lincoln was a "loyal" member of the working class (*SDH* 10).

There were two indications that Sandburg was not entirely comfortable as a worker in the Milwaukee movement. One was personal in nature. Lilian Steichen clearly had some problems with Berger and one comment by Sandburg suggested his resentment of Berger (*Poet and Dream Girl* 59, 66, 86, 216). Furthermore, according to Niven, Berger had a romantic interest in Steichen and at one time proposed to her that she bear his child so his "genius" could be perpetuated (159–60, 729). A second involved an effort by Sandburg and his fellow writers on the *Milwaukee Leader* to unionize the paper in early 1912. In theory, of course, having its writers unionize should have presented no problem to Berger and the Social-Democratic Publishing Company. Milwaukee's socialist leaders stood solidly behind the right of workers to organize, and in return they received considerable support from the city's powerful unions. But whether because the writers were considered differently because they were "professionals" and therefore not really workers, a constant theme in the history of American unionization, or simply because the fledgling paper was not yet on a sound financial footing, the *Leader*'s management refused to recognize and to negotiate with the new union. This, incidentally, was not the first time that a socialist newspaper management hypocritically took an antiunion position. In 1903 workers at the *Appeal to Reason* struck and were met by an assortment of strikebreaking management tactics (Shore 115–37). But unlike this earlier incident, which yielded broad recriminations, charges, and countercharges, nothing much came of the *Leader* situation. The writers did not strike, and the owners did not lock them out. Instead, the writers continued to work while the owners, at least according to the account given by Sandburg in a letter of complaint he wrote to Emil Seidel's secretary in early August, spread rumors about the writers' antisocialist attempt to gouge more money (*Letters* 93–96). Whatever his private misgivings about Berger and other leaders, though, Sandburg was publicly a loyalist. This was true in his *Herald* and *Leader* articles, though he would not have continued publishing in those organs had he been anything less than absolutely loyal. It was also true, however, even after he left Milwaukee in August 1912, when he spoke of Berger in the warmest, most admiring terms. Writing in the first issue of the *Western Comrade,* which had been started in Los Angeles by people connected with the Milwaukee movement, he bemoaned Berger's loss to a political hack in the March 1913 congressional race in Milwaukee, summarizing his feelings by saying, "The Socialist party has been in luck to have in congress a man with two unusual qualifications for the place (1) a wide knowledge of existing economic conditions and (2) ability to express his knowledge in straight English, 'language that a bricklayer can understand,' to use Berger's own phrase" ("What Happened"). Coming from a writer who soon would show every indication that he prided himself on his sociological and economic knowledge and his ability to write in the language of workingmen, this was high praise indeed.

More perhaps than any previous year, 1912 was a turning point in the history of the modern American left, a year in which, among other events, some of the key disputes within the Socialist Party of America were played out publicly and the Industrial Workers of the World seemed to be beginning an ascendancy with potential revolutionary implications. As any historian who has written about them knows, these were extremely complicated events involving personalities, assessments of the meaning of recent national and international tendencies, assessments of the revolutionary potential of the American working class, tactical and methodological assessments, and bureaucratic disputes within and between left organizations.

However complicated by history, alternative historiographies, and so forth, the tensions within the Socialist Party of America that crested in 1912 were in many respects a direct result of the position regarding tactics taken by the Industrial Workers of the World, though it needs to be immediately added that even without the challenges thrown up by the IWW, the party would likely have erupted and fractured of its own accord because it was too ideologically diverse and too decentralized. Founded in 1905, four years after the SPA, the IWW had in its first several years struck an uneasy accord with socialists of various kinds. But the famous "Preamble" to its constitution, revised in 1908, stressing class struggle to the exclusion of other strategies, attacking trade unions as outmoded, and calling for broad-based, militant industrial unionism seeking the overthrow of capitalism rather than "a fair day's work for a fair day's pay," was too radical for many Socialist party members.

Through the first half dozen years of the organization's existence, Big Bill Haywood, who usually sounded more like a European syndicalist or anarcho-syndicalist though he continued to refer to himself as a socialist, continued his membership in the SPA and even served on its Executive Council. In 1911, though, Haywood along with Frank Bohn published *Industrial Unionism,* a pamphlet in which he argued that "capitalist law" should not be obeyed and that capitalist property rights should not be respected. The implications of this position were not lost on many socialists, and before long the party was involved in an extended public discussion of the morality and potential results of sabotage and other forms of class war violence. Haywood's position was not that limited, as readers of the *International Socialist Review* discovered in the February 1912 issue, which printed a speech he had given at Cooper Union in New York City in December (with audience reactions inserted). Embedded in the speech was Haywood's comment that "do you blame me when I say that *I despise the law* (tremendous applause and shouts of 'No!') and I am not a law-abiding citizen. (Applause.) And more than that, no Socialist *can* be a law-abiding citizen." These comments were incendiary enough. In addition, though, Haywood launched a pointed attack on party intellectuals ("when a person becomes intellectual he doesn't understand socialism"); an attack on socialists who got elected to public office ("it is decidedly better in my opinion to be able to elect the superintendent on some branch of industry than to elect a congressman to the United States congress") which was a veiled reference to Victor Berger, who was increasingly a target of far left vilification; an attack on gradualists, "the step-at-a-time people whose every step is just a little bit shorter than the preceding step"; and a discourse on why lawyers and preachers could not be socialists. All of this was aside from various celebrations of hard-nosed, hard-fisted working-class militancy as evidenced in recent great strikes and other events, including the heroic actions of the Western Federation of Miners, Haywood's original union (Haywood, "Socialism the Hope").

Haywood, an imposingly big man with one eye (he lost the other in a childhood accident), often sounded like a legendary tough westerner who knew how to do and get justice and he obviously knew all of the great populist traditions of vilifying effete, unmanly, cerebral elites. To respond to him officially, the party chose Eugene Debs, whose article "Sound Socialist Tactics" the *International Socialist Review* also printed in its February issue. Predictably, Debs took the high ground, arguing for constructive as opposed to destructive tactics, for the toleration of ideological differences within the party, for a pragmatism that recognized that at present the working class would be defeated in an armed confrontation with capitalists, and, finally, for a clear recognition of working-class attitudes. Regarding this crucial issue, Debs wrote that "the American workers are law-abiding and no amount of sneering or derision will alter that fact. Direct action will never appeal to any considerable number of them while they have the ballot and the right of industrial and political organization." All of this was stated in a manner that suggested reasonableness, clarity, and restraint (Debs, "Tactics").

None of the implications of Bill Haywood's position or of the threatening changes within the Socialist party were lost on the leaders of the Milwaukee movement. In late December 1911, before the publication of the Haywood-Debs articles, the *Leader* published a commentary by Robert Hunter, one of its regular writers, on what he called the "growing and irresponsible power of the Charles H. Err Publishing Company," the publisher of the *International Socialist Review,* and Kerr's payment of exorbitant fees to Haywood to plug the magazine during his speeches. Two days later the *Leader* printed a translation of an extremely harsh editorial from the *New Yorker Volkszeitung* denouncing what it claimed was Haywood's call for class violence in the Cooper Union speech and suggesting that he resign from the party. Over the next several months, there were more such *Leader* as well as *Social-Democratic Herald* commentaries (Hunter, "Comrade"; "What"; "More"; "Violence"; "The I.W.W."; "Sabotage"). Oddly enough, however, on one occasion the hated and feared Haywood was given front-page space by the *Leader* (Haywood, "Murderous").

If any members of the party in Milwaukee or elsewhere were so sanguine or naive as to expect Debs's appeals to calm things down, they were of course proven wrong. Heated debates about political or direct action, sabotage or "sound socialist tactics," angry, galvanic working-class action or carefully considered gradualism, the role of intellectuals in the movement, who could be a socialist and who could not, and so forth, continued to shape left attitudes and allegiances as well as the internal history of the movement for years to come. With strong involvement by Victor Berger and others from Milwaukee, Haywood was "expunged" from the SPA Executive Council in 1913 and from then on became one of the party's sharpest and most influential critics.

The tactical dispute was not abstract. While the *International Socialist Review* was preparing to go to press with its February issue featuring the Haywood-Debs debate, what would turn out to be a watershed event in the IWW's organizational history began in Lawrence, Massachusetts. On January 11, the first of twenty-two thousand mostly foreign workers walked out of that city's textile and woolen mills, initiating a series of events that tested IWW theories of direct action as they had not been tested before, measured the militancy of foreign-born unskilled workers, and demonstrated the lengths to which the state and corporate interests would go to repress efforts to ameliorate abject workplace and living conditions such as were experienced by the vast majority of Lawrence's workers.

On each issue, the IWW came out far ahead. As if seeking to fulfill all of the left's most nightmarish assessments of capitalist brutality, the state and Lawrence's mill owners did not hesitate to use the crudest methods possible, including militarization of the city, massive arrests and imprisonments, harsh police measures, and the framing of two strike leaders, Joseph Ettor and Arturo Giovannitti, on murder charges. The militancy of the Lawrence strikers and their families, however, was so great and usually so disciplined that they rapidly became mythicized in a surprisingly large part of the nation's press, which printed story after story about the long-suffering immigrants who nevertheless possessed simple grace, solidarity, and an almost otherworldly perseverance in the face of the tremendous force arrayed against them.

Although the general strike Haywood and others called for at one point did not occur, the IWW's most basic positions—its belief in direct action, in the irresistible power of the masses, in the conservatism of the American Federation of Labor, some of whose local members crossed picket lines, and that the country was nearing a revolutionary stage— seemingly were validated in Lawrence. In addition, the organization became famous across the country as it had not been before (despite its best efforts in the Far West, where it had concentrated its attention until Lawrence), and, perhaps most important in the long run, was now increasingly seen either as an inspirational organization backed by formidable theories and talents or as a dangerous, foreigner-based, lawless, anarchistic evil that was hell-bent on destroying America. After Lawrence, the IWW, flush with its new reputation as a two-fisted fighting organization, a labor union, and, it often seemed, a social movement, continued to expand, using its direct-action tactics in some of the most important strikes in a period famed for the frequency and fierceness of its strikes. Lawrence, which was for years afterward often spoken of as a grand metaphor for everything that was wrong with class relationships in America, turned out to be just one of the opening bars in a crescendo of conflict as workers over the next several years conducted pitched battles with capitalists and, often, their surrogate armies. Strikes in the Pennsylvania coal fields and steel plants, the Paterson, New Jersey, silk mills, the other textile mills in Massachusetts, and the Colorado mines, to name just the most famous, confronted the country, it was often said, and not just by radicals, with the real possibility of revolution.

Sandburg left Milwaukee for Chicago in August 1912 to work as a reporter for the socialist *Evening World,* the only paper in the city that continued to publish during a general strike of the city's newspapers. This job, though, did not last long, for when the strike ended and newspaper competition resumed, the *Evening World* folded, an apparent victim of its own opportunistic (and, arguably, unsocialist) expansion. Out of work in a city in which he had not lived for several years, Sandburg began a long hunt for a steady job. In late 1912, he applied for a position at *La Follette's* in Madison, Wisconsin, but nothing was available there, though the managing editor told him there might be an opening in the next year and put him in touch with the editor of the *St. Paul News* (CS Coll: La Follette's folder, January 9, 1913). A short while later, he found a position in an unexpected place, the business magazine *System.* There he wrote persuasive articles on such subjects as the costliness and inefficiency of government, how a rural clothier could retain business, and workplace safety, most of them printed under the pseudonym of R. E. Coulson (*Sys* 17). At the time, Sandburg told his friend Reuben Borough that the job was good because he was learning firsthand about how the world was controlled, but his explanation suggested some embarrassment, perhaps because the articles were so pro-business and perhaps because of leads supplied by the editors, including one stating that one of his articles on workplace safety was about "the easy way to evade workmen's compensation laws" (*Letters* 99–100). Too much can be made of his short involvement with *System*—he was let go by the editors in November—and he and his family *did* have to eat and pay the bills. But read in the light of other dramatic changes he underwent a few years later, the episode could be seen as a troubling indication of an ability to change his politics to suit his employer all too easily and adeptly.

While he worked for *System* and, a bit later, for the *American Artisan and Hardware Record,* he also wrote for a small tabloid aimed at a workingman audience. The *Chicago Day Book* had been started by the newspaper magnate E. W. Scripps in 1911 as an experiment aimed at testing his idea that it was possible to publish a paper that did not take commercial advertising but could be self-sustaining by selling it for one cent per copy. At times, the *Day Book* sounded like another of the era's anticommercial, cooperative, or vaguely socialistic enterprises. But though Scripps clearly wanted, as he said, to see if a paper could avoid "being assisted or trammeled by advertisers," he was also interested in profits and got part of his inspiration for the venture from the success of the Salvation Army's adless *War Cry,* which he believed made $60,000 a year (Scripps 208–9). Scripps, however, was not the usual newspaper magnate. He believed in the necessity of capitalists and in the need to develop powerful armed forces to extend and protect American hegemony. But he also had maverick—and not altogether coherent— social and political ideas.

Although capitalists must exist, Scripps maintained in a 1907 document dealing with his wire service but applicable to his chain of newspapers, they were a dangerous class whose influence needed to be checked by "constant attacks and public ill will" molded by his newsmen. It would not be harmful, he claimed, if the present class of plutocrats were swept away through "perfectly lawful and moral ways," to be replaced, presumably, by a new class of capitalists who would serve the people for a while. So the Scripps news organ was to have an educational function: "The people of the United States should be taught that there should be a revolution in the country, a lawful revolution, a revolution by laws, and they should be taught how best to obtain this revolution." Furthermore, organized labor represented a "healthier individualism" than the "low form" of individualism represented by capitalists. Union men obtained "power and influence" by "force of character and intellect and by the greater force and the nobler one of justice and goodwill toward their fellows." So labor organizations were to be vigorously supported (Scripps 231–37).

Sandburg worked for Scripps's *Day Book* from 1913 until 1917. The job paid the bills, but in two other respects it was a crucial experience. First, as a reporter for the newspaper he learned about Chicago working-class and street life, something he apparently never did during his earlier time in the city, when he was involved with the left gentry. Second, his *Day Book* experience reinforced what he had learned in Milwaukee about writing prose, for Negley Cochran, Scripps's hand-picked editor, was apparently a stickler for getting his reporters to write for the workingmen readers who were targeted in the experiment.

Sandburg fulfilled all of Scripps's desires about promoting organized labor, teaching people to rebel, attacking capitalists, exposing corruption, and so forth. His *Day Book* articles and some uncollected poems he contributed (Nash; Reid) made for good, lively, informative reading. There were, though, limitations to how much he could do in the newspaper and, more important, how far he could go. The paper was good at exposing local corruption but offered no solutions beyond electing the right people and passing legislation; the issues it took up were local, not national or international; and, finally, articles in the *Day Book* were usually very brief, allowing few opportunities for development by their writers.

# II

# *The Emergence of a Radical Journalist*

Founded in 1900 by the Chicago-based Charles H. Kerr and Company, the *International Socialist Review* was for its first several years a magazine whose interests were mostly theoretical. It was devoted to the task of interpreting Marxism and describing and debating contemporary social and economic tendencies with the stated goal of teaching the teachers of the working class. It was a showcase for the international movement, publishing articles by nearly every European and American left intellectual of note. Its tone and format were scholarly. In 1908, its editor, Algie M. Simons, was replaced by Charles Kerr himself and a number of associates, and the *Review,* mirroring the intraparty wrangling of the American movement, took a sharp turn to the left, becoming far less interested in Marxist scholarship and, most important, fully supportive of the industrial unionist, direct-action philosophy of the IWW and the left wing of the party. Styling itself as the magazine "of, by and for the working class" (later its masthead would announce it was "The Fighting Magazine of the Working Class"), in its post-1908 phase, during which it multiplied its circulation several times over, going from a few thousand to some fifty thousand in May 1912, the *Review* articulated its belief in the American masses, or at least the majority who had not been organized and thus ruined by the conservative craft unions of the American Federation of Labor. From the editors' perspective—during Sandburg's time, the driving force among the editors was Mary Marcy, though Bill Haywood also served as an associate editor—the American working class was natively intelligent, requiring no vanguard to lead it and in fact serving as the instructor of intellectuals. It was profoundly powerful, though often induced to sleep by its capitalist masters (as well as by trade unionists and gradualist socialists). It was mythic, Promethean in its potential, and always near the brink of revolution. What one recent scholar writing about the turn-of-the-century left's propensity to inflate and romanticize the masses into a "Proletarian Myth" was for the *Review* a given, a self-evident truth rarely relaxed or modified (Kraditor 113–53).

Sandburg's first metamorphosis from a homespun prairie-town boy into an educated, cultivated socialist-artist was documented in letters and in the autobiographical *Ever the Winds of Chance*. His second metamorphosis into an organizer, bureaucrat, and propagandist for Milwaukee socialism was likewise well documented. Next to nothing, however, is known about how he metamorphosed into a radical propagandist for the *Review*. A comment he made in 1907, near the end of his first stay in Chicago, indicated an early attraction to Bill Haywood. Writing to Reuben Borough, he remarked that he had seen Haywood and that "he looks very much like presidential timber, a Whitmanic type—raw, strong, canny, and yet with the flavor of romance we want in our heroes" (*Letters* 51). But if he had earlier had IWW sympathies, he either restrained himself because of his employment or was restrained by the pressures for orthodoxy within the Milwaukee movement. Certainly nothing in the articles he wrote about the Lawrence strike in the *Leader*, for example, in which he argued that Lawrence and other such strikes were caused by the rising cost of living, suggests that in mid-1912 he was ideologically close to the IWW, though one article made it clear that in the dispute between the IWW and the local AFL affiliate, he favored the former (*Lead* 13, 26, 34, 51, 54).[1] Nor does an article he published in the *International Socialist Review* in August 1912, just as he was leaving Milwaukee, suggest that at that point he had moved closer to the IWW. Written in high cultivated style, "The Wops of Kenosha" registered surprise that unorganized Italian workers in a Wisconsin mill could do anything for themselves, concluding in typical Milwaukee socialist fashion that what they needed now was organization according to "tried methods and principles," by which he no doubt meant craft union methods (*ISR* 1).

In the spring of 1915, in any case, Sandburg's pieces began appearing regularly in the *Review*, giving him for the first time in his career a national and international political audience as opposed to the local audiences for which he had written earlier. Within a few months, he became a major contributor—many of his articles were magazine leads—whose articles, fundamentally different in style from his earlier work, focused on the horrors of capitalism, national and international trends in the labor movement, and prospects for a working-class revolution. And perhaps most important for his development as a poet, on several occasions he took up issues having to do with the relationship of art and politics.

Given the *Review*'s critique of craft unionism and its support of revolutionary industrial unionism, it was not surprising that the first series Sandburg wrote for the magazine was an exposé of the class treason of conservative union leaders. "Fixing the Pay of Railroad Men," three articles published in April, May, and June 1915, was a wholehearted application of left-wing labor theory to the situation within the four western brotherhoods of skilled railroad workers. Taking as his premise the idea that even these "aristocrats" of the American labor movement had revolutionary desires and potential—at best, as he was to learn, an optimistic view—Sandburg argued that the brotherhoods' leaders had been corrupted and had become the tools through which the railroad corporations held the union rank and file in check. If it were not for their leaders, Sandburg said, repeating a standard Wobbly explanation of why some workers were not radical, the membership would launch a crippling transportation strike of the ninety-eight railroads on which they worked, an event that could stimulate strikes in related industries and, finally, revolutionary cataclysm. The brotherhoods' conservatism was, then, caused by union leaders who cozied up to management and thereby served themselves, gaining perquisites, Sandburg implied, in return.

The arbitration of labor disputes was in this period one of the means by which cooler heads hoped to avoid strikes—*arbitration* had become a magic word over the past two decades, Sandburg accurately said at the beginning of the first article (*ISR* 2: 589)—and in 1914 and 1915 the brotherhoods, as they had done before, availed themselves of the device. By itself, that was enough for Sandburg. Arbitrating disputes, he said, was a fatal sign of weakness which displayed a naive trust in capitalist law, an incomprehension of the fundamental, overriding fact that capitalists were inevitably able to purchase the votes of any "unbiased" arbitrators they did not already own: arbitrators were, after all, lawyers and politically connected members of the ruling class. The "fixing" in the series title, then, referred both to the goal of arbitration, the fixing or setting of contract terms, and to the idea that arbitration was by definition a corrupted procedure, a fix.

His experience with the *Milwaukee Social-Democratic Herald* and *Leader* and the *Chicago Day Book* had made Sandburg a skillful reporter with a superb sense of detail, an ability to read and understand

complicated economic and legal documents, and a developed understanding of how to use on-the-record information to his advantage.
His attacks on arbitration and on the brotherhoods' leadership were
not mere applications of left theory. Rather, they were based on hard
evidence drawn from the stenographic record of the Chicago arbitration
hearings and on research into the previous careers of the arbitrators. In
a later *Review* article he commented on this technique of investigative
reporting, claiming, "If we want to prove this is a hell of a country to live
in for workingmen, all we have to do is point to government records"
(*ISR* 26: 737). That was not quite all, of course, but it sometimes served
him as a good beginning.

Warren S. Stone, the president of the Brotherhood of Locomotive
Engineers, was one of Sandburg's two prime targets in the series, the
chief fixer among the other fixers, and the evidence against Stone was
to be found in his own words to the board of arbitrators. At the
beginning of the first article, the smoking gun was displayed when,
in an epigraph under the ironic banner of "A Craft Union Official's
Confession of Faith," Stone was quoted as saying that the brotherhood
leaders represented the forces of "conservatism," that their function
was to "keep the brake on" their members "instead of taking the lid
off." Remarkably, Stone had told the chairman of the arbitration board
that "if any fault has been found with the executive officers of the
organization it is because they have been too conservative and *have
allowed the railroad to capitalize that conservatism and have not got the
results that the rank and file think they should have gotten*" (*ISR* 2: 589).
Of course, Stone may have been using a standard good cop-bad cop
bargaining tactic, saying that he was backed by a demanding, militant,
powerful membership and that management would find it best to make
a reasonable settlement with him, but not for a moment did Sandburg
allow his readers to draw that conclusion. Stone's "confession" became a
hangman's noose, to be alluded to again and again, to be quoted in later
years whenever Sandburg returned to the subject of the brotherhoods
and labor fakers.

The other fixers, the other corrupters, were the allegedly unbiased
arbitrators themselves, and in the series Sandburg documented the
business connections and antiunion personal histories of the two who
he believed would tip the six-member arbitration panel toward the
interests of the railroads. One of the suspects was Jeter C. Pritchard,
a Virginia judge known for his pro-business decisions. The other was

Charles Nagel, who had been secretary of labor in the Taft administration. Sandburg summarized Nagel's social connections: "Nagel is chummy with steamship capitalists. All his friendships are in the world of corporation lawyers and the whole range of capitalistic interests that were tied up with the Taft administration. When he goes out for a dinner or a concert or a game of golf, he doesn't pick up any 'old rail' of an engineer or fireman. They are outside his social fences" (*ISR* 2: 590–91). After the arbitration decision was handed down—it was, as he predicted, entirely favorable to the railroads—Sandburg returned to Nagel, reporting his discovery in old newspapers that years before the former secretary had headed an infamous strikebreaking military contingent in St. Louis and that a number of strikers had been killed by his troops (*ISR* 5).

Documenting how the arbitration fix worked made interesting reading, but broader issues were involved. The upshot of the series, hammered home again and again, was that engaging in polite talk with the enemy was a waste of time and, more to the point, a sellout. Talk, Sandburg said, beginning to play on one of the basic themes in his *Review* articles, was cheap; language as used by corporation lawyers and their ilk—and that now included the brotherhood leaders—was as stretchable as rubber (*ISR* 3: 658). Rather than talk, there should be action; rather than politeness, there should be force; rather than the slithery bargaining or conciliation process, there should be old-fashioned directness. Near the end of his third article, he explained the situation in folksy terms. Watching the union leaders "patiently going along month after month trying to squeeze a drop of justice for workingmen" out of the arbitrators, Sandburg said, reminded him of some folk adages about

1. The man who locked the barn after the horse was stolen.
2. The man who built a boat in his barn and made it so big he couldn't pull it out through the barn door.
3. The waiter who spilled the soup and then turned his back to the patron, touched the seat of his pants and said, "Kick me right here, sir—right here, sir."

The Warren Stones were, in other words, the same damn fools commonsensical folk had always known and scorned, though these fools were really asking their patrons to kick their members, not their own well-protected rear ends. But, Sandburg said, the rank and file was beginning to wake up. There was now, he reported in his last paragraph in the series, "talk running strong in the rail brotherhoods for a newer and a bigger brotherhood that will take in all rail workers—and which will strike to enforce its demands instead of going through the farce, the mummery, the inexpressible monkeywork of arbitration" (*ISR* 5).

The final installment of the railroad arbitrations series appeared as the lead article in the June *Review*. In the same issue, the editors applauded Sandburg's work, writing that it "was making a hit with the rank and file of the railroad boys" and reporting that over the past few weeks they had received "hundreds of letters" asking for copies as well as requests for yearly subscriptions ("News and Views"). A month later Sandburg published the first of three articles on the work of the Commission on Industrial Relations, the congressionally sponsored investigation of labor-management relations in the United States. Although it continued some of the same themes as the railroad series—most prominently, the need to avoid conciliation, the need to avoid slithery ruling-class language, the need for direct action—this new series was far more significant. Getting the assignment to write the *Review* articles on the work of the commission, which was of overriding importance in the period, was sure to enhance his reputation as an up-and-coming radical journalist. Furthermore, the series was crucial for his intellectual development because on many future occasions he used elements of the investigation as a basis for his propaganda and, especially in *Chicago and Other Poems,* his first big book, as a source for his poetry.[2]

Created by Congress in 1912 at the urging of newly elected President Woodrow Wilson, the Commission on Industrial Relations was intended to be the official government response to the unprecedented "industrial unrest" of the past few years and especially to the bombing of the *Los Angeles Times*. Nine "nonpartisan" commissioners had been appointed by Wilson, three to represent management, three for labor, and three to represent the "public." The latter were by no means ordinary citizens, however; they were famous, well-to-do people who, cynics might have thought, tipped the commission toward management's interests. To chair the group, Wilson first selected Louis Brandeis and then, when Brandeis refused, University of Wisconsin historian John R. Commons, the author of major work on the American labor movement. Commons also refused the chairmanship but agreed to serve as one of the commissioners. Finally, Frank P. Walsh, a liberal senator from Kansas, was selected as chair.

The commission's investigation was in part public. In a series of well-publicized, sometimes dramatic hearings held in different sections of the country, the testimony of several hundred witnesses was heard. Witnesses included economists and labor market analysts, academics, spokespersons for trade unionism, IWW revolutionaries such as Bill Haywood and Vincent St. John, and spokespersons for capital including, most notoriously, as it would turn out, John D. Rockefeller, Jr. Beyond public view, the commission's work was conducted by a large staff that gathered and analyzed data and, later, formulated policy options. In mid-1915, three years after it was established, the commission issued an eleven-volume study containing testimony, technical analyses, policy statements and recommendations to Congress, a "Final Report" written by Basil Manly of the Bureau of Labor Statistics and signed by Senator Walsh and the three labor representatives, and a series of dissents.

Internal politics were involved in the commission's conclusions. The "Manly Report" or "Walsh Report," as contemporaries were more likely to call it, was in reality a minority report. The majority of the commissioners split into two groups, each of which issued its own report, so that for all intents and purposes the Walsh minority of four became the "majority." The dissenting groups did not, however, disagree with the basic factual conclusions of the "Walsh Report"; rather, they differed over what should be done to cure the problems.

The political infighting among the commissioners about the path of reform was of little interest to the public in any case. It was the factual findings of the commissioners—authoritative, seemingly unprejudiced, sensational—that riveted the country's attention. Any radical cynics who had believed that the commission would turn into a whitewash of capitalism were proven wrong. Perhaps more significant, Americans who had grown used to dismissing radical analyses of the country's ills as heated rhetoric by foreigners and malcontents were also proven wrong, for in most respects the "Walsh Report" as well as the dissents gave a congressional imprimatur to all of the standard radical descriptions of American capitalism. This was true of the commissioners' broadest conclusions. "Industrial feudalism," the commissioners said, echoing every soap-boxer who had spoken in recent years, was characteristic of American industry. There was deeply concentrated wealth and widespread poverty. Capitalists consistently abused the human rights of their workers. The country was dangerously close to revolution. It was also true of the hundreds of particular, focused, data-based descriptions of the circumstances in which the vast majority of Americans lived, labored, and died, including everything from high infant mortality rates, at least among the working class, to woefully inadequate educational systems (three-quarters of urban youth dropped out of school before the seventh grade), to the breakdown of traditional family structures (too many women forced to work), to hazardous working conditions (an average of thirty-five thousand on-the-job deaths per year), to high incidences of pauper burials.

The conservative press, led by the *New York Times,* predictably despaired over such conclusions, sometimes implying or actually saying that the commissioners had been bamboozled by radicals. Other elements of the mainstream press responded with solemn editorial shock, as if this was the first news about such things. The left press, in contrast, found itself in the peculiar position of applauding a document produced by the despised capitalist system. After the "Walsh Report" was published, as could be expected, there were admiring comments, many in a superior we-told-you-so tone, in *Solidarity,* the IWW newspaper, the *Masses,* even in Emma Goldman's rigorously antistatist *Mother Earth* (Ashleigh, "Momentous"; "Industrial Relations"; Comyn). Although the commissioners' findings receded from mainstream attention after a few months, displaced by other aspects of the class war and, later, by the war in Europe, they continued to be used by radicals long afterward. Years later the "Walsh Report" was still cited by Wobbly and other radical organizers to recruit new volunteers for the class war; "Even the U.S. government admits" apparently began more than a few exhortations to revolution. Needless to say, arming the warriors of one of the combatant armies had not been among the intentions of Wilson or Congress. But that was the most tangible result of the commission's work.

Of the testimony given before the commission, that of John D. Rockefeller, Jr., was easily among the most sensational and compelling. The Rockefeller family and its holdings had long been the subject of national concern and had led to two of the previous generation's blockbuster exposés, Henry Demarest Lloyd's *Wealth Against Commonwealth* (1894) and Ida Tarbell's *History of the Standard Oil Company* (1901). Stories of the Rockefellers' ruthlessness, their corruption of the political process, and their stealthy, unfair business practices were legion. In more recent years, despite the famous antitrust case brought against Standard Oil, the family had fared much better in press coverage, largely because of the public relations efforts of Ivy Lee and the clean, upstanding public image maintained by John D. Rockefeller, Jr., who had ascended to the head of the family empire. The younger Rockefeller struck many as a new breed. He was seemingly more forthcoming than his tight-lipped father. He did not have his father's eccentricities, never, for example, taking up the aged scion's health food diet of graham crackers and mother's milk supplied by imported wet nurses. He was concerned about such respectable causes as white slavery. He had developed the Rockefeller Foundation and assorted charities. He taught Sunday school.

In the winter of 1913–14 the young Rockefeller's carefully cultivated public image began to disintegrate when the family's Colorado Fuel and Iron Company was struck by miners. The epic conflict that ensued, as titanic as any labor event of the era, included a classic lockout, armed confrontation between miners and company-sponsored police, a declaration of martial law—the twelfth in Colorado since 1894, as the Industrial Relations Commission reported—and, finally, an attack on a miners' tent encampment by the military. The Ludlow Massacre, as the attack came to be called, which resulted in the killing or wounding of several dozen women and children, was of course exactly the sort of event the Commission on Industrial Relations had been established to investigate. Occurring midstream in its work, the massacre became a focus of attention, a dramatic contemporary event that seemed an emblem of everything that was wrong with the country. How much the Colorado Fuel and Iron Company orchestrated the strike violence, to what degree the Ludlow Massacre was an unplanned, undirected military "riot," or to what degree the Rockefeller interests were responsible for it became the central subject of John, Jr.'s, testimony.

Sandburg's first article in his commission series, titled "The Two Mr. Rockefellers—and Mr. Walsh," began by reviewing the exposé literature on Rockefeller the elder, noted the son's efforts at pious appearances, then quickly turned to the real character behind the public relations image. The young Rockefeller was two-faced (that was the "two" of the title). People may have thought he was not "a chip off the old block," but during his testimony before the commission, Chairman Walsh, who Sandburg called a "two-fisted Irishman from Kansas City, Mo., a lawyer of courage, intestines, and democratic ideals," had shown that he was "the same ruthless, cruel type of the American business man as his father." During his testimony Rockefeller "had a chance to go on record as a real guy, a living, red-blooded human entity." Instead, he had been effetely evasive, the opposite of Walsh's stand-up manliness.

Rockefeller embodied, Sandburg concluded, "all the covert, left-handed stealings and killings of the capitalist system of industry"; Walsh, Sandburg said, had succeeded in bringing an arraignment for the murder of the women and children at Ludlow against the billionaire (*ISR* 6).

This was partly wishful thinking. Rockefeller's testimony *was* evasive. At some moments his lapses of memory were transparently defensive, and he was abundantly pretentious about his charity and generosity toward his employees. His appearance before the commission tarnished his polished image. But he was not shown to be indictable for murder. In the end, the commission had to rest its case with a sharp comment in the "Walsh Report," including quotation of a statement in which Rockefeller maintained that he had entire sympathy and empathy with his long-suffering workers. "My appreciation of the conditions surrounding wage earners and my sympathy with every endeavor to better those conditions," he said, "are as strong as those of any man." Twisting their rhetorical knives, the authors of the "Report" juxtaposed Rockefeller's fatuous remark against a statement by a feudal tyrant of an earlier time, Louis XVI: "There is none but you and me that has the people's interest at heart" (Manly I: 34). A seething commentary, certainly, but not a legal indictment.

Though the commission did not produce any arraignments for murder, its conclusions were an indictment of the entire economic and moral structure of American capitalism. In many respects a masterpiece of complex analysis, organized to allow space for dramatic narrative, quotations of authorities, inferences, and counterinferences, the "Walsh Report" was nevertheless simple and comprehensive at its core. An introduction established the importance of the subject, providing a general assessment of the conditions in which the majority of the country's 25 million workers and their families lived and describing management-labor relations in general terms. Then it proceeded to its sensational conclusions. American society was failing—that was the significance of the "industrial unrest" it had been called upon to study—because of the unjust distribution of wealth and income, because of high unemployment and blacklisting, because workers were denied justice, and because they were undemocratically denied the right to unionize.

This picture of the abject state of the country was nowhere more startling—or bracing to radicals like Sandburg—than in the discussion of wealth distribution. Laid out in elaborate detail, the "Walsh Report" analysis was based on two sets of statistical data. One had to do with the typical circumstances in which the great majority of the labor force lived. Bare subsistence for a family of five was $750 per year (the poverty line at the time), but a minority of families, barely one in ten, could live on the earnings of the father only. Women were therefore forced to work, as were children, for pitifully small wages. The result was a breakdown of family structures, a shredding of the social fabric, and enormous social cost especially as measured by the ignorance of the nation's youth (this was the significance of three-quarters of urban children leaving school before the seventh grade), their physical deformity, and their destiny to age prematurely.

At the top of the social scale, in contrast, were a relatively few rich people, a concentration of capital, social, and political power that made a mockery of democratic ideals. The focus of the description was the income earned from investment by the wealthy, that is, income earned without what the commissioners defined as socially productive work, and the comparisons with the impoverished were designed to dramatize social injustice: "We have, according to the income-tax returns, forty-four families with income of $1,000,000 or more, whose members perform little or no useful service, but whose aggregate incomes, totalling at the least $50,000,000 per year, are equivalent to the earning of 100,000 wage earners at the average rate of $500" (Manly 1: 32). Though the commissioners had heard the usual defenses of the wealthy from witnesses, they were clearly unimpressed by arguments about how the rich created jobs or about "trickle-down" effects.

The commissioners provided readers with a perspective on the forest of facts and figures they had created. Anyone who still doubted the seriousness of the problem, the country's drift toward "feudalism," or the basic facts of inequality in the Promised Land could study a graph on wealth distribution. The authors were careful to point out that the breakdown did not come from a dissident with an ax to grind. It was from the work of a "statistician of conservative views":

> The "rich," 2 per cent of the people, own 60 per cent of the wealth.
> The "middle class," 33 per cent of the people, own 35 per cent of the wealth.
> The "poor," 65 per cent of the people, own 5 per cent of the wealth (Manly 1: 33).

The passage was low-key. It spoke loudly, though, and memorably, as a general explanation of the causes of the nation's conflicts.

For left propagandists and organizers, all of this represented a mother lode of useful information, a series of congressional confessions that could supplant guesswork, abstract ideological theory, and hellfire and brimstone denunciation. But the information still had to be interpreted and, just as important, put into language that could be understood by ordinary workers. That was precisely the task Sandburg undertook. In a note placed at the beginning of the second and, slightly changed, at the beginning of the third article of the Industrial Relations Commission series, he told his readers what he was doing:

> Bankers, Corporation Lawyers, Capitalists, and Their Officers of government have a language their own. They talk and write in long words. We hear old priests in Egypt spoke a mumble-jumble about the sacred white cows in the temples. So the spokesmen of the Big Thieves and Big Murderers of today have their long words and mumble-jumble which the working class does not understand. Now when Frank P. Walsh and those with him on the United States Commission on Industrial Relations made their report as government officers, they spoke some big and tremendous ideas of the working class. As government officers, they had to use the language of the government. This article puts in working class language some of the high spots of the report (*ISR* 11: 198; *ISR* 13: 265).

Others, then, would not have to face the task of wading through the commissioners' economic and sociological prose. In ways that paralleled Wobbly translations of abstract ideology into simple songs and poems, Sandburg would extract the meat from the dressing and rewrap it for the plain people. If, as was very likely, his readers were not the plain people themselves, then they too would be spared the time and trouble while they were taught how to express themselves in proper proletarian language. In any event, Carl Sandburg would be put on display as a real red-blooded, straight-talking working-class husky.

Sandburg's "translation" of the main points of the "Walsh Report" typically substituted plain English for jargon, simple sentence structure for complex structure, slang for bookish, technical diction. The sensational findings on wealth distribution, for example, were rewritten to cleanse them of their plodding quality. The commissioners' description of the wages earned by adult men bristled with facts and figures: "Between one-fourth and one-third of the male workers 18 years of age or older, in factories and mines, earn less than $10 per week; from two-thirds to three-fourths earn less than $15, and only about one-tenth earn more than $20 per week. This does not take into consideration lost working time for any cause" (Manly 1: 31). Sandburg's rewrite was "One out of every ten gets more than $20 a week. About two out of three gets less than $15 a week wages. One out of four gets under $10 a week. Only one out of ten gets close to a living wage with over $20 a week" (*ISR* 11: 198). The commissioners wrote sentimentally about how far a typical woman's wages would go: "Six dollars a week—what does it mean to many? Three theater tickets, gasoline for a week, or the price of a dinner for two; a pair of shoes, three pairs of gloves, or the cost of an evening at bridge. To the girl it means that every penny must be counted, every normal desire stifled, and each basic necessity of life barely satisfied by the sacrifice of some other necessity" (Manly 1: 31). Sandburg's version was "And say, bo, how far do you think a working girl can go on $6 a week? It's way under the inside limits of a living wage. If she pays more than fifteen cents for a dinner, she's lifting nickels out of the money that ought to go for clothes. If she goes a little too far on clothes, she's taking nickels off her lunch money. Six dollars a week wages for one-half the wage earning females of the United States is a fierce proposition when we look at the middle and upper class people who blow $6 for an opera seat, $6 for a week's automobile gasoline, $6 for a restaurant dinner for two, $6 for a pair of shoes or two pairs of gloves" (*ISR* 11: 198–99). The commissioners wrote about the "heavy toll in ignorance, deformity of body or mind, and premature old age" that resulted from child labor (Manly 1: 31). Sandburg's translation said that there was "a big army of children of the working class worn to the bone. Thousands never learn to read or write their names. Hundreds of thousands are short winded, played out, and no good when they grow up. And because the kids work, the father's wages have been cut" (*ISR* 11: 199). In a passage quoted earlier, the commissioners registered their shock at wealth concentration and income from investment. Sandburg's version said that "44 families pull down $1,000,000 or more. Most of these people don't work. They don't have to. The working class brings them everything they want and more than they can use" (*ISR* 11: 198).

So it went with the other main findings of the "Walsh Report." The second section, dealing with unemployment and blacklisting, was the result of painstaking analysis which suggested that a typical American worker could expect to be unemployed for one-fifth of each year. The concluding paragraph warned of the results of unemployment, saying that "hundreds of thousands of otherwise productive citizens" were annually driven into "poverty and bitter despair, sapping the very basis of our national efficiency, and germinating the seeds of revolution" (Manly 1: 38). Sandburg, obviously excited by the revolutionary potential, rewrote it as "These hundreds of thousands of men who want jobs and can't get jobs, who shake their fists in despair and rage at whoever and whatever it is that shuts them out of a job—here is danger. Look out!" (*ISR* 11: 199). The third section of the "Walsh Report" was about the breakdown of the nation's judicial system. It was organized into a list of ten "charges" against the courts, evidence and inferences on each, and a conclusion (each charge was sustained) on each. In Sandburg's translation, legal language was replaced by an English plain enough to satisfy the harshest critics of lawyerly obfuscation. The commissioners' statement, for example, that "it is charged by the workers that after wholesome and necessary laws are passed they are in large part nullified by the courts either upon technicalities of a character which would not be held to invalidate legislation favorable to the interests of manufacturers, merchants, bankers, and other property owners, or thrown out on the broad ground of unconstitutionality, through strained or illogical construction of constitutional provisions" (Manly 1: 42) became "When a good law goes on the books the courts generally wipe it out" (*ISR* 11: 199). The commissioners said that the "ordinary legal machinery provides no adequate means whereby laborers and other poor men can secure redress for wrongs inflicted upon them through the nonpayment of wages, through overcharges at company stores, through exorbitant hospital and other fees, fines, and deductions through fraud on the part of private employment offices, loan offices, and installment houses, and through the 'grafting' of foremen and superintendents" (Manly 1: 50–51). Sandburg broke the statement into component parts, including sentences like "There ain't no law and there ain't no government office where a working man can go when some corporation or grafter has skinned him" and "Company stores cheat him with rotten goods and high prices." That part of the passage ended with the notable addition of "It makes men clench their fists at the rotten system that lets it go on" (*ISR* 11: 199).

Turning to the central issue of collective bargaining, the commissioners found that "during strikes, innocent men are in many cases arrested without just cause, charged with fictitious crimes, held under excessive bail, and treated frequently with unexampled brutality for the purpose of injuring the strikers and breaking the strike." They also concluded that "in many localities the entire system of civil government is suspended during strikes and there is set up in its place a military despotism under so-called martial law" (Manly I: 54, 56). Sandburg rendered the first sentence as "When strikes are on, men who have not been mixed up in pulling any strong stuff are arrested, booked under a wrong name, held for high bonds, and sometimes given the third degree or worse. This stunt has been worked in many places for breaking a strike." The second came out as "When strikes are on, in many places, the regular government goes out of business, a new government of soldiers, detectives and strike breakers is set up. They call it 'martial law'" (*ISR* II: 200). The commissioners were deeply disturbed by the erosion of constitutional protections and wrote that "sections of the Constitution framed primarily to protect human rights have been perverted to protect property rights only and to deprive workers of the protection of rights secured to them by statutes" (Manly I: 47). Sandburg's version was "That piece of paper called the Constitution of the United States is some joke. It was made for men and against dollars. It is used for dollars and against men." In a short sentence summarizing his beliefs about legal protections, he added a disgusted and definitive "Constitutional right—huh!" (*ISR* II: 199).

In some respects, the section of the "Walsh Report" on unionism was more sweeping and conclusive than the previous sections on wealth distribution, unemployment and blacklisting, and the failures of the judicial system. But it was also the most controversial, the point at which the commissioners split into factions. No one disagreed that the often brutal tactics used by employers to break unions were among the chief causes of industrial conflict. The disagreement was about the means by which the situation could be corrected, with one group, led by Walsh, saying that the future of the working class lay in collective bargaining and another, led by John R. Commons, arguing that the future could be better secured by political action through a European-style labor party.

Walsh and his followers did not propose unionism "pure and simple." From their perspective, unions did not exist merely to provide better wages and working conditions; rather, unions were "part of the age-long struggle for liberty." Without unions, employers ruled in absolute terms; even employers who treated their nonunionized workers with respect and concern, they argued, were dictators, benevolent dictators but, nonetheless, dictators. The testimony of Supreme Court justice Brandeis (reproduced in Manly I: 991–1011) was quoted at length to support this position. Brandeis and the Walsh group said that the nation could not stop with securing political democracy. There must be "industrial democracy." Furthermore, if the nation decided to improve only the physical and material conditions of workers, there would be a great risk of "reducing their manhood." The nation must remember, Brandeis said, "that we must have above all things men; and it is the development of manhood to which any industrial and social system must be directed" (Manly 1: 61–64).

To some readers, this may have sounded curiously close to radical rhetoric, but by "industrial democracy" neither Brandeis nor the commissioners meant anything like "worker control" or a workers' state. Rather, they meant a *measure* of worker involvement in management decisions, a collegial system of governance that would bring about the diffusion of power within large, bureaucratic organizations. "Industrial democracy" was simply an application of classical checks and balances theory to the workplace and allowing unionization a way of avoiding the spontaneous revolts and "mob action" of unorganized, angry workers. The goal, in short, was industrial peace, not revolution. As Brandeis said, when the power of labor and management was balanced, "agreements are nearly always reached by negotiation; but, even if this fails, the strikes or lockouts which follow are as a rule merely cessations of work until economic necessity forces" a compromise (Manly 1: 61–64).

The Walsh commissioners proposed statutory and constitutional changes to institutionalize collective bargaining. Twenty years later, when Franklin Roosevelt did as much in the collective bargaining section of the National Industrial Recovery Act, a more mellow Sandburg celebrated it as a great victory for American labor, an emancipation of Lincolnesque proportions. In the fall of 1915, however, adhering to fundamental left-wing faith and distancing himself from the commission's Progressive reformism, he summarily dismissed legal, peaceful gradualism. At the end of his October article, he wrote that there was not "much use in trying to organize" workers "by a slow steady route. Revolts, flare-ups, count here," a remark that did not remotely resemble anything the commissioners or Brandeis ever said (*ISR* 11: 201). The opening paragraph of his November article made his position still clearer: "If the fat man who runs a factory doesn't run it right," he said, "pass a law and make it right. That's the notion in the heads of some working men. Well, this is all right, only it doesn't work in most cases." He underscored his point by quoting Eugene Debs's famous quip, "You can no more regulate a corporation with laws than you can tangle an elephant with cobwebs" (*ISR* 13: 265).

In a *Review* article published two months later, he was less politely metaphorical. A new session of Congress had just begun, or, as he put it, the "Bunk Mills" in Washington had reopened and the bunkshooters were back at work:

> Washington, D.C., is the one place in these United States where they spill more bunk than anywhere else. Bunk? Take most any senator or congressman in the bunch of them and his first name is Bunk. A few exceptions, yes. A few men with the nerve and the backbone to face real issues and tell the facts as they are. But mostly bunkshooters, Hiram, mostly bunkshooters. Less common sense, less ordinary human gumption displayed on the floor of the senate and the house of representatives and more hypocritical palavering than anywhere else on the map.

The commissioners' high-minded reforms, in other words, would be buried in an avalanche of words, and the bunkshooters would send out copies of their speeches to their constituents. "But how much real action from these gents strikingly notorious for much gab and no action?" (*ISR* 17). None.

The arbitration series and the commission series established Sandburg as an important radical journalist, and in the months that followed (and even while the commission series was still appearing) he was assigned to write some of the *Review*'s crucial monthly roundups of class war events, capitalist atrocities, battlefield progress reports, and theories. Usually a few thousand words long and made up of anywhere from six to fifteen "takes" or quick reports, many of these articles set the *Review*'s tone and, sometimes, its substance. In his earlier series, Sandburg had to stay close to the record and to write with some degree of restraint and reportorial distance. In his new assignments, however, he was freer to bang away at the enemy, at liberty to be a bare-bones slugger for the working-class cause.

His September 1915 lead article, like several others called "Looking 'Em Over," was a typical combination punch made up of a report on the latest capitalist atrocity and a couple of quick takes on working-class action. The atrocity was the sinking of the passenger ship *Eastland*, full of Western Electric employees headed for a company picnic, at its dock in Chicago, a tragedy in which about a thousand of twenty-five hundred passengers drowned. As he reported it, the ship had been overloaded, the government's safety inspection system, a corrupted, graft-ridden mockery, had not worked, and the disaster was still another indication of business profiteering. Why, he asked, had so many people been put aboard "a cranky, unstable ancient hoodoo tub like the *Eastland*"? He provided a three-word answer: "Business required it." What did the disaster prove? That "grim industrial feudalism stands with dripping and red hands behind the whole Eastland affair" (*ISR* 8).

The article also attacked Warren Stone, this time called the "$10,000-a-year bonehead" leader of the Brotherhood of Locomotive Engineers, and the sellout always involved in "peaceful" arbitration. Stone was just a foil in this article, however. The real subject was the lesson to be learned from a recent Chicago strike. During contract negotiations, public transportation car men had been offered arbitration by management. Their union leaders wanted to accept the offer, but the rank and file rose up and overcame its false leaders. The union had struck. And the strike was won. Labor militancy, ran the moral, could produce dramatic results.

The article also contained a thinly veiled appeal for a first step toward armed revolution. Theodore Roosevelt had recently suggested that to prepare for its possible entry into World War I the country should adopt the "Swiss system" by which all men were given military training and provided with rifles. Sandburg was no Roosevelt fan. As he said, he found it "hard to say yes to anything coming from the horse-teeth patriot and politician from Oyster Bay." But, he allowed, at last Roosevelt had a decent idea. Facetiously, he said that because of Roosevelt, now "every wop working in the steel mills shall have a rifle in his house and be trained to shoot straight." Then, sensing the possibilities, he became more serious. The "Swiss system" would produce greater equality among the class war combatants: "Every striking workingman under these conditions will be more dangerous to scabs, strikebreakers, gunmen and thugs than now. When compulsory military service is suggested for the people of this country, let the working class stand solid for the Swiss system, whereby each workingman is given his own gun and belt of cartridges to keep in his home for 'mobilization' " (*ISR* 8).

The fall strike by fifteen thousand Chicago members of Sidney Hillman's Amalgamated Clothing Workers of America, another dramatic labor event of the period, was exemplary in that regard. Sandburg covered the strike for the *Day Book*, and some of the material he gathered on that assignment was recycled into his *Review* article, which appeared as an unsigned lead in the November issue, just before his last commission piece. The article featured descriptions of Chicago police brutality, with several photos to prove the point, as well as photos of the pitifully small pay envelopes of two garment workers ($2.66 for thirty-five hours of work, $3.01 for forty hours, figures that made the "Walsh Report" averages seem high). "The Garment Workers Strike," however, stressed what other workers could learn from the Amalgamated. The strike was a lesson in the value of solidarity, for it was largely successful, it illustrated the power of industrial unionism, for that was how the Amalgamated was organized, and it also exemplified AFL treachery, for Samuel Gompers had forbidden his union members to support it in any way ( *ISR* 12).

Pretty much the same lessons were taught in two articles in the *Review*'s January issue. "Railroad General Strike" said that the men of the brotherhoods had finally learned about the fix of arbitration, were in the process of repudiating their leaders, especially Warren Stone, and were possibly headed toward a general strike ( *ISR* 18). The lead roundup for the month included the piece on the Washington "Bunk Mills," another take on the Industrial Relations Commission, and one on capitalist war profiteering in which labor was told to seize the moment of high employment by "strikes and direct action" to "force those capitalists to divide those profits, those withheld wages" ( *ISR* 17).

Sandburg's *Review* articles of the period recorded concerns other than those having to do with the nature, tactics and strategy, progress, and ultimate outcome of the class war. The other war, the Great War in Europe, which over the coming months and years increasingly absorbed his interest—and changed everything—was discussed from time to time, as we shall later see. His other primary subject, which had far more immediate effects than the Great War, had to do with the relationship between his new politics and his art as a poet.

On occasion, as if to say to his readers that in this new revolutionary world there were no differences between the two, he carefully worked poetry into his agitation. Among the many times he did this, the most interesting were when he placed his own poems at the end of two of his *Review* articles. In both instances there was a seamless transition between prose and verse. In both instances, as well, immediate contexts were established for the poems while new slants were given to the articles. The poems did not function as simple, one-dimensional summaries of the prose. Rather, they were complex counterpoints to the prose so that even an educated *Review* reader would have had a good deal of difficulty understanding some of the connections and ironies.

His last piece on the Industrial Relations Commission ended with a sentence about the power of collective action which reiterated his thesis:

"A thousand workingmen who know what they want and will take action are hard and costly for any boss to handle." This was followed by a poem titled "A Million Young Workmen," signed "C.S." Beginning "A million young workmen, straight and strong, lay still on the grass and roads," it then briefly described the insane slaughter of workers by fellow workers on Europe's battlefields. In a bizarre, cynical reaction to the slaughter, the poem went on, the kings, the kaiser, and the czar "grinned" and continued to live their obscenely lavish lives. The poem ended with Sandburg's description of his dream:

> I dreamed a million ghosts of the young workmen rose
>    in their shirts soaked in crimson and yelled:
> God damn the grinning kings. God damn the kaiser and
>    the czar. (*ISR* 14; *Poems* 141)

Here, in other terms, was an answer to the bitter facts about class conflict marshaled by the commissioners, and here was also a recognition that the American industrial barons were kin to European aristocrats. The lords of Europe grinned while workers fought their wars; the industrial barons, as the "Walsh Report" said, pretended that they did not know the conditions in which their workers suffered and sometimes died. The final, enraged line of the poem said that beyond social analysis there was an appropriate human response, a "God damn," and an arising, it might be, to take revenge.

An even more complicated juxtaposition occurred in a *Review* article in January 1916. "Railroad General Strike" took up the situation of the brotherhoods and their leaders again, with still another attack on Warren Stone. The article ended with the refrain that had run through it: "WILL THE RAIL MEN GO THROUGH ON A GENERAL STRIKE? IF THEY DON'T, WHO HAS PUT THE BRAKES ON?" Printed below was Sandburg's "Child of the Romans," a poem playing on the differences between an Italian railroad laborer and the aristocratic people who rode in a railroad dining car:

> The dago shovelman sits by the railroad track
> Eating a noon meal of bread and bologna.
>    A train whirls by, and men and women at tables
>    Alive with red roses and yellow jonquils,
>    Eat steaks running with brown gravy,
>    Strawberries and cream, eclairs and coffee.
> The dago shovelman finishes the dry bread and bologna,
> Washes it down with a dipper from the water-boy,

And goes back to the second half of a ten-hour day's work
Keeping the road-bed so the roses and jonquils
Shake hardly at all in the cut glass vases
Standing slender on the tables in the dining cars. (*ISR* 19; *Poems* 12)

Appearing in the avant-garde *Little Review* of April 1916 or bound among other poems in a book, "Child of the Romans" would read like a fairly obvious contrast of the well-to-do and laboring classes, leisure and grueling work, flowers and the dirt of the roadbed, the taste for rich food and a diet of rough food. Here, though, the contrasts were additionally entangled with the main contrast of the article, the allegedly militant rank and file of the brotherhoods as opposed to the conservative leadership. If a reader knew, as most readers of the *Review* no doubt did, that the brotherhood members considered themselves not workers but "professionals," the "aristocracy" of American labor, and had a long history of hostility toward unskilled and immigrant labor, then both the poem and the article took on further meanings and deeper ironies. Three aristocratic groups, the diners, the union leaders, and the union members, were being contrasted with one person, a "dago" who represented the quiet, simple dignity of the lowly and who was also, ironically, the only one—because he was the child, the descendant of the Romans—who had any claim to aristocratic lineage.

Although that sort of mutual enrichment and complication of poems and articles occurred only twice in this period, other *Review* pieces suggested that the linkage of art and politics was very much on Sandburg's mind. His August 1915 "Looking 'Em Over" included a take on the rise of working-class art amid the industrial grime of prewar Belgium. The blackened, blistered Belgian environment might appear to have precluded the creation of art—here Sandburg could easily have drawn the analogy to Chicago—but miraculously, or perhaps inevitably, great literature, painting, and sculpture had accompanied the development of a great working class movement for liberation (*ISR* 7: 71–72). His February 1916 "Looking 'Em Over" included a recommendation (Sandburg said, "it stacks up good") for a poem about dismal workplace conditions written by a "roughneck" member of the Transport Workers of America (*ISR* 20: 466). Two takes in a roundup published in December 1915 also dealt with vernacular expression. One, a quotation of an old song and an invitation to readers to send in others if they knew any, indicates his early interest in "plain people's" music, an interest that would develop a decade later into *The American Songbag*. A sardonic verse was quoted:

> My mother she takes in washing
> My father he fiddles for gin
> My sister she works in a laundry
> My God! how the money rolls in!

The other was a paragraph on Charley Chaplin in which he expressed his interest in the comedian (that interest, too, would develop in the 1920s when he became a movie reviewer for the *Chicago Daily News*), his understanding of Chaplin's art, and his interpretation of a recent Chaplin film as an illustration of "non-violent" sabotage at work: "Charley Chaplin has his knockers. They say he ain't high class art. I don't care. Especially I like him in that comedy 'Work,' where he does a bum job of paperhanging and slathers buckets of paste all over the gazaboes who took him for a mutt" (*ISR* 16: 325).

Sandburg's efforts to meld art and politics reflected the general concerns of left culture of the moment. Earlier left interests in art and social change had in the past few years developed apace with deepening class conflict, and by 1915 there were indications that hopes for a mature social literature were being fulfilled. Emma Goldman was near the height of her career as an orator on the capacity of art to energize individuals and whole cultures. The *Masses* had taken off after its somewhat shaky beginnings under its new ownership and was near its height, while its spin-off magazine, the *New Review*, was publishing distinguished cultural and literary criticism. In one remarkable article in the *New Review*, the no-nonsense Louis Fraina, who several years later was to be one of the founders of the Communist party in the United States, caught the general sense of the overriding importance of art when he announced that "poetry is more interesting even than war. Each bends to its ends the finer and deeper things of life. But the one is transitory, the other permanent. War will one day cease: poetry begins and ends with man." Fraina then went on to discuss new books by Robert Frost, Edgar Lee Masters, James Oppenheim, and Vachel Lindsay, discovering that they "have a quality in common—a rugged democracy, an effort to get to the reality and beauty of crude American life." Several new little magazines, most prominently the *Little Review*, founded in Chicago in 1914 by two anarchist women, Jane Heap and Margaret Anderson, were sponsoring what was said to be, in matters of aesthetics at least, revolutionary literature. At the beginning of 1915, the IWW's *Solidarity* printed a short poem by Ralph Chaplin; as a labor song, which it soon became, "Solidarity Forever," based on the tune of "John Brown's Body," was to live on into the present. A few months later, Edgar Lee Masters, previously a law partner with Clarence Darrow, published *Spoon River Anthology,* the sales of which broke all records for a book of poetry.

In short, in late 1915 and early 1916 there was within left circles, as perhaps never before, no doubt about the intertwining of art and revolution or the idea of the poet as revolutionary. Furthermore, an object lesson of many aspects of these issues, an extended metaphor of sorts, could be found almost daily in the press in the case of Wobbly songwriter and poet Joe Hill.

In 1914 Hill, who had written some of the most famous Wobbly songs after his emigration from Sweden as a young man, had been arrested for the murder of a Salt Lake City grocery store owner during a holdup. Thus began a national passion play, one of the truly great public causes in a period that produced more than its share.

Eyewitness accounts tying Hill to the holdup and murder were somewhat short of convincing, and the preliminary hearing and other proceedings were, arguably, legally flawed. Finally, though, the case against him apparently turned on one set of details. During the holdup one of the storekeepers had fired at the robbers, and when Hill was arrested he was nursing a gunshot wound in his arm. But, perhaps believing that the legal system could not convict him on such skimpy evidence—a strange belief for a true-blue Wobbly revolutionary, as his defenders pictured him—Hill refused to give an accounting of how he had sustained the wound. All he would say was that it was in a dispute over a woman and that he would not name her because her honor was involved. This Byronic touch, the first of many, was not, however, convincing to the judge and jury. Hill was convicted.

Predictably, the state of Utah argued that the case was a straightforward criminal proceeding. The IWW, joined by liberals and even the AFL leadership, however, argued that Hill had been framed and convicted by the Utah plutocrats and Mormons because he was a Wobbly revolutionary, that is, the trial was political, not criminal. In much the same manner as the trial and execution of the Haymarket "martyrs," the Moyer-Haywood extradition and trial a decade earlier, the ordeal of the McNamara "boys" (at least up to their pretrial confession), the Giovannitti-Ettor case in Lawrence, and prefiguring the Sacco and

Vanzetti case of the 1920s, the Hill case was from the left perspective about the capitalist system's use of the courts to repress the working class and ultimately about "judicial murder."

Before and during the trial, as Gibbs M. Smith's *Joe Hill* describes it, the case received widespread national attention. After the conviction on June 28, 1915, the attention, if anything, was greater. When an appeal to the Utah Supreme Court failed—Hill and his lawyers decided not to appeal through the federal courts—and as it became clear that Hill would be executed, demonstrations, speeches, and magazine and newspaper articles reached a virtual crescendo of anguish and recrimination. Prodded by Samuel Gompers of the AFL and Helen Keller, the inspirational folk heroine (Keller also had radical political convictions), President Wilson appealed to the governor of Utah to reexamine the case. That appeal, like all the others, was stillborn. Hill was finally executed by firing squad in the early morning hours of November 19, 1915.

Hill's case served the left as an illustration of capitalist vengefulness and judicial murder. It also illustrated, as Hill himself recognized in his last days, how a rebel and poet should die. By all accounts, Hill met his executioners with superb self-containment and grace. His last telegram to Bill Haywood was studiously forward-looking about how the IWW should use his martyrdom to advance the revolution and even contained a touch of good-natured irony in its last sentence: "Goodbye Bill: I die like a true rebel. Don't waste any time mourning—organize! It is a hundred miles from here to Wyoming. Could you arrange to have my body hauled to the state line to be buried. I don't want to be found dead in Utah." His last writing, handed to a guard, intended as a will, would later do stalwart service as one of the most quoted of left poems:

> My will is easy to decide
> For there is nothing to divide
> My kin don't need to fuss and moan
> "Moss does not cling to a rolling stone."
> My body?—Oh!—If I could choose
> I would to ashes it reduce
> And let the merry breezes blow
> My dust to where some flowers grow.
> Perhaps some fading flowers then
> Would come to life and bloom again.
> This is my Last and Final Will
> Good luck to All of you.

The self-consciousness of this and other of his statements—it was as if Hill were reciting his lines from a popular melodrama about the death of a romantic poet—was picked up in most of the accounts in the left press. The editorial in *Solidarity* was typical. Titled "Like a True Artist," it spoke of Hill in terms that made clear that he had perfectly combined art and revolution, and in case any reader did not understand "artist," the editors provided a definition: "When we speak of 'artists' we do not mean dilettantis, who put daubs on canvas according to approved rules, or actors, who feign moral qualities they do not possess. We mean MEN who live and act true to their convictions and their declarations."

Hill's wish to be cremated was honored, but not so simply were his ashes spread to the wind. Small packages were made up and distributed to IWW locals around the country so that their disposal became an organization matter that, in a peculiar way, illustrated the Wobbly belief in local control. Strictly speaking, Hill's instructions to organize rather than mourn were not followed, but the mourning that took place became a spectacular IWW organizing drive. Hill was given two funerals, the first in Salt Lake City, the second an extravaganza in Chicago. The Chicago funeral included the usual denunciations of capitalist law, judicial murder, and so forth. But its most impressive aspect was that Hill was given a poet's funeral that no other American poet has ever been given or even dreamed of having. Hill's songs were sung before the orations. After the service the casket was carried into the street that news photos showed to be packed with thousands of people. Ralph Chaplin described the scene for readers of the *International Socialist Review:*

> Slowly and impressively the vast throng moved through the west side streets. Windows flew open at its approach and were filled with peering faces. Porches and even roofs were blackened with people, and some of the more daring were lined up over signboards and on telephone and arc-light poles. The flower-bearers, with their bright colored floral pieces and wreaths tied with crimson ribbons, formed a walking garden almost a block in length. . . . Songs were sung all along the way, chiefly Joe Hill's, although some of the foreign-speaking workers sang revolutionary songs in their native tongues. As soon as a song would die down in one place, the same song or another would be taken up by other voices along the line. (Chaplin, "Joe Hill's Funeral")

The capitalists of America, Chaplin seemed to say, knew how to murder our poets, legally and unmercifully, but the righteous citizens of the country knew how to honor them.

The same issue of the *Review* in which Chaplin's description appeared was led off by Sandburg's short summary of Joe Hill's execution and its meaning. Calling Hill "one of the gamiest ([*sic*]—and a delicious one from a different political perspective), gladdest, brawniest, big-hearted rebels the American working class has flung forward into historic action," Sandburg printed some snippets of the "straightforward, simple letters" Hill had written from prison, including his last telegram to Haywood. Big Bill's telegram back to Hill was also printed. "Good-bye, Joe," Haywood had said, "You will live long in the hearts of the working class. Your songs will be sung wherever the workers toil, urging them to organize." The article ended on the same note, with Sandburg providing the final moral, in a poet's language for another poet: "The working class can look back at the short flash of his scarlet life, can remember the heroic nerve of him, can learn better to sing his songs and live up to the daring and ironic quality of his songs" (*ISR* 15).

As the Wobblies told it, the Joe Hill story was another lesson about corrupt capitalism. It was also about the agony and martyrdom that awaited the radical artist in America. Finally, it was about the ability of song and poetry to inspire the masses. In some respects this story was a variation on traditional literary understandings of the role of the poet as prophet and seer, the murder (or neglect, more accurately) of artists in America, and the theory that poetry and song would show the way to social salvation, perhaps, as Sandburg intimated, when the masses learned to imitate art.

# III

# *Politics and Art*

I n March 1914, Sandburg attracted considerable attention when he published nine poems in Chicago's *Poetry,* then a major standard-bearer for the "new" art, and won the Levenson Prize for the best poetry published by the magazine during that year. In the summer of 1915, as his star was rising among radicals because of his *Review* work, his poetry began to attract further attention among literary people. Edgar Lee Masters, who had recently achieved national fame with his *Spoon River Anthology,* on which Sandburg had given him some help, first showed some of it to Theodore Dreiser, then tried to interest the publisher John Lane in bringing out a collection. During the fall, as the Joe Hill drama was unfolding, Alice Corbin Henderson, an associate editor of *Poetry,* put Sandburg in touch with Alfred Harcourt of Henry Holt and Company in New York. Unlike the John Lane contact, this one paid off. In December, Sandburg told Henderson that he was "slaving" away on the manuscript of what would soon be *Chicago and Other Poems.* Soon afterward, he sent a 260-poem manuscript to Harcourt ( *Letters* 103–7).

According to the sense of the world he expressed in the *Review,* Sandburg should not have received any encouragement from Henderson or any other members of the bourgeoisie, nor should a capitalist publisher have shown the slightest interest in his work. Left theory maintained that the "capitalist press," like other social and political institutions, suppressed the working-class point of view, and in *Review* articles he was to write over the two years following the publication of *Chicago,* Sandburg sometimes waxed outrageously vituperative on this subject. So, presumably, he would face a predictable effort to suppress his politics as soon as he began dealing with Harcourt.

At least for his own poems, the theory proved wrong, for a short time after he sent his manuscript off, he struck a deal with Harcourt, beginning a publishing relationship that lasted his entire life. This is not to say that Harcourt accepted Sandburg's manuscript completely. Rather, he responded with several suggestions, including cutting its length by some two-fifths. But far from being motivated by politics, most of Harcourt's proposed cuts were apparently based on his belief that the poems in question had lost their contemporaneity, for in his rejoinder Sandburg took exception to only one deletion, saying that "Murmurings in a Field Hospital" had "a present time value above that of others" and should therefore remain in the book. A second group of poems Harcourt proposed cutting were about "living people referred to by name," by which he probably meant that they exposed Holt and Company to libel suits. How many such poems there were is unclear. In his response, Sandburg referred to only one, but there were no doubt more. Finally, Harcourt questioned the expletive "by Christ" in "Buttons" and the inclusion of "Dynamiter" in the volume (CS Coll: Holt folder 1).

Harcourt's response was a model of how an editor could help to put together a collection of poetry that, because it had been written over some fifteen years, included a number of stylistic changes. He was concerned with avoiding libel suits, cutting the book down to a marketable length, ensuring even quality, and making it more topical. In addition, he went well beyond editorial norms in shepherding the book through Holt and Company. As he was to recall years later, "There was something of a skirmish to get it past the inhibitions and traditions of the Holt office, for its middle-western atmosphere, its subject matter and strength seemed to them rather raw for their imprint." But Harcourt proved to be an adept (or sneaky) office operative, removing some of the potentially troublesome poems before editorial board approval—perhaps, after all, Sandburg *did* have something to fear from the "capitalist press"—and, on the assumption that board members would never look at the book again, reinserting them for the printer (Harcourt).

No doubt anxious to have a book issued by a major publisher but not falling all over himself, Sandburg accepted much of the professional advice offered by Harcourt while persuasively but politely arguing other points. Two poems became major issues. From Harcourt's point of view, "Billy Sunday," an attack on the famous evangelist, was inviting a libel suit, but for Sandburg it was a central statement. After an exchange of views, a compromise was rapidly struck, and Sandburg agreed to retitle it "To a Contemporary Bunkshooter." "Dynamiter," in some respects the most radical poem in the book, brought forth a vigorous defense from Sandburg. It also brought forth a couple of comments which indicated that he thought *Chicago* was going to be a success precisely because of its politics. Sandburg told Harcourt he thought "the backing for this book will come from the younger, aggressive fellows, in the main," and clearly "Dynamiter" would be one of the most appealing poems to that audience. In this connection, he also said, "Without tying it up to any special schools or doctrines, the intellectual background of [*Chicago*] takes color from the modern working class movement rather than old-fashioned Jeffersonian democracy" (*Letters* 107). If, in fact, Harcourt had been trying to deradicalize his new poet, "Dynamiter" would have been a good place to start, but he did not pursue the issue. Sandburg won his case without any further discussion, and, like the Billy Sunday poem, "Dynamiter" was printed.

Although among some readers *Chicago and Other Poems* made Sandburg's reputation as a radical writer, parts of the book had little connection to the class war or to anything remotely public and topical. That was because five of its seven sections showcased his development over fifteen years. Reflecting his new politics, "Chicago Poems" and "War Poems (1914–1915)," the two up-to-date sections, were in Sandburg's tough, assured, direct new voice. It is possible that the core of the "Chicago Poems" section was written between the spring of 1914 and the winter of 1915, for only three of the nine "Chicago Poems" Sandburg published in the March 1914 *Poetry,* "Chicago," "Lost," and "Harbor," were included in it; the others were placed in other sections of the volume. Nearly every poem in these other five sections—"Handfuls," "The Road and the End," "Fog and Fires," "Shadows," and "Other Days"—read like a step, often a halting and self-consciously "poetic" step, toward maturity. Reflecting the dreamy "idealism" of his earliest phase, a substantial number of these poems were shrouded in soft palls, fogs, and twilight hazes. Always acutely sensitive, always soft and warm, the speaker was typically troubled and melancholy; themes of mutability, death, and decay dominated.

The poems were not poorly executed. To the contrary, many of them demonstrated a secure command of trope, image, and rhythm. The section called "Handfuls," for example, contained eleven very brief imagistic exercises that showed Sandburg's grasp of poetic minimalism. "Fog," destined to be widely anthologized and memorized by schoolchildren, managed its intensity in one trope, the dense Lake Michigan fog rolling in on "little cat feet," twenty-one words worked out in alternating three- and four-word lines. Though Sandburg later remembered "Fog" as a "free-going American Hoku" (Corwin 32), the twenty-one words were exactly the number of "syllables" contained in traditional Japanese *tanka,* then a high literary fashion (*Poems* 33). "White Shoulders" memorialized a woman and an intense moment with her in eighteen words, "directly treating," as Imagists said, an occasion that would have produced gushing sentiment in a less well-schooled poet (*Poems* 35). Other sections of the book showed distinctively different stages in his development as well as the range of his interests. Landscape poems showed his sensitivity to color and mood, the seasons, and the power of natural forces. The section called "The Road and the End" was stylistically gnomic and philosophically expansive. The pieces in this section questioned fundamental meanings in the universe and the long drift of history, sought big answers to big questions, and received a good deal of irony and silence in response. His domestic life was recorded in poems about flowers in the backyard garden, his wife, and child.

Some poems in the book's earlier sections were not all sweetness and light, flowers, delicate nocturnes, and moonbeams. Several linked poems in "Shadows" showed that Sandburg had long been interested in prostitution, though, more significantly, they also showed that in this earlier poetry he had not quite figured out how to present character and situation without sounding like a superior observer from another world. "It Is Much" depicted painted women of the night "skulking" in the shadows to the refrains of their own "heart-deep laughter" and the observer's dramatic (or bathetic) "It is much to be warm and sure of tomorrow." "Harrison Street Court" began in a formal tone, with "I heard a woman's lips / Speaking to a companion / Say these words." Then the "lips" spoke in overdone vernacular about how " 'A woman what hustles' " always had her money taken by pimps and cops. "Soiled Dove" had a similar superior tone, with Sandburg declaiming "Let us be honest, the lady was not a harlot until she married a corporation lawyer who picked her from a Ziegfield chorus." A personified bawdy saloon spoke about debauchery in "Jungheimer's." And, at the end, there was "Gone," about a beautiful small-town girl, a "Dancer, singer, a laughing passionate lover," who had left for greener and, presumably, more remunerative pastures (*Poems* 62–64).

"Other Days (1900–1910)," the last section, included four pieces that also suggested how he had translated his earlier social interests into verse. "Old Woman" pictured a homeless old "waif" trying to sleep in a doorway, though it succeeded better at picturing the observer, comfortable in his room, melancholically looking out: "Against a pane I press my forehead / And drowsily look on the walls and sidewalks." Like this and the prostitute poems, "The Junk Man" and "Noon Hour," about a woman who made cigars for a living, were stiffly formal and distant. "Boes" had the observer looking at some hoboes in a railroad yard but became an occasion for Sandburg to tell the story of how he had once been arrested for riding a freight train. Finally, there were "I Am the People, the Mob" and "Government." The first, apparently one of Sandburg's earliest poems about the potential power of the masses, offered conventional advice about the need for the people to remember the lessons of the past so they could shape the future. "Government" was more interesting and considerably more surprising, mainly because its litany of the abuses of the state—police brutality, militia action against strikers, political corruption—was inclusive. That is, Sandburg did not say that when socialists were elected, everything would change. The form of government did not matter, he said, sounding more like a philosophical anarchist or Wobbly than a "constructive" socialist, because governments were made of men, and men in power were all the same (*Poems* 69–72, 75).

Sandburg was a wonderfully gifted poet, and if *Chicago and Other Poems* contained only lyrics, it might still have become an important book in the history of modern verse. The Imagist and minimalist poems were accomplished and could stand comparison to much of the verse then being published in avant-garde magazines. And however rhetorical and distant, stiff and formal, the more political and social poems of his earlier phases were distinguished in comparison to much of the work of other radical poets. "Government" was a good example, for, though it apparently came from an earlier stage in his development, it continued to be used by Sandburg and the editors of the *Review* to express the magazine's stance on the hopelessness of "political" action. But the sections of the book showcasing his development were overshadowed by "Chicago Poems," in which he wrote with tremendous power and persuasiveness about the contemporary class war, and, most impressively, about Chicago street scenes and people, the pain and indignities they suffered as well as their gestures of dignity. Here, and to a lesser extent in "War Poems," he came into his own.

The majority of poems in those two sections melded what he had learned about art—but not the homespun art of Joe Hill and other left poets—with his new politics. Very few were in the characteristic modes of other radical poets and verse propagandists. They were, in many respects, modernistic, intense, and direct in form and language while politically radical.[1] Only three of the poems could be said to have arisen directly from contemporary events and to have been absorbed with ideology. Two of those three struck later readers (not radical readers) as vintage Sandburg. "Chicago," the lead poem of the section, was to become an American schoolroom poem, taught as a great work about a great city by a great son of the people, memorized, along with "Fog," by generations of children. "To a Contemporary Bunkshooter" was to become a favorite as a poem that talked persuasively about "false religion." The third, "Dynamiter," was not famous in later years but was apparently meant as a central ideological statement.

Appropriately, the creation of wealth and power, the source of economic well-being, was the subject of the famous lead poem. As in capitalist theory, this was the most basic issue in radical theory, the issue from which everything else flowed, including the issue of who and what were the people.[2] Sandburg's answers to these questions were, of course, predictable; they could be found on every page of his *International Socialist Review* articles, or, for that matter, on practically every page of every left magazine. But in "Chicago" he also took up some of the major issues raised in contemporary discussions of the American city, what it represented, and what it gave its residents.

The poem thus unfolded as alternative views of the city, a device that probably had something to do with its being remembered and taught in schoolrooms as a booster statement. The beginning, for example, sounded like a chamber of commerce blurb, its capitalized words suggesting the advertiser's craft. In this version of the city, catchy phrases defining Chicago's economic functions and character said everything:

> Hog Butcher for the World,
> Tool Maker, Stacker of Wheat,
> Player with Railroads and the Nation's Freight Handler;
> Stormy, husky, brawling,
> City of the Big Shoulders.

Then, in the second part of the poem, Sandburg turned to another version of Chicago, referring to the typical complaints of reformers, antiurban crusaders, and suburbanites. From their perspective, the city was "wicked," "crooked," and "brutal." Sandburg answered these "sneers" ironically. Yes, Chicago *was* wicked, "for I have seen your painted women under the gas lamps luring the farm boys." Yes, Chicago *was* crooked, for "it is true I have seen the gunman kill and go free to kill again." And yes, Chicago *was* brutal, for "on the faces of women and children I have seen the marks of wanton hunger."

What was Chicago if it was not a commercial center or, alternatively, Sodom and Gomorrah? Getting to his point, Sandburg said it was a powerfully built, lusty, joyful myth-man—the archetype of the worker. Declaring, "Under his wrist is the pulse, and under his ribs the heart of the people," he pictured his mythicized Chicago as the essence of manliness. Sweating and "half-naked," he loomed above the skyline as a defiant roughneck, "with lifted head singing so proud to be / alive and coarse and strong and cunning." He was "a tall bold slugger," primal, elemental. He stood with "dust all over his mouth, laughing with white teeth." History's hero, he was not cowed by the "terrible burden of destiny" but was joyful, brimming over with coarse energy, "Laughing even as an ignorant fighter laughs who has never lost a battle." This proud, charismatic workingman-hero was what made Chicago "a tall bold slugger set vivid against the soft little cities." At the end, Sandburg repeated the opening. The city was indeed "Hog Butcher, Tool Maker, Stacker of Wheat, Player with Railroads and Freight Handler to the Nation." But now the answer to how it had become those things was clear, for the sentence was introduced with a phrase saying that the myth-man was "proud" to be these things (*Poems* 3–4).

Thematically, "Chicago" was an orthodox radical statement about labor as the creator of wealth. Visually, Sandburg's myth-man was a perfect replica of the Adonis-like American worker depicted in cartoon and poster art in left magazines and organizing propaganda. Sometimes, looming heroically above industrial landscapes, this familiar figure— powerfully muscled, square jawed, grinning, or looking resolute—was pictured as already victorious over his circumstances. Other versions stressed the potential of victory, with the worker tensed to catapult into a future beyond wage slavery, his broken chains dangling from his powerful wrists. Needless to say, these images of working-class heroism were the exact opposite of the images depicting capitalists and their lackeys as Rockefeller-like rails of men, slimy octopuses, or grotesquely obese, top-hatted blobs that decorated left magazines and newspapers.

Sandburg's poem about Billy Sunday was not analogous to a visual cartoon, but it was the poetic equivalent of the cursing, up-against-the-wall, finger-in-the-chest damnations of capitalists and their lackeys he published in the *Review*. When he wrote to Alfred Harcourt justifying its inclusion, he emphasized Sunday's hypocrisy, saying he had heard rumors of Sunday's financial involvement in the disreputable Hotel Morrison in Chicago. Sunday, he also said, was a demagogue, "the most conspicuous single embodiment in this country of the crowd leader or crowd operative who uses jungle methods, stark voodoo stage effects, to play hell with democracy" (*Letters* 108). This was not an unusual description. It could be found in some mainstream newspapers and was especially prevalent among more traditional Protestant ministers, for whom Sunday's emotionalism and vaudeville antics—he was a former professional baseball player who liked to wow audiences by jumping, somersaulting, and sliding into home plate, Jesus' home plate, he said— were revolting and embarrassing.

"To a Contemporary Bunkshooter," which originally appeared both in the *International Socialist Review* and in the *Masses* in September 1915, also grew directly out of contemporary events. Along with radical rhetoric, labor militancy, congressional concern, and the Joe Hill passion play, antirevivalist feeling crested in 1915, when the Chicago-based Sunday went to the East Coast on one of his campaigns to save souls. In April, after several stops marked by controversy, he arrived in Paterson, New Jersey, the site of the 1913 IWW-led strike and, just two years later, already a sacred place in left folklore. The Wobblies were not about to step aside while Sunday converted the mill workers, and, perhaps drawing on the ordeal of Hill in Utah, they quickly pictured Sunday's Paterson campaign as a contest between pie-in-the-sky religion and the IWW for the hearts and minds of the local workers. *Solidarity* reported in two issues on the new Paterson struggle by reprinting articles from mainstream newspapers. The first, picked up from the *New York Press* and printed under the sardonic headline "I.W.W. Gives Billy Sunday Pain: Evangelist Meeting Cold Reception from Paterson Slaves, Who Were Previously 'Converted' by Chief Bimson," told of how the crowd who heard Sunday was apathetic and announced that the Wobblies, led by Carlo Tresca and Frank Tannenbaum, were soon coming to Paterson to lead an anti-Sunday campaign. A week later, under the title

"Billy Sunday Has Hard Row in Paterson," *Solidarity* reprinted a report from the *Philadelphia Ledger* which said that the IWW was denouncing Sunday as an employee of the despised mill owners and threatening to parade. But it was clear that no parade would be necessary, for the report concluded by saying that though Sunday had impressed some old people with his antialcohol message, he had made no inroads among the mill workers. The Wobbly agitation was working, and "every cabaret in town is featuring songs, parodying the well-known revival hymns and the city is flooded with anti-Sunday newspapers."

People with very different dispositions and interests could unify in opposition to Billy Sunday, and likewise Sandburg's poem about him reflected a wide spectrum of opinion. It recounted standard denunciations of Sunday as a cheap, overwrought performer, a distorter of Jesus' social gospel, and a con man whose main business was frightening people out of their wits and money. It also rehearsed Wobbly denunciations of Sunday's pie-in-the-sky promises to the suffering. Its originality, however, did not lie in the content of its arguments; rather, it lay in its hard-boiled tone and its insulting language, for "To a Contemporary Bunkshooter" was a poison-pen letter, an up-against-the-wall, ripsnorting denunciation that echoed all the traditions of literary and oratorical cursing. Sunday was pictured as out of control, "squirting words at us, shaking your fist and calling us all dam fools so fierce the froth slobbers over your lips . . . always blabbing we're all going to hell straight off and you know all about it." His friends were the enemy: "I say the same bunch backing you nailed the nails into the hands of this Jesus of Nazareth. He had lined up against him the same crooks and strong-arm men now lined up with you paying your way." He took from the poor and helped the rich: "You tell $6 a week department store girls all they need is Jesus; you take a steel trust wop, dead without having lived, gray and shrunken at forty years of age, and you tell him to look at Jesus on the cross and he'll be all right" (*Poems* 29–31).[3]

Of the poems in "Chicago," only "Dynamiter" was so closely tied to contemporary events and so immediately related to Sandburg's *Review* prose. It was about sabotage as a tactic, dynamite as a weapon of choice in the class war. Anton Johannsen, who Sandburg knew well and who he identified as the real-life name of the subject of the poem, had for several years been reputed to be a fearsome saboteur and had at one point been thought to have been behind the *Los Angeles Times* bombing.[4] So in writing and publishing the poem, Sandburg was in a difficult area.

He settled his difficulty with ease. His poem about Johannsen recounted a dinner conversation with him in a saloon, but Sandburg was careful to say that during the conversation "not a word was said about his deep days and nights as a dynamiter," so the poem did not actually wrestle with the wisdom, necessity, or utility of sabotage as a tactic. But Johannsen was lauded. "His name was in many newspapers as an enemy of the nation and few keepers of churches or schools would open their doors to him," yet he was warmly, passionately human. He was a good husband and father. He was loquacious, telling "stories of his wife and children and the cause of labor and the working class" over a dinner of steak and onions. Like the mythic Chicago figure, he laughed a lot. In one brilliant metaphor, his laughter "rang like the call of gray birds filled with a glory of joy ramming their winged flight through a rain storm." Twisting the conventional image of the saboteur as a cold-blooded murderer, Sandburg played on Johannsen's sense of life as a "rich and red-blooded thing." The last line of "Dynamiter" put the point succinctly, its repetitions and summary statements ennobling Johannsen and, in effect, explaining his vocation: "Only I remember him as a lover of life, a lover of children, a lover of all free, reckless laughter everywhere—lover of red hearts and red blood the world over" (*Poems* 21). The conventional left description of Debs throughout these years was "Lover of Mankind." Was Sandburg saying that the dynamiter was Debs's equal? Probably. In a very short poem called "In a Back Alley," which was placed on the page before "Dynamiter," Sandburg described Lincoln as a "Dead lover of boys" who had become just an image engraved on the pennies newsboys pitched (*Poems* 20). Johannsen was a "lover of children." Was he saying that Johannsen was Lincolnesque? Probably this, too.

A poem placed almost immediately next to "Dynamiter" clarified Sandburg's attitude toward sabotage and violence as tactics in the class war. In some respects, the character portrayed in "Ice Handler" was very nearly Johannsen's double. He is proud and hard, "his head in the air and a hard pair of fists"; he is pictured in a saloon, first lugging a hundred-pound cake of ice, then helping himself to a free meal; he has a sort of family, or at least he sees on Saturday nights a big woman who washes dishes in the Hotel Morrison, Billy Sunday's hotel. Most important, though, the ice handler is also a hard-fisted union man and a saboteur. He has created havoc by loosening the wheels of ice wagons that were running during a strike. He has beaten up scabs without remorse: "All he was sorry for was one of the scabs bit him on the knuckles of the right hand so they bled when he came around to the saloon to tell the boys about it." His matter-of-fact, joking manner (he did not punch the mouths of the scabs; one bit him on the fist) comes as easily as his "flannel shirt with pearl buttons the size of a dollar" is worn or his comment to the bartender that "it's hotter than yesterday and will be hotter yet tomorrow, by Jesus" (*Poems* 21–22). Without the benefit of theory and without any dramatic rhetoric, the ice handler did what came naturally. Violence and sabotage, the poem seems to argue, are as much a part of working-class culture as saloons, raucous laughter, and liver and onions.

Perhaps inevitably, the ripsnorting attack on Billy Sunday and the dramatic statements about sabotage so commanded the attention of Sandburg's readers that other parts of the section were obscured. But "Chicago," far from being that limited, was made up of fifty-five poems. Four unmarked but distinct parts organized the poems into a tight structure based on the point of view, the angle and distance, from which the subjects were seen. The first, following the poster-poem "Chicago," presented wide-angle, general views of the cityscape. The second narrowed the focus to working-class street life. The third focused still further to present group and individual portraits of ordinary working people. The fourth presented portraits of heroes and antiheroes, including "Dynamiter," "Ice Handler," and "To a Contemporary Bunkshooter," and was followed by "Skyscraper."

Reflecting the widespread contemporary interest in describing and assessing the circumstances of ordinary Americans, and also reflecting the common belief that poetry was a documentary instrument, within this four-part structure Sandburg took up the nature of workers and working-class culture. Who ordinary workers were, how they behaved, what they believed, their aspirations, their strengths and weaknesses, and their social relationships were his primary subjects. The abstraction of Chicago-the-mythic-worker was, in other words, complemented and given specificity by a series of street scenes and portraits of ordinary Chicagoans.

Any attempt to write about workers and their culture was extremely challenging. Centering on the telling details, avoiding projecting one's desires and values onto the subjects, accounting for variables and variations, choosing the valid representative sample, drawing reasonable inferences, in short, all of the pitfalls of sociological description and all of the ethnographic problems that could be imagined, was as difficult in the early decades of the century as it still is. Sandburg was not naive about these problems. As a reporter, he faced them every day. Nor was he unaware that a great deal of what passed as contemporary description of working-class culture and workers as individuals was inadequate. On occasion, he remarked on the difficulties involved. "Halsted Street Car," a short poem placed in the street scene section of "Chicago," used the device of challenging newspaper cartoonists to get their subjects right while presenting his own interpretations of a group of people on a trolley in the immigrant district made famous by Jane Addams's settlement house. "Try with your pencils," Sandburg said to the cartoonists, to capture the "crooked faces," the "tired empty faces," the faces "Empty of dreams" (*Poems* 6–7). "Onion Days," a portrait of an Italian woman who worked as a picker for a farmer just outside the city, included a sharp comment on the artistic difficulty (or impossibility) of capturing her character: "I listen to fellows saying here's good stuff for a novel or it might be worked up into a good play. / I say there's no dramatist living can put old Mrs. Gabrielle Giovannitti into a play with that kindling wood piled on top of her head coming along Peoria Street nine o'clock in the morning" (*Poems* 14).

As it was for other artists, and, it should be added, as it was for sociologists, settlement house workers, investigative journalists, and the like, the most important issue Sandburg faced was how to create a convincing illusion of adequacy and accuracy in dealing with his workers and their culture. How he dealt with the issue, the methods he used, the posture he adopted, was a combination of a number of the elements of his previous experience. First, there was his organizing device, his reliance on a photographic analogy as his fundamental structural principle. Sandburg was very familiar both with photography as an emerging art and as a documentary method. He had probably looked at thousands of social investigation photos over the years, starting with his first contact with Jacob Riis and including the uses of exposé photographs in the *International Socialist Review,* a few of which accompanied his own contributions to the magazine. Edward Steichen, his brother-in-law and one of the great photographic portraitists of the period, exercised a continuing influence on his life and work. His contact with photographic technology reached back to his college years, when he had sold stereopticon views in the hinterlands. So it is not surprising that in a series of poems that purported to be documentary he used a structural device that emphasized an analogy to photography, the standard, it was then commonly thought, for authentic social documentation.

The photographic analogy created a loose framework suggesting authenticity. Other devices contributed to the general effect. For the most part, Sandburg adopted the sincere, restrained tone of an objective reporter of "facts" who spoke in the trustworthy, understated language of hard nouns and verbs and let the story tell itself.[5] "Halsted Street Car," in which he suggested personality through a few physical details, was typical of his minimalism. On a few occasions he used the reporter's device of presenting purportedly unedited extended quotations, creating the illusion that his subjects were speaking for themselves, but with none of the condescension of the earlier "Harrison Street Court." In "Mag," a husband spoke of his wish that he and his wife had never found each other—making ends meet was tough—and concluded, "I wish to God I never saw you, Mag. / I wish to God the kids had never come" (*Poems* 13). The speaker in "Blacklisted" declared the convenience of changing names, wondered, "Why does God Almighty or anybody else care whether I take a new name to go by?" and never for a moment suspected that a name and a self-identity were intertwined (*Poems* 7). Though from time to time it was interrupted by some hot radical rhetoric, there was, in short, a consistent reportorial tone in most of the poems and, on occasion, a direct reference to covering the daily events for the newspapers. In "Fellow Citizens," most obviously, Sandburg told how he had spent his day interviewing a rich manufacturer, listening to a speech at the Advertising Association, and, in a detail telling his audience how important and trusted a correspondent he was, interviewing the mayor of Chicago. This set the stage for the real point of the poem, his talk with a lowly—but happy—accordion and guitar maker near Hull House (*Poems* 22–23).

Finally, the seeming authenticity of the poems derived from Sandburg's use of specific names, places, dates, events, wages earned, working conditions endured, and so forth. At times the poems sounded like passages out of realistic novels or rewrites of sociological data. In "Onion Days," most prominently, the woman portrayed was named Mrs. Gabrielle Giovannitti; she left for work at 5:30 in the morning, returning home at 9:00 or 10:00 at night; she worked ten and sometimes twelve hours per day; last week she had been paid eight cents per box of onions, this week the price had been dropped to six cents;

the farmer she worked for was named Jasper; he had seven hundred acres along the Bowmanville Road and went to Episcopal services in Ravenswood; he advertised for his pickers in the *Chicago Daily News,* and, when he had attracted a surplus labor force of women and girls, he lowered their wages. The immigrant couple in "Population Drifts" was described in case-study terms. They haggled with "landlords and grocers." Their six children, who "prowled in the garbage cans," had constricted destinies: "One child coughed its lungs away, two more have adenoids and can neither talk nor run like their mother, one is in jail, two have jobs in a box factory" (*Poems* 15). The Italian laborer in "The Shovel Man" was pictured in terms of his dirty clothes and his wages of "a dollar six bits a day" (*Poems* 9). In "Graceland" there was a description that echoed the findings of the Industrial Relations Commission on the conditions of women's work, girls who did not have the nickel to go to the movies, women working the tables in a saloon, "In a hundred furnished rooms is a girl who sells silk or dress goods or leather stuff for six dollars a week wages" (*Poems* 11–12). One poem grew directly out of a *Chicago Day Book* front-page story. On January 15, 1913, the newspaper printed "The Death of Anna Imroth in Riordan's Factory Fire Was Plain Murder," a short exposé of how the woman's death resulted from improper door installation in a Chicago factory. Sandburg's "Anna Imroth" described how she was carried out, concluding, "But all of the others got down and they are safe and this is the only one of the factory girls who wasn't lucky in making the jump when the fire broke. / It is the hand of God and the lack of fire escapes" (*Poems* 16). In all of these examples—and many others could be cited—a reader with expectations that poetry was a means of being transported to other worlds, other states of consciousness, would have been mightily disappointed, if not thoroughly outraged. But the point of "social poetry" was engagement, and engagement, for Sandburg at least, started with facts, data, wages, hours, and working conditions.

Sandburg declared in "They Will Say" that the worst that could ever be said of Chicago was that it mercilessly exploited its children, and in "Mill-Doors," a surrealistic companion poem, he wrote that in the mills the blood was tapped from the children's wrists, "drop by drop, / And you are old before you are young" (*Poems* 5–6). As poems like "Graceland," "Mag," "Onion Days," and many others made clear, the children, though the most pitiful, were not the only sufferers.

Low wages, awful working conditions, low emotional and intellectual horizons, loneliness, fatigue, and broken families were the lot of many.

But his preoccupation in "Chicago Poems" was not simply with documenting the travails of the lowly; it was to affirm and glorify them. Some of the portraits in which this occurred have already been discussed: "Dynamiter" and "Ice Handler," where he suggested something of the virility and lustiness of two strong men, "Child of the Romans," where he spoke about the dignity of the railroad laborer in contrast to the illusory delicacies of the dining car riders, and "Onion Days," where he spoke of the quiet endurance of the Giovannitti woman. Many others had similar outcomes. The fascination with Italian immigrants he showed in "Onion Days" and "Child of the Romans" was also evident in "The Shovel Man," a poem that indicated how much his portrait art depended on broad, bold lines combining with sociological detail to uncover the sweet, precious humanity that lay behind appearances. Here was "A dago working for a dollar six bits a day" walking begrimed down a street with his shovel slung across his shoulders while "a dark-eyed woman in the old country dreams of him for one of the world's ready men with a pair of fresh lips and a kiss better than all the wild grapes that ever grew in Tuscany" (*Poems* 9). Rough-hewn nobility and tough, swaggering, graceful ease defined the characters in "Dynamiter" and "Ice Handler." Likewise, "Jack" pictured a man who had worked ten-hour days for thirty years on the railroad, had hands that "were tougher than shoe leather," had eight children with his "tough woman," had seen her die, watched his children leave, and ended in the poorhouse. When he died, though, he still had his joy, was still a "swarthy, swaggering son-of-a-gun" (*Poems* 22). In many cases, the poems involved a two-step process. First, very often, Sandburg began by stating the typical grounds, the ethnic slur or the political caricature, for example, upon which the individual was dehumanized in ordinary discourse: the dynamiter was first presented as the legendary mad bomber, the shovel man and the railroad laborer were "dagos," a poem about a fish peddler began "I know a Jew fish crier down on Maxwell Street," a poem involving the death of an immigrant child included the statement that "I shall cry over the dead child of a stockyards hunky," one poem was even titled "Nigger." After that was done, he provided his own substitute images of the characters, humanizing them, ennobling them, rescuing them from the stereotypes to which they had been consigned (and, arguably, creating substitute stereotypes).

In his earlier *International Socialist Review* articles and, as we shall see, in later ones, Sandburg often addressed the issue of what workers wanted, one of the two fundamental questions that drove public debate in early twentieth-century America. His answer was conventionally radical: workers, or at least workers who had learned to see through the trickery of politicians and trade union leaders, wanted revolutionary unionism. In "Chicago Poems" he addressed the other of the two fundamental issues—who workers were. Though equally radical, his answers were considerably more complicated, more provisional, and more open to interpretation. But, still, there was an answer, one that went a step beyond the many assertions of workers' dignity, integrity, physical and spiritual beauty, lustiness, and so forth.

At the beginning of the section, the myth-man Chicago loomed over the cityscape as the fundamental force of creativity, the source of all wealth. At its end was "Skyscraper," which proclaimed that the "soul" of the grand symbol of modernity was the workingmen who made it and the ordinary people who worked in it. Between these bookends, there were many occasions when he again insisted that his workers, as downtrodden as they might be, as long-suffering and lowly, also stood for creativity, for art, for the joy of creation. The worker as builder of the city was memorialized in "Muckers" and "A Fence," the latter a poem that involved considerable irony because the fence being built was going to serve to keep out the brothers and sisters and children of the creators (*Poems* 10, 16). The joy of groups of plain people was associated with music in "Picnic Boat," which ended with "the rhythmic oompa of the brasses playing a Polish folk-song for the homecomers," and in "Happiness," where the speaker learned the meaning of that word when he "saw a crowd of Hungarians under the trees with their women and children and a keg of beer and an accordion" (*Poems* 10). The creation of music—vernacular music, of course—was a subject in several poems. The people who passed by in "Clark Street Bridge" left behind them

> . . . Voices singing, singing,
> . . . Silver voices, singing,
> Softer than the stars,
> Softer than the mist. (*Poems* 7)

The person in "Nigger," who was perhaps the most stereotyped character Sandburg created (but all of his portraits were of character types, not individuals as such), was also known as the "Singer of songs" (*Poems* 23–

24).[6] Individual human happiness was the subject of two of Sandburg's most impressive portraits. As if he were talking in Morrisite terms, in "Fish Crier" he portrayed one of the lowly, a Jew, who plied his trade with the joy and grace of a modern dancer, a "Pavlowa dancing." His face, Sandburg said, was "that of a man terribly glad to be selling fish, terribly glad that God made fish, and customers to whom he may call his wares from a pushcart" (*Poems* 9–10). In "Fellow Citizens," he discovered humanity, integrity, and joy in another lowly person. Beyond any others, this portrait was so warm, detailed, and extended that it may have represented his most positive statement in "Chicago Poems," the place where he realized not just the ideological abstraction of the worker as creator or as the "soul" of modernity but its full human meaning. The person, apparently another Italian, was discovered in the immigrant district near Hull House; with "his jaw wrapped for a bad toothache," he appeared as one of Sandburg's typical street people. He was a great creator, making beautiful guitars which he sold, stating the price "in a sorry way, as though the music and the make of an instrument count for a million times more than the price in money." Sandburg was unrestrained in his admiration: "I thought he had a real soul and knew a lot about God," he said. "There was light in his eyes of one who has conquered sorrow in so far as sorrow is conquerable or worth conquering" (*Poems* 22–23).

The creativity, integrity, joy, and sweet simplicity of ordinary people which was the upshot of such poems as "Fellow Citizens" and "Fish Crier" and, beneath the surfaces of exploitation and violence, of most of the other portraits in "Chicago Poems," was a testimony of Sandburg's hope and faith in common humanity. Doubt was no part of the equation. Nor were the burdens of the historic past, or the countervailing power of capital, human perversity, or evil.

The other up-to-date section of the book, "War Poems (1914–1915)" was, on the contrary, a testimony of Sandburg's shock and unabated sadness about the first bloody year or so of the Great War in Europe. Here there were few if any tonal highs or lows, no moments of personal epiphany or anecdotes about heroic surmountings of circumstances. Appropriately meditative, contemplative, most often brooding, the eleven short poems gathered together in the section recorded only killing, death, blood running in endless streams, the absolute absence of hope. Common humanity had been reduced by the war to one function. "Killers," the opening poem, said that sixteen million men had been turned into a colossal death machine. "Fight" put the point in different words, but the outcome was the same. Here the pitiless war god lived its "red joy." A "child cries for a suck mother," Sandburg wrote, "and I cry for war."

Did anyone resist participating in the slaughter? Was it possible, as radicals and others had hoped before the outbreak of war, that ordinary people out of class solidarity would say no, would refuse to spill their brothers' blood? If Sandburg ever had such hopes, they were not apparent in "War Poems." One poem, indeed, may have arisen from such questions. One stanza said that workmen and citizens were commanded to build "factories and cathedrals, warehouses and homes / Into buildings for life and labor." Its other stanza said that soldiers were commanded to reduce it all to rubble (*Poems* 40). The poem was titled "And They Obey."

Was there any redemption to be discovered in the slaughter, any sign that the world would be a better place after the killing was over? Some observers, including Sandburg a couple of years later, saw silver linings in the bloody clouds. But not here. In "Salvage," Sandburg wrote about reading William Morris's chapter on the great churches of Europe that were now being blown to smithereens and remarked, "I'm glad you're a dead man, William Morris, I'm glad you're down in the damp and mouldy, only a memory instead of a living man—I'm glad you're gone" (*Poems* 41). At least Morris did not have to bear witness to man's bloody fate. And in the final poem of the section, "Wars," Sandburg made it clear that there would be no redemption. Wars would go on and on. Only the technologies of warfare and the forms of death would change (*Poems* 42).

As fine a group of poems about home-front reactions to the European killing as any published by an American, written in a severe minimalist idiom such as others would discover only years later, Sandburg's "War Poems (1914–1915)" were nonetheless only the beginning of his intellectual engagement with the Great War. Set among the other themes and preoccupations of *Chicago and Other Poems,* they seemed relatively minor (reviewers and later critics would rarely even comment on their existence). But, as we shall see, the war, its significance, the proper attitude toward it, the politics of dissent and repression, would soon become for Sandburg, as for nearly every other American, *the* essential issue, overshadowing and changing everything else.

* * *

The major, up-to-date sections of *Chicago and Other Poems* were complex and, very often, subtle and nuanced, the work of a first-rate poet who had come a long way since his beginning fifteen years earlier. Individual poems, central themes having to do with the worker as creator, matters of technique, and political matters demanded attention to detail. Dismissed by the vast majority of later critics as simple or crude, work best suited to schoolchildren, *Chicago,* like Sandburg's later poetry, was destined never to get the attention it needed and deserved. What was true later was also true of contemporary commentary on *Chicago,* which split along clear ideological lines and, no matter the ideology, reduced the book to issues having to do with political and aesthetic correctness.

The most enthusiastic review appeared in the IWW newspaper *Solidarity.* Written by Victor Basinet, " 'Chicago Poems': Echoes of the Revolt in Verse" proclaimed that of all the recent poetry having to do with the social rebellion, *Chicago* was the "most radically thought compelling." Basinet, reflecting the usual Wobbly concern with manliness in their heroes and artists, called Sandburg "one of the few really big men in American literature." His work showed a true understanding of the contemporary struggle: "The future will speak of him as a poet who understood; who felt and knew; a people's poet; one who pictured with strokes of truth their existence—in all its sordidness and its beauty, its misery and its joy, its pain and its pleasure, sympathetically and without fear. His songs are of the dirt, the water, the air, of men and women red-blooded and alive."

Sandburg's message was abundantly clear, according to Basinet. The poems flashed "the 'Red Challenge' to the world's oppressors from the clenched fist of the oppressed!" To prove his point, Basinet used "Child of the Romans," projecting the sweetest Wobbly dream of revolution into the poem: "As we read, we picture somewhere in the distant future the shiny pick of the 'dago' crashing through the table top—we see him crush with his heel the 'dry bread and bologna' into the dirt and reach out a gnarled, sweaty hand to take that which belongs to him. The lines ring out with harsh, metallic sounds that this will come—we wonder, when?" Other poems had similar, if less violent messages. "Muckers" was said to contrast the joyful rebelliousness of wage slaves to the contemptuous respectability of the bourgeoisie. "Blacklisted" would be understood by every worker who bore the marks of the "Mailed Fist of Capitalism" on his throat. In conclusion, Basinet called Sandburg's poems "fiery beacons, burning scarlet on the horizon of the Revolution."[7]

69

There were other indications that *Chicago* became something of a Wobbly favorite. Years later, Ralph Chaplin wryly recalled that in 1918, when he along with other Wobbly leaders was on trial, he spent his time in the courtroom reading *Chicago Poems* and, perhaps as appropriately, Mark Twain's hilarious *Joan of Arc* (*Wobbly* 243).[8] Charles Ashleigh, another Wobbly poet who was also tried in 1918 and, like Chaplin and the others, convicted and sent to prison at Leavenworth, recalled in his 1930 autobiographical novel *Rambling Kid* how the tough bindle stiffs with whom he traveled had hotly debated the merits of Sandburg, Dreiser, and Sherwood Anderson. There were, according to Ashleigh, "tremendous arguments" over steam beer in a San Francisco saloon about whether "Sandburg, Dreiser, *et alia* were revolutionary writers. Mort said yes, Phelan stoutly, amidst magnificent gulps, protested they were not." Joe, the "Kid" of the book's title, said that, revolution aside, they were still great writers. Another speaker responded by asking, "What the hell's that got to do with it?" The issue, he said, was not whether they wrote well "but whether they're revolutionary writers, in the working-class sense" (207–8).

Literary professionals were considerably less enthusiastic about Sandburg's politics than Victor Basinet or some of the stiffs in Joe's gang. Writing in the *Boston Transcript,* the aristocratic William Stanley Braithewaite, a leading literary tastemaker at the time, conceded that Sandburg had some lyric strengths but maintained that *Chicago* was a "book of ill-regulated speech that has neither verse or prose rhythms." The reviewer for the little magazine the *Dial,* anticipating the ploy used by a great number of Sandburg's later critics, tried to separate the truly "poetic" Sandburg from the vulgar, political Sandburg. The one who wrote "highly sensitized impressionist poems" was worthy. The other he called a "rather gross, simple-minded, sentimental, sensual man among men, going with scarcely qualified gusto through the grimy business of modern life, which, mystical mobocrat, he at once assails and glorifies" (Bradley). Conrad Aiken, writing in the *Poetry Journal,* sounding very much a schoolmaster, lectured Sandburg on proper poetic form, language, and sentiment. Similarly, though more respectfully (she had, after all, "discovered" him for the literary avant-garde), Harriet Monroe said in her *Poetry* magazine that Sandburg had tremendous talent as a poet. She was virtually silent, though, about political matters.

William Marion Reedy of *Reedy's Mirror,* writing in the *International Socialist Review*—and no doubt Sandburg approved—argued that

*Chicago* was "utterly undecorative free verse" appropriate to Chicago's environment. For him, the book was in this respect a great success: "He sings Chicago by showing us Chicago crude, cruel, vast. He damns Chicago from its own point of view, not from that of culture. He damns it with a mighty passion of seeing and saying what he sees. Imagine 'The Jungle' put into an ascetic [*sic*] form of imagism—that is 'Chicago Poems.' " Reviewing the book for the *Masses,* Louis Untermeyer, then a young socialist poet, later a famous anthologist, recognized the tendency for literary people to depoliticize Sandburg, a tendency that, among American academics, would continue well into the future. Untermeyer countered by stating orthodox left beliefs about the connection between great art and social commitment. Sandburg, he said, was both an artist of substance and a socially engaged man, a writer whose art arose from a Whitmanesque interest in democracy. This was, arguably, as balanced a judgment as any reviewer made. Printed in the pages of the *Masses,* though, it was not likely to prove persuasive to Sandburg's harsher critics because it completely missed their point. To them, poetry was supposed to be cultivated, refined, and delicate. The poet was supposed to be a superior craftsman who minded his own business—that is, the business of producing beautiful poems—and not become involved in the mundane businesses of politics and sociology.

Sandburg should have expected the more high-toned, formalistic literary critics to deplore his politics. Drawing from his own work, he could have responded with any number of quips about the art of the people, the class war playing itself out in literary wars, and so forth. Alternatively, he might simply have said that his critics were irrelevant. He wrote for the "younger, aggressive fellows," people who took their cues from *Solidarity* and the *Masses* and the *International Socialist Review.* They wrote for the bourgeoisie and, in any case, they had about as much power to shape working-class opinion as, say, Charles Ashleigh's Joe and his gang of bindle stiffs had of dragging William Stanley Braithewaite into a saloon, treating him to a bucket of steam beer, and educating him on the fine points of direct action and sabotage.

Amy Lowell, one of the grand doyennes of literary haute couture, presented Sandburg with a perfect target when she reviewed *Chicago* for the *Poetry Review.* As a Massachusetts Lowell whose brother was then president of Harvard, she was clearly of the ruling class; her literary criticism was rigorously bound by purely aesthetic considerations, or so she maintained; her poetry refused to acknowledge the vulgar and mundane. In her review, Lowell did not say anything different from other commentators: Sandburg was sometimes a gifted artist, but he was also, unfortunately, a propagandist; real poetry, of course, must be judged as poetry; and that is why so much of his work came up short. But perhaps because he thought Lowell's opinion carried more weight, Sandburg responded to her.

He did not, however, launch an assault, declaim about democratic art, or even tell her that she was irrelevant. Rather, he calmly told Lowell that, while he had a "thousand points of defense or counter-offensive against the antagonisms you voice," she had written a "pippin of a review" (*Letters* 113–14). This comment was, needless to say, curiously restrained. Was he using "pippin" ironically? Was he feinting? He said that one day he would write her a long letter laying out his arguments. Was he planning to give Lowell a piece of his mind at a later date?

# IV

## *Zigzags in Wartime*

After the publication of *Chicago,* Sandburg continued earning his living at the *Day Book* and continued to write for the *International Socialist Review.* As in his earlier *Review* pieces, the objects of his plentiful wrath continued to be capitalists, their various retainers, and union leaders who sold out their members; manly direct action continued to be urged as the only way to create meaningful social change. Following the practice he adopted in late 1915, he continued to sign his articles with pseudonyms. But he also published signed poems in the magazine. "Government" was reprinted in the May 1916 issue; "Ready to Kill" appeared in June under a silhouette showing Sandburg looking pensive but tough alongside three pictures of rotting battlefield corpses in Mexico; "Wars," printed under a Robert Minor cartoon from the *Masses* and facing a lead roundup authored by Sandburg under his pseudonym Jack Phillips, appeared in July (*ISR* 23, 25, 27).

A great deal of his venom was spent on Warren Stone and the other leaders of the western railroad brotherhoods and the sellout of arbitration, while the potential for militancy to develop in the rank and file and the possibility of the railroads being struck occasionally energized him. Month after month he flogged away at the union leaders and speculated on if and when the workers would rise up. In March 1916, as *Chicago* was being published, he succinctly put his hope in the railroad rank and file. He reported that there had been some talk of the United Mine Workers combining in a strike with the rail workers, and this set him off on a vision which, not coincidentally, printed out like a free-verse poem:

> But look at it!
> How could the combination lose?
> If the 500,000 railroad brotherhood men join hands with
> the 250,000 men of the mines, who can stop them from
> winning their demands?

The fires would be banked in thousands of factories
without coal.
Great cities would lose food supplies.
Warehouses would be stormed by mobs.

But, he added, Stone and his cronies, joined by the overlords and the
press, would probably be able to stop the combination from happening
(*ISR* 21). The pattern of the article—hope for militant action, breathless
anticipation of colossal destruction, hope dashed—repeated the pattern
he was to fall into whenever he wrote about the western rail unions
(*ISR* 24, 26: 733–35, 28: 10, 30: 138, 31, 35: 402–3, 36: 476–77, 37:
547–48, 38). In the end, early in 1917, Sandburg came to the conclusion
that, like their leaders, the rail rank and file were hopeless. The leaders
continued to believe that they could "out-talk and out-argufy and out-
speechify the railroad lawyers and managers, so as to whipsaw them into
granting the brotherhood demands." The majority of the members,
who had inherited a union built through heroic sacrifice and manly
force by the dead heroes of an earlier generation, had gone soft from
never having to fight (*ISR* 37: 548, 38: 604).

Following the *Review*'s position, Sandburg preached deliverance
through sacrifice, force, and massive direct action in nearly every one
of his articles. A conversation he reported having with Irish Republican
Army fugitive Jim Larkin about a new Chicago law that had been passed
to control police riots—"Jim had tea and we took java," he said, stressing
the difference between an Irishman and an authentic American husky—
ended with Larkin saying that capitalist laws were unnecessary because
"the working class can enforce any laws it wants" (*ISR* 20: 466). A
discussion of union negotiating tactics ended with a recommendation
to use the ultimate bargaining strategy: "Why shouldn't the working
class TAKE what it needs and wants" (*ISR* 28: 6). An article that began
by noting that during the summer of 1916 the country had come as close
to revolution as it had since the Civil War—strikes had come fast and
furiously that summer—described what would happen when workers
took to the barricades. Sandburg's vision was similar to his dream of
a coal and rail worker combination, though grander: "Get enough
strikes going in transportation, fuel, and food supply industries, and
the bottom falls out of national life. Chaos arrives. A condition results
where all the machinery of government by which the propertied class
ordinarily controls labor and drives the working class to its orders—
all that elaborate machinery of courts, police, newspapers, soldiers,

detectives, gunmen and strike-breakers—all goes to pieces" (*ISR* 30: 137). Out of chaos would come a fresh beginning. That, in short, was the core lesson to be learned. As he put it a few months later, drawing on orthodox left traditions about the golden age to come after the revolution, when the working class awoke from its slumber, there would be "rising wage scales and the shortening workday and the deepening values and valuations of man as man" (*ISR* 36: 478).

These straightforward statements about how profound social change would occur were sometimes complemented by remarks about working-class heroes, people like Matthew Schmidt, one of the convicted conspirators in the *Los Angeles Times* case, and quotations of ordinary workers.[1] But usually Sandburg was far more interested in portraying capitalist villains, and through these articles ran a stream of curses and damnations to everlasting perdition of these subhuman beasts. Every radical orator and writer had a ready stock of stories about the meanness, hypocrisy, and murderousness of famous members of the ruling class. They were homilies about the degraded, and in that regard they were deadly serious, but they were also entertainments, howlers, and thigh-slappers in which the target's false grandeur was reduced, if not obliterated. Sandburg was a good practitioner of the art, though not the best (Oscar Ameringer, the left's "Mark Twain," was unbeatable), who, when he took up a victim, usually stopped at nothing.

He had attacked some of his targets earlier. Rockefeller the younger, for instance, was regularly abused as a liar and hypocrite, as when he appeared with Warren Stone at a YMCA convention and "prattled" about settling labor disputes by remembering the doctrine of the brotherhood of man while Stone talked about settling the problems through "spiritual forces" (*ISR* 26: 735). As if he had decided to write a series of political cartoons to complement his famous poem, Sandburg turned again and again to Billy Sunday, lambasting him with glee and gusto. In his February 1916 article, the "famous bull-slinger" was burlesqued because of a recent tirade against evolution in which he had shaken his fist at a scientist and yelled, "Stand up, there, you bastard evolutionist! Stand up with the Atheists and the Infidels and the whore-mongers and the adulterers, and go to hell!" (*ISR* 20: 465–66). Another take pictured Sunday as a money-grubbing huckster who got people to pay him a "free will thank offering" for bringing them to Jesus (*ISR* 34: 2). A sermon Sunday preached to an audience of women in Kansas City produced comic outrage:

He went after the assemblage of skirts hammer and tongs and said there wasn't enough of Jesus in the lives of men and women and for that reason men with rotten diseases were infecting women with rotten diseases, and if they would all get more of Christ in their lives everything wouldn't be so rotten as it is.

At the high peak of this sermon there were fourteen women keeled over in a dead faint.

At other points in the sermon more women keeled over. A total of thirty-five (35) went down for the count, slimpsy and exhausted. The thirty-five (35) mothers and daughters were carried away in stretchers to the tabernacle emergency hospital.

He ended this humorous description on an altogether different note, issuing a war taunt: "Some day this foul-mouthed, ruthless savage whose regular game is to knock women silly with rotten talk, will get what's coming to him" (*ISR* 28: 7).

The only capitalist mentioned by Sandburg to escape his wrath was Henry Ford, labeled a "traitor" to his class, a "Man of Property" who was, surprisingly, a "Human Being" because he paid the famous wage of five dollars for an eight-hour day and had recently promised he would not call for troops if his plant was struck (*ISR* 29: 69–70). Every other was a target for his rage and cartoonist's talents. On one occasion he commented on the "world's greatest strikebreaker, Jim Waddell" and the armies of thugs he gathered to do his evil (*ISR* 32: 207). More typically, his attacks were launched against famous rulers. Robert Lincoln, chairman of the Pullman Palace Car Company's corporate board, was pilloried in terms of how his father might be reacting to his brutality: "If people ever turn over in their graves and groan after they're dead, then Abraham Lincoln surely moves his bones in the grave and wonders to God how he was ever connected with the shrimp who's the head and front of the thieving, iron-handed Pullman Co" (*ISR* 20: 467). Judge Elbert Gary, head of United States Steel, was slammed for a Rockefelleresque sermon on how capital and labor should respect each other (*ISR* 29: 73). Marshall Field III, the heir to the Chicago department store fortune, was whacked as a "cheap imitation . . . of his brainy, cunning, brutal, two-fisted fighting grandfather" (*ISR* 28: 6). John Steger, the Illinois piano manufacturer, came in for heaps of abuse. One of several such pieces Sandburg wrote in these years, the Steger take was a burlesque obituary that broke all of the taboos about treating the recently dead with respect. It began, "A Feudal lord is dead. An

American Stars and Stripes feudal lord," then described how Steger's "Twentieth Century slavies," long used to having their lives controlled in his company town, had come to pay their last respects to their master who was, though, "buried in a coffin and laid in common dirt of the earth like any one of the 1,300 slavies who are to die and be laid away." As in a number of his poems, death was here the great equalizer, the great avenger. But Steger's work, Sandburg said, would go on, carried forward by his newspaper, which would praise him as a friend of labor because he fought unions: "The local editors of his local newspaper will say that he always fought for the rights of labor, that when a strong labor union appeared, he rose like a noble gladiator and crushed it and thus preserved the right of any and every man to work without being forced into membership in an organization" ( *ISR* 28: 7–8 ).

This remark about the capitalist press was similar to others. Next to the take on Steger was a comment about the *Chicago Daily News,* run by a "Christian gentleman" named Victor Lawson, which had responded to a dynamite attack on the home of a Chicago contractor, recently acquitted of murder, with an editorial blaming the labor movement ( *ISR* 28: 6). His August roundup began with an attack on William Randolph Hearst as one of the country's great slave drivers and traitors. Sandburg indulged in some wishing thinking, saying that now "the working class has got his number" and that Hearst had "less influence in proportion to his circulation than anybody that ever printed a newspaper or magazine in this country" ( *ISR* 29: 69). Some months later, Hearst editors were lambasted for writing "daily editorial psalms of peace" about the war in Europe while their boss was trying to get the Wilson administration to invade Mexico to protect his million-acre ranch from the people's revolution ( *ISR* 36: 477). A clear indication of what he thought about the liberal press was contained in a take on the *New Republic,* then and for many years afterward a restrained, reasonable sponsor of progressive reform. The magazine had published an editorial dismissing the IWW as a social movement mired in the past, an expression of ideas appropriate to earlier times. Sandburg did not argue. Rather, he simply called the magazine a "goo-goo and a holier-than-thou" mouthpiece ( *ISR* 30: 139).

Sandburg appeared certain about the class war, certain about friends and enemies, tactics and strategy, and ultimate victory. He was considerably less certain about the other war then under way, the Great War in Europe. In earlier, pre-*Chicago* articles in the *Review*, he had begun to take notice of the home-front implications of the Great War. On one occasion in 1915, he ended a roundup with a series of short paragraphs on the war in an uncharacteristically meditative tone:

> The vast swirl of battling human atoms is not understood except by a small remnant of philosophers, poets and humorists. . . .
>
> Twenty-one million men in uniform with guns trying to kill each other. "Why?" is the one pointed word that burns in the hearts and heads of workingmen who think. It's the most terrible "Why" that has ached at their hearts in all of history.
>
> Big, easy-going men like the new mayor of Chicago say the world "has gone mad" (*ISR* 7: 72).

This was an honest statement which said he had no reasoned assessment of the war in Europe or what it meant for the class war at home. The job of a *Review* propagandist, though, was not to point to ambiguity; it was to tell readers why, what, and how to think. This Sandburg tried to do on several occasions, with thoroughly confusing results.

In 1915 and early 1916, the primary war issue that dominated left discussion was the production by American workers of matériel for use in Europe. In some respects, of course, war production was as much a boon to American workers in providing high employment and higher wages as it was to the profit margins of some American corporations; and the high employment in the early war years was also, arguably, responsible for increased labor militancy. But Sandburg saw the war at this stage in terms of moral issues. It was clear to him, he indicated in his August 1915 *Review* roundup, that American workers bore some indirect but tangible responsibility for the death and destruction in Europe. That assertion, however, led him toward little more than confusion.

In the August piece, he first asked what would happen if the American working class refused to engage in war production. Responding to a widely quoted speech by U.S. congressman Stephen G. Porter which precisely counseled that approach, Sandburg attacked pacifists like Porter. "Some of you pacifists . . . make us tired," he said, adding that "these men in the workshops whom you call murderers would have their places filled from an unemployed army if they went on strike and would be clubbed and shot if they tried to keep scabs from coming to take their jobs" (*ISR* 7: 70). Apparently, then, the working class was to continue war production so that jobs could be protected and picket line violence avoided.

Other earlier articles registered similar contradictions. Sandburg applauded as heroes two legendary European socialists who had refused to support their country's war efforts, Karl Liebknecht of Germany and George Bernard Shaw of England, but he said Victor Berger of Wisconsin, who was also resisting, was becoming a German sympathizer. The war was a grotesque evil, an orgy of murder, and profiteering American capitalists, like the German Junkers, were bloodsucking monsters, but he told American workers to use direct action tactics to see to it that they got their share of the bloody profits. Workers of all nations were killing each other, but, Sandburg claimed, the war might finally bring about international solidarity because the workers of all the nations might rise together to repudiate the war debts of their nations. "Preparedness" for American entry might by "bunk," but, then again, "Maybe it ain't." The kaiser should be fought because he suppressed free speech. In America, according to one surprising concession, there was free speech, but, still, the war was "worse in a thousand ways than any reporter had been told" and the news was censored by the American government because "it was too stinking fierce and shocking rotten to be printed" (*ISR* 7, 8, 16: 335).

Although the Great War still did not dominate his *Review* articles as it would dominate all of his work after April 1917, it cast a wide shadow over everything he said. Now, owing to the country's gearing up for entry into the war, the pervasive discussions about "preparedness," pacifism, conscription, and so forth, he was much more attentive to the war and its home-front implications than he had been earlier. Some of what he wrote about the war was a logical extension of other elements of his articles. His attacks on corporate profiteers were similar to his standard attacks on industrial despots and slave drivers (*ISR* 20: 467, 26: 736, 29: 70–71, 30: 138–39, 33: 266). Likewise, his descriptions of how workers fared at war were similar to his descriptions of how they fared in "peace." Orators might talk of the glory of war and the glamour of soldiering, but Irwin Cobb, a popular lecturer, had set the record straight in a recent Chicago speech— the men in the trenches looked like "a bunch of sewer diggers after a hard day's work in mud and water" (*ISR* 28: 5). Some might talk of men returned from the front as heroic survivors, but the returnees were likely to be crazy from the "colossal madhouse" they had witnessed (*ISR* 35: 404). Other takes stressed the human cost of the conflict, the loss of young working-class lives, the sheer insanity of the fighting.

One summarized the haunting questions that were involved for every working person:

> Why is a flag? What is a uniform? Is a soldier any use? Who wants war? Do American workingmen feeding munitions and supplies to the European armies understand that they are taking part in the war the same as the men in the trenches? Are American workingmen thinking and thinking hard and deep as to where this nation called the United States is headed? How far do we want the crazy-sickness of war to sink into the hearts and minds of the people of this country? War! war!!—br—brrr!!!! (*ISR* 30: 138).

Through the second half of 1916, preparedness discussions, demonstrations, and parades became part of the American scene. Some businesses, including Swift meat in Chicago, began to organize military companies among their workers as part of preparedness, though Sandburg claimed that they were really going to use them to crush strikes (*ISR* 26: 735–36). A huge preparedness parade was held in Chicago in early June, leading Sandburg to say that though it had been orchestrated by the city's "economic masters," what it proved was the power of the working class. Seeing the miles and miles of marchers was so inspiring that a viewer could say to himself: "Here's power! This is a human Niagara. If we can only harness this up to a solidarity of action! Look at 'em. They can tear the town down and build it again. These moving masses of mechanics and day laborers, they can pull the skyscrapers to pieces and stick up new skyscrapers any time they want to" (*ISR* 28: 9). A similar parade in Milwaukee, headed by that city's socialist mayor, led him not to reverie but, quoting Eugene Debs's disgusted remarks on the occasion, to a denunciation of the Milwaukee party's sanctioning of "bourgeois patriotism" and "betrayal of socialist principles and ideals" (*ISR* 33: 267).

There were, however, some indications during these months that Sandburg was not a wholly convinced or comfortable opponent of American participation in the war. On several occasions he wrote that Germany was a repressive state, exactly the sort of state that ought to be wiped off the face of the earth. He also repeatedly slammed American pacifists and antiwar radicals, magazines, and newspapers—William Jennings Bryan, Victor Berger, Walter Lippmann of the *New Republic*, the Hearst-owned *Chicago Tribune*—for not being sufficiently tough on the kaiser or for simply being irrelevant (*ISR* 30: 140, 33: 267, 35: 404, 20: 466, 37: 548). Furthermore, on one occasion he presented a remarkable defense of Woodrow Wilson as the man of the hour, the president who had kept the working class out of the war. Some socialist papers, Sandburg said, naming only the *Milwaukee Leader,* had grown suspicious of Wilson's intentions. But Wilson was to be trusted. He was a "peace fool instead of a war fool," and to "howl suspicions of militarism" against him was "a species of treachery to the working class that does no good" (*ISR* 29: 71).

When the United States formally declared war in early April 1917, Sandburg's brave and fulsome devotion to the left principle of opposing capitalist wars, and, as it would turn out, his devotion to most of the principles he had been proclaiming evaporated in a twinkling. With the American declaration, he abruptly did an about-face, announcing his support of the war in several straightforward, patriotic, anti-kaiser, make-the-world-safe-for-democracy comments in the *Day Book.* This was the first of several about-faces, self-repudiations, and worse that he was to do in the next couple of years, the opening episode of what was to become an extremely confusing period. His support of the war blossomed several months after his *Day Book* pronouncements, reaching an especially aggressive and destructive low point the following fall. Before that happened, though, he did a second about-face, this one on his literary front.

A year or so earlier, after he read her review of *Chicago and Other Poems,* he had written to Amy Lowell to protest that he had defenses to her charge that he sometimes wrote propagandistic verse and promised that he would someday write her a long letter. Now, in June 1917, a couple of months after his emergence as a patriot, he wrote the promised letter and followed up shortly afterward with another. He explained himself by telling Lowell about how some of his earlier political beliefs had unfortunately "crept" into his poems. He had taken another look at some "old and genuinely propaganda material of mine of ten years ago," he said, as if he were no longer thinking and writing such things— and he was probably thanking his lucky stars that he had taken to using pseudonyms in the *Review*—and now "I got a sneaking suspicion that maybe you're right and maybe I have struck a propaganda note rather than a human note at times." Lowell thought that *Chicago* had some violent moments. Sandburg responded that he did not believe in violence, that he agreed with her on the subject. What violence there was in *Chicago* should not have been taken as his own philosophy, he said. He had just been trying properly to present the "motives and character" of his human subjects, not to further the IWW cause, though he did prefer the IWW to its opponents. Sandburg also remarked that he thought Lowell and Anton Johannsen of "Dynamiter" were "really kinfolk" (*Letters* 117–18, 119–20).

Lowell recorded what Sandburg told her about his politics in her *Tendencies in Modern American Poetry*, the book she published a few months later. Sandburg, Lowell said, had once worked for the socialists in Milwaukee, but he had split with those "Parliamentary Socialists." Rehabilitation had followed, and since those early days "he has been a free lance, allied to no party, and passionately believing in the dreams of his own imagination, and in action—the action prompted by those dreams" (217).

She did not, however, give him a completely clean bill of health. She still objected to the "propaganda note" that had "crept" in. Whatever Sandburg thought of her kinship with Johannsen, "Dynamiter" still caused her to say that "propaganda is the pitfall of poets. So excellently endowed a poet as Mr. Sandburg should beware." "The Right to Grief," the poem contrasting the agony of a rich and a poor father who had lost children, brought forth a condemnation that included a remark about the "reformers" hurting their own cause (221). And she thought that, in general, Sandburg was too concerned with "entirely ephemeral phenomena": "Art, nature, humanity, are eternal. But the minimum wage will probably matter as little to the twenty-second century as it did to the thirteenth, although for different reasons" (231).

Lowell said that she only made aesthetic judgments and deplored the yoking of poetry and politics, but her preface to *Tendencies in Modern American Poetry* made it clear that she was in fact deeply involved in claiming a social purpose for literature. The war, she said, was proving to be a great event for poetry. Because the war was "welding together" all Americans into a "strenuous endeavor," Americans were claiming their nationality as never before. The "new movement" in American poetry testified to the rise of a "native school" (v). Elsewhere in her book Lowell measured the Americanness of her poets, providing genealogies for each. Edwin Arlington Robinson came of "good Anglo-Saxon stock" (10); Robert Frost was from "New England stock on his father's side and Scotch descent on his mother's" (81); Edgar Lee Masters could trace his ancestry all the way back to the American Revolution (178). Sandburg, by contrast, came from "the strong immigrant class which comes yearly in boatloads to our shores." He and his "ilk" were bringing to the country "points of view which are working so surely, if insidiously, upon the whole body of the people" (201). She of course did not explain the connection between nationalism, lineage, and aesthetics. Given the times, though, no explanations were necessary.

The war became the greatest test—of principles, of resolve, of character—yet faced by American radicals. Some, among them some of the most famous, passed with flying colors, holding to their beliefs in the face of severe repression, risking and often receiving long jail terms for speaking and acting against the war, losing careers (Giffin). Others failed the test.

For all intents and purposes, the class war on the home front accelerated and deepened with the American declaration. The IWW did not take a formal stand on the war, but by their actions and words the Wobblies clearly indicated that they did not intend to put aside their plans for revolution. Led by Emma Goldman, anarchists began to speak forcefully against the war, as did various pacifist and Christian groups. The response of the Socialist party to the declaration of war, a response that was to have a major effect on Sandburg, was immediate. Meeting in emergency session in St. Louis a few days after the declaration, two hundred delegates, led by Morris Hillquit of New York and Victor Berger of Wisconsin, after considerable parliamentary jockeying, issued a proclamation declaring the party's "continuous, active, and public opposition to the war through demonstrations, mass petitions, and all other means within our power," vowing "vigorous resistance to all reactionary measures, such as censorship of press and mails, restriction of the rights of free speech, assemblage, and organization, or compulsory arbitration and limitation of the right to strike," and pledging to resist conscription (Baritz 114–15). The Socialist Party of America, then, carried out its promise to resist capitalist war and thus joined the socialists of Italy and Serbia as the only parties which, faced with the fact of war, did not crumble into nationalistic support of the slaughter. Months later, the membership was asked to approve the St. Louis *Proclamation,* which it did overwhelmingly by a margin of 21,639 to 2,752. Remarkably, this lopsided vote took place after vicious press and government attacks on the party—Hillquit and Berger especially—as pro-German, unpatriotic, and treasonous.

Soon after the declaration of war, the government passed several emergency laws. In late April adequate financing for the war effort was addressed in the Liberty Loan Act, which called for citizens and companies voluntarily to purchase long-term bonds. In May, apparently recognizing the unpopularity of the war—in the first six months there were relatively few voluntary enlistments and some signs of mounting resistance (Weinstein)—the personnel needs of the armed services were addressed in the Selective Service Bill, which inaugurated a draft. In June the Espionage Act was passed, which made it a criminal act to speak or write against conscription or otherwise to counsel resistance to the war.

Its title implied that the Espionage Act was aimed at protecting the country from German spies, and in the hysteria following the declaration, that was, arguably, its purpose. Quickly, though, it became the government's legal instrument to stifle dissent, now, in a crucial move, defined as prima facie evidence of pro-German sympathies. The July arrest and indictment of Kate Richards O'Hare for an antiwar speech was the first indication of how the act would be used in the months and years to follow. The assault on dissent also took place on several other fronts. By midsummer, radical publications were being denied second class mailing privileges under provisions of the act. Government-supported "citizens committees," in many cases local gangs of toughs, meted out vigilante justice to dissidents. Surveillance of radicals began in earnest with increased activity by the Department of Justice's Bureau of Investigation (the predecessor of the FBI) and the new Military Intelligence Division of the U.S. Army. Meanwhile, the mainstream press poured out articles, cartoons, and editorials attacking leftists, pacifist objectors, slackers, and those who failed to meet the newly coined test of "100 percent Americanism," the same test Amy Lowell used, in somewhat more dignified language, in her book.

War hysteria, intolerance, and repression reached its first but not its final crescendo during the summer of 1917. So too did strike activity by American workers. Between April and October 1917, a new record was set for labor militancy when more than six million workdays were lost because of strikes. Industries directly or closely related to war production were among the most severely affected, with the metal trades, shipbuilding, coal mining and copper mining topping the list. Strikes by the IWW were among the fiercest and longest and, because it was involved in fully one-sixth of the April to October strikes, it seemed both to the organization and to its opponents that the Wobblies had finally come into their own. This confidence caused the IWW to step up its agitation and its rhetoric about revolution. It also caused the Wilson administration, joined by state and local authorities, to increase

84

surveillance of the organization and to begin looking to Espionage Act prosecution of Wobblies as a final solution. Acts of violence against the organization also became commonplace during the summer. The roundup of some twelve hundred Wobbly-organized copper miners in Bisbee, Arizona, and their "deportation" to the desert, where they were unceremoniously dumped from boxcars, and the early morning kidnapping of IWW organizer Fred Little from his rooming house in Butte, Montana, and his castration and hanging from a railroad trestle were dramatic illustrations of vigilante justice.

In July, Sandburg lost his bread-and-butter job with the *Day Book* when Scripps decided to close the newspaper down, apparently for reasons unrelated to the war (Scripps 209). He found work as an editorial writer for Hearst's *Chicago Evening American,* but he soon discovered that he and the job were a "mismatch" and resigned (Niven 291–92). Shortly afterward, he went to work as a labor reporter for the *Chicago Daily News* where he would stay until the early 1930s. The *Day Book* had been a lively, interesting place to earn a living, but its small distribution created limitations. With 350,000 daily sales, the *News* was the largest afternoon tabloid in the country. It was also among the very best. Its coverage of local politics was thorough and penetrating, its national and international coverage distinguished. Its book review section, published every Wednesday, stayed abreast of currents in modern literature and published many noteworthy reviews of and by Conrad Aiken, Ezra Pound, Sherwood Anderson, Louis Untermeyer, Wallace Stevens, Amy Lowell, Ben Hecht (who also worked on the paper), and the like.

But Sandburg's initial work at the *News* was in no way cultural. Very significantly, his first assignment was to cover the convention of the recently formed American Alliance for Labor and Democracy, an assignment that involved recent events within the Socialist party as well as the government's efforts to repress dissent.

When the party took its strong antiwar stand, there was, quite naturally, a vocal minority that broke with the majority and, proclaiming themselves the pro-war, loyal socialists, began a rear-guard action. Most notable among this group were some key party intellectuals: John Spargo, A. M. Simons, Phelps and Rose Pastor Stokes, Charles Edward Russell, Harry Slobodin and William English Walling. Their reasons for supporting the war were complicated. Sometimes they seemed to argue for patriotism, or at least that they were Americans first and socialists second. Sometimes they appeared to base their disagreement with the majority party position on the antipathy for Victor Berger many of them had developed in a dozen or more years of interparty squabbles. At other moments they calculated that the war issue was the place to take a stand about the fundamental direction of the party; that is, they claimed, support of the war could provide the occasion to "Americanize" the SPA by replacing the "foreign" idea of class struggle with the presumably more "native" idea of cooperating with others interested in the "democratic movement of the time." Pragmatically, they argued that the war was a fait accompli, that resistance was futile, and that it should therefore be seen as an "opportunity" for socialists. A public demonstration of socialism's Americanness could bring about new political alliances and, as a result of gratitude or clever horse-trading, advances for "democratic collectivism" and "industrial democracy."

The American Alliance for Labor and Democracy, funded by the government but professedly independent, was designed to show American Federation of Labor support of the Wilson administration's war policies. As it evolved during the summer of 1917, it also became the organization through which prominent pro-war socialists could demonstrate their loyalty. From their point of view, there were obvious gains to be made from participating in the alliance. They would be brought closer to the AFL trade unions and thus advance their program of building a new "American" socialism through cooperation with others, and they would gain credibility with the administration. From the point of view of George Creel, the real power behind the alliance as head of the administration's Committee on Public Information, the central propaganda bureau, their participation could provide major dividends. AFL backing could be expected, he reasoned, but pulling radicals into the fold would further the administration's claims that leftists were not united and that the Socialist party majority were subversives. Because of their long history of personal and ideological animosities, there was of course considerable mutual suspicion between Gompers and the socialists. But Creel controlled Gompers and the socialists with a strong hand, leaving those peculiar bedfellows little opportunity to rupture their marriage with old arguments and accusations (Grubbs 40–43, 58–71; Hendrickson; Vaughn).

Creel's hand was hidden from public view. But both Gompers and John Spargo, the spokesperson of the socialists, received detailed instructions from him on exactly how the organizing convention was to proceed and to what ends. Before the proceedings began, Creel supplied the two leaders with the wording of major resolutions which would later be reported in the national press. Lest the convention be seen as a transparent administration fix, he also provided instructions on how radical rhetoric was to be orchestrated in adopting resolutions reflecting traditional left causes and war policy alternatives. These "radical" resolutions would, presumably, steal the thunder of the antiwar left and say in effect that radicals were still, after all, radicals but that some smart radicals understood that the kaiser must be defeated if radicalism was to triumph. Totally co-opted, Gompers and Spargo fulfilled Creel's instructions to the letter. The convention dutifully passed major resolutions supporting the war as well as resolutions demanding free speech, the right of peaceful assembly, the conscription of wealth to fight the war, taxing excess war profits, and government takeovers of key industries.

Sandburg's four articles on the alliance convention were written with all the gusto and just as much attempt at objective distance as his *Review* articles denouncing capitalist exploiters and political fixers. The first article, which appeared in the *Daily News* on September 3, spoke glowingly of prospects for the convention. A "Red, White and Blue special train" had left from New York for Minneapolis, the convention site, and was due to arrive that evening in Chicago, where local labor leaders would climb aboard; the joining of radicals and AFL unionists was "smashing precedents." An alliance preconvention declaration was made the article's centerpiece by quoting a Chicago delegate who said, "We shall strip the mask from those who in the name of democracy, antimilitarism and peace are engaged in the nefarious propaganda of treachery in all that those noble words represent. We indignantly repudiate the claim that this propaganda—which, be it remembered, brings joy and comfort to the German autocracy—has the support of the labor movement of America." Sandburg predicted that the work of the alliance would help to bring about industrial democracy, then revealed the alliance slogans to his readers—"Labor and Democracy" and, more to the point of the administration's real intent, "Crush the Traitors" (*DN* 1).

His second article, a very brief one, was mostly a description of the tumultuous welcome given to the patriotic delegates by the people of Minneapolis (*DN* 2). The third started with a litany of names of delegates and their statements supporting the administration. At the end, John Spargo was given ample space to denounce the People's Council, the umbrella organization under which various antiwar groups took shelter, Morris Hillquit, who a few months later would come

87

close to winning the New York City mayoralty race, and Victor Berger. Spargo asked, according to Sandburg, "Is it possible to imagine a record which could be of more service to Germany? Could the People's Council have served the Hohenzollern dynasty better if its members had gone into the trenches to kill Belgian soldiers and into Belgian and French homes to violate Belgian and French women at the command of German officers?" (*DN* 3). In case a reader missed the point of Spargo's rhetorical questions, the *News* editors placed a cartoon next to the article. It showed a "pro-German pacifist" killing the goose of free speech with the ax of treason while the golden eggs of constitutional rights tumbled from his basket.

The final article in the convention series was a selection of human interest stories under the headline "Varied Forces Unite in Labor War League." Here Sandburg told about the alliance having brought together millionaire socialists, high church people, Zionists, and Clarence Darrow, a recently reconstructed pacifist. Sounding a bit like Amy Lowell, he also told how Winfield Gaylord and John Spargo were pure Americans: both could trace their lineage back to the Revolution, both could be members in the Sons of the American Revolution. Sandburg followed this pedigree by quoting the various convention resolutions, including the "radical" ones about the need for the government to control food prices, the need for the alliance to reach out to the revolutionary workers of Russia to create a united front, and the need to protect free speech, a free press, and free assembly.

This resolute announcement of loyalty to the First Amendment, however, contained significant caveats, for, Sandburg reported, there were distinctions to be made. Free speech was a fine ideal, but if statements "are plainly calculated to embarrass the government in the conduct of the war" or if they gave comfort to the enemy, then they should be "vigorously repressed" and harsh punishment should be meted out to the offenders (*DN* 5). After the convention, Sandburg continued writing *Daily News* articles attacking the antiwar socialists. The alliance idea of limiting the free speech rights of some people was carried forward in a postconvention article published on September 12, when, quoting pro-war socialist Charles Edward Russell's statement that in these times "I have no friends, I have no brother, I have nothing but the republic," he once again wrote approvingly about how loyal radicals wanted to restrict the free speech rights of disloyal radicals (*DN* 6). A day later he published an interview with Fred Warren, editor of the *Appeal to Reason,* the old socialist newspaper that had recently declared itself to be pro-war. The interview laid out what Warren said were the only options available to socialists and other "lovers of peace." They could choose to be antiwar, and in that event they would suffer and accomplish nothing. They could choose to be passive spectators. Or they could support the war, help to win it, and then inaugurate world socialism. Sandburg left no room for readers to wonder about which was the best course (*DN* 7). During the early fall, he also joined the alliance and very shortly thereafter made a further contribution to its work with a long patriotic poem called "The Four Brothers," distributed by George Creel to newspapers across the country.

The American Alliance invitation to the government to repress the rights of disloyal leftists was accepted even before it was formally made into an alliance resolution. For on September 5, just as the Minneapolis doings were getting under way, the Department of Justice conducted raids on IWW headquarters in Chicago and twelve other cities. Files and publications were confiscated, arrests were made, and office equipment destroyed. Warrants were also issued for the arrests of almost two hundred Wobbly leaders—the first level of leadership, the second, and then some—who were to be brought to Chicago and indicted for some ten thousand separate crimes, most of which had to do with sabotage and other efforts to stop the efficient production of war matériel. In one fell swoop, as it would turn out, to the accompaniment of the ringing rhetoric of the alliance loyalists, the beginning of the end had arrived for the Wobblies.

There is no record indicating that George Creel, Samuel Gompers, or any of the loyal socialists worked with the Department of Justice in timing the raids on the IWW to coincide with the convention. But the coincidence seems too obvious and the payoff too great to the various parties to have been the result of mere chance. As an administration insider and as the head of government propaganda production, Creel of course could have easily planned the linkage with his counterparts in the Department of Justice. Samuel Gompers, whether he knew about it beforehand or not, would have savored anything that would help to destroy the IWW; the organization had long been a thorn in his side and because of its recent successes it posed serious challenges to the AFL. The pro-war socialists, on the other hand, many of whom had been involved in the expulsion of Bill Haywood from the SPA

Executive Council in 1913, would have welcomed the destruction of the Wobblies for reasons having to do with their notion that a truly American movement needed to give up class struggle tactics. And George Creel would have understood entirely the propaganda value of having the alliance resolution come at exactly the same moment as the raids.

A day after the raids, the *News* indicated its editorial attitude toward the Wobblies and especially toward Bill Haywood when it published a cartoon titled "In the Kaiser's Gallery" on its front page. It showed Kaiser Wilhelm working on his war map, apparently planning more assaults on the Allies. On his wall were four portraits. Three were of long-familiar enemies, Ludendorff, Hindenburg, and the crown prince. The fourth was Bill Haywood, sneering.

Despite his work for the alliance, Sandburg was still a Wobbly devotee, and, remarkably, the *News* editors permitted him to have his say about Haywood and the prosecutions. On October 2, he published an interview with Bill Haywood, then behind bars in the Cook County jail. The first interview that Haywood had been allowed to give since his arrest, it was in many ways an extraordinary piece for a mainstream newspaper to publish at the time and, as well, one which demonstrated that what he now felt about the Socialist party had nothing to do with his feelings about the Wobblies.

Sandburg's entirely sympathetic Big Bill appeared "through the square holes of the steel slats" of the "cage door" of his cell. He was calm and collected, speaking in "the voice of a man who sleeps well, digests what he eats, and requires neither sedatives to sooth him nor stimulants to stir him up." Addressing the ten thousand IWW crimes alleged in the government indictment, he spoke "with the massive leisure of Hippo Vaughn pitching a shutout." He manfully denied all the charges. The IWW, he said, was not antiwar. Its strikes were for better wages, not to interfere with the war effort (and not, apparently, to create revolution either). It was not against conscription. Some of its members had registered for the draft; some were already serving. Sandburg reminded Haywood of some of the particulars contained in the indictment, instances of sabotage, burning wheat fields, destroying machinery, and so forth. More denials followed. The impression the interview left for *News* readers was that Haywood and the Wobblies were guilty only of serving the working class, which, as Haywood noted, was suffering from severe wartime inflation. And, like the true man he was, Haywood asked for nothing from his accusers except that the "other boys" in jails across the country should be brought to the Cook County jail. "We'd like to have them from all over the country together here," he said. "It would be homelike for us all to be together" (*DN* 8).

The next Sandburg piece on the IWW the *News* printed was even more remarkable. "Sabotage 'Knockout Drops' for Industry: I.W.W. Leaders So Define Word Used in a Different Sense by Zimmerman" took up the "real" meaning of the word *sabotage* to teach readers that German tactics and Wobbly tactics were altogether different. Sandburg treated the word poetically, saying that it was "one of the mystic and many faced words of our speech," that "it is like those other words 'democracy,' 'liberty,' 'poetry.' " Zimmerman, the foreign secretary of Germany, had used the word one way when he gave instructions for the destruction of railways and munitions plants in Canada and the United States. The IWW, though, according to Sandburg, did not use sabotage to destroy but only to cripple industry and, more usually, only meant that workers should slow down on the job. Wobbly sabotage (which never happened anyway, according to the Haywood interview) was, therefore, not violent. It was simply a tactic for labor to secure a better living (*DN* 9).

None of this was new. The Wobblies, when pressed about the issue, had been saying these same things for years, without impressing very many observers. But for the editors of the *News* it was too much. Two days later, they published "Defining Sabotage" as their lead editorial. Thoroughly rejecting the attempt to relieve the word of "some of the odium now attached to it," refusing to acknowledge that sabotage was ever innocently employed, and thereby repudiating their own reporter's article, the editors maintained that sabotage was always murderous and destructive. It was always "heavily overcast with crime" and "the salve of smooth words will not serve to beautify its foul and malicious countenance." Why the editors hadn't killed Sandburg's story before it was printed is not clear, though an educated guess can be made that after it was published they heard a good deal of protest from the Department of Justice and the various surveillance agencies which, as Sandburg himself would learn before long, were very active in Chicago at the time.

Logically, the changes recorded in his private correspondence with Amy Lowell and, more to the point, in his public support of the war and the American Alliance for Labor and Democracy should have caused

Sandburg to stop writing for the *International Socialist Review* or, alternatively, should have caused the editors of the magazine to fire him. But logic (among other things) did not prevail. Jack Phillips took on a life of his own, did not participate in his master's dissembling, faking, and feinting, and continued as a *Review* writer, producing articles in which, among other themes, he attacked the government for its persecution of the Wobblies, argued that the war should be supported not for patriotic or any other conventional reasons but because it promised to lead to a worldwide working-class revolution, and saw the overthrow of the czar by Russian workers in the spring of 1917 and then the Bolshevik Revolution of October as portents of the wondrous world to come. For their part, the *Review* editors, who must have known about Sandburg's pro-government activities, recorded no hesitation in publishing his offspring Jack Phillips, perhaps because Sandburg's virulent attacks on the pro-war socialists were compatible with their own distrust of Berger and the party's right wing and center.

In an August statement, the editors laid out their theories of the war and its potential results as well as their understanding of the repression of radicals. Avoiding the question of the correct left position, which may also help further to explain why they continued publishing Sandburg, they instead discussed what they called "The Great Issue," whether "when the war does end, it will end with the working class of the world strong enough to stop future wars, and to demand and take control of the processes of production." They noted the recent events in Russia, the workers' revolt in Germany, the financial panic in France, the rise of the liberal David Lloyd George in England, and the recent growth of the IWW "by leaps and bounds." All of these happenings implied, they claimed, that the paradise of American capitalism might soon be a "Paradise Lost," for the United States government was in the process of becoming a huge employer and that would lead to socialism and a new world order. The other major issue touched upon in this editorial, the government's repression of radicals, produced a similarly sanguine statement. Like every other radical magazine and newspaper that did not pitch in with the government, the *Review* had begun to come under pressure soon after the Espionage Act was passed, but, inexplicably, the editors maintained that censorship and repression were "annoying but not dangerous."

Jack Phillips anticipated the *Review*'s editorial position on the war by a few months, arguing consistently that the war might be a grand opportunity for the working class. He, of course, understood that the working class would make sacrifices, that workers who fought would suffer and die, and that there would be hardship on the home front. But then there were the wonderful things that workers—the ones who were still alive or unmaimed, he should have added—would get in return. Phillips typically phrased his thoughts as questions. If the federal government took emergency control of food supply and distribution, would it "hand back to the meat and bread lords the same powers which they had when the war started" or retain control when the war ended? If the war needed to be financed by billions of dollars, "Will the money and property of the possessing class be confiscated with a direct ruthlessness?" Those questions were asked in May (*ISR* 39). In June, Phillips became even more visionary when he wrote about the potential of the war to bring about "socialization of the food supply of the world." He conceded that such thoughts were perhaps "the dream of a rarebit fiend and a pipe smoker." But that did not prevent him from carrying his notions to their nether limits in his July article, when he asked, "Will the chaos of this war result in any situation where the government or military power will co-operate with the working class of the nation toward throwing off the yoke of industrial oppression?" (*ISR* 42).

Entertaining these wild possibilities in June and July was a direct result of recent events in Russia, specifically the spring revolution that had overthrown the czar and installed the short-lived provisional government of the Mensheviks. In June, Sandburg published a lead article in the *Review* titled "The Russian Revolution." Though it consisted almost totally of news reports quoted from Isaac Don Levine of the *New York Tribune,* he indicated his recognition of the great possibilities when he remarked in his introduction that "the one fact which stands head and shoulders above all others is that organized labor, hand in hand with the Social Revolutionists, precipitated the revolution which overthrew Czarism in spite of the Duma." That same month, quoting Georges Clemenceau, the former prime minister of France, as his authority, Jack Phillips claimed that the revolution had occurred precisely because of the war so the idea of the conflict as a great opportunity for radicals was no longer just a theory. More important, the defeat of the Romanoffs by the Russian workers might, he dreamed, be like the coming defeat of U.S. Steel by American workers. The Russian workers had awaited their opportunity, then an "enormous, volcanic explosion of revolution" had occurred, and they had been delivered from centuries of oppression. The news, he said, "fairly trembles, glitters, and coruscates with the chaos" of what was going on (*ISR* 41, 42: 742–43). A month later, again with sketchy information, he reported on strikes and agitation in Germany. Perhaps, he remarked, what millions of socialists had hoped for since Marx and Engels, a worldwide revolt, was now actually happening. Perhaps, also, the reports of battlefield fraternizing between German and Russian soldiers were true, perhaps the war was about to end because the working classes had rediscovered their kinship. Again, he used highly charged poetic language to describe his feelings. There was "an incalculable magic of suggestion" about the reports from Europe. Anything was possible. But he was not entirely a visionary. The July article included a comment in an entirely different vein:

> "See the World," said the recruiting sign.
> And the hungry young workman eager for adventure walked in, passed the exam, and became an enlisted man in the United States army.
> Now he is with Pershing's corps on the western battlefront.
> They will be shot off the horizon and form a pyramid of skulls.
> They will never understand just what the recruiting sign meant by "See the World" (*ISR* 43).

At least here there was a willingness to confront the meaning of the war in more realistic terms.

Unlike the *Review* editors and unlike Carl Sandburg of the American Alliance, Jack Phillips understood how radicals, especially the Wobblies, would be hurt by government repression. In September, as Sandburg hatcheted the pro-war socialists in the *Daily News,* Jack Phillips reacted to the Bisbee "deportations" and the Fred Little lynching of the previous month. His theme was the unfairness of the attacks on the Wobblies, who he pictured as fighters for democracy and enemies of German autocracy, and the silence of the nation's press—the *Chicago Tribune,* the Hearst papers, the *Los Angeles Times,* and the Associated Press— about war profiteering corporations. Those hypocritical patriots, Phillips said, because they paid less than subsistence wages, were responsible for the "human deterioration" that aided the kaiser. His seething anger at the situation was apparent in every line of the article, reaching a pinnacle in the obituary of Harrison Gray Otis, the owner of the *Los Angeles Times,* he included near its end. Death, the great leveler, had come to seize Otis, the "slave-driver and advocate of slavery—dictatorial and foul-mouthed champion of industrial kaiserism and czarism—death came at last and took Harrison Gray Otis with the same peculiar silent certainty that it takes a wop or a hunky or a rag-head." If there was no justice, this suggested, then we could at least look forward to death's triumph and curse our enemies as they crossed the bar (*ISR* 45).

There were limitations to how far Sandburg could go in using the *Daily News* to boost the fortunes of the Wobblies. There were even greater limitations at the *International Socialist Review,* because by October, although the magazine still existed, which is more than could be said for most other left organs, it did so just barely. Earlier, the editors had announced that "censorship and repression are annoying but not dangerous." They soon learned otherwise. For unspecified reasons the July issue was ruled unmailable by the postal authorities, and they permitted mailing of the August issue only after the editors agreed to delete some paragraphs from a book review written by the French writer Romain Rolland, which, ironically, had been published earlier in the *Chicago Daily News.* The editors tried the tactic of avoiding the postal authorities and the inevitable delays or declarations of unmailability that followed the submission of issues for inspection by using expensive express delivery companies to get the magazines to subscribers. But even that expedient failed when the Espionage Act was extended to prohibit the express companies as well as newsdealers from handling publications that had not been judged mailable. As indicated by the reduced size of the magazine, the quality of its layout, the use of reprints in place of fresh articles, the issuing of a double number, and so forth, it was soon clear that the *Review* had become another victim of government censorship and was about to fold. It did so in February 1918.

A desperate, funereal tone characterized Sandburg's last several contributions, beginning with Jack Phillips's September remarks on the Wobbly persecutions and his seething obituary of Harrison Gray Otis. In that same issue, Sandburg's poem "Grass" was reprinted from the avant-garde *Seven Arts* magazine. Here, wartime deaths, whether at Austerlitz, Waterloo, Gettysburg, Ypres, or Verdun, meant nothing except that the grass grew in those places again. Far from being preludes to revolution, war deaths had been forgotten by everybody in the past and would be in the future. "Shovel them under and let me work," said the grass. "I cover all" (*ISR* 44; *Poems* 136). In the October *Review,* there was another reprint of "Government," in the context of late 1917 more pointedly cynical than ever (*ISR* 46). The combined November-December issue, showing all the signs of editorial wear and tear, reprinted Sandburg's early October *Daily News* interview with Bill Haywood, though with a couple of significant changes: the last several paragraphs of the *News* version were lopped off and a new paragraph substituted, with Haywood now saying that "not a dirty German dollar has ever come into our hands" and "before the war ever started we were in favor of slashing the Kaiser's throat." This reprint served as a lead into the following anonymous piece, an appeal for money for the IWW defense, which, stylistically, sounded much like Jack Phillips. Following this piece, according to the table of contents, there was to be a Sandburg poem titled "Knucks," but for some reason the poem was pulled and the table of contents not modified. Instead of "Knucks," a piece of gallows humor was laid in, an announcement of a "Grand Entertainment" to be given by the Wobbly "Class War Prisoners" at the Cook County jail, complete with a list of songs, skits, and recitations. This piece was not even typeset; rather, it was a photo reproduction of a manuscript done in Sandburg's unmistakable handwriting (*ISR* 47, 48).

In January and again in February, as the *Review* was shutting down, there were two more Jack Phillips pieces on the ordeal of the Wobblies, whose mass trial in Chicago was about to get under way. Both spoke angrily about the IWW's tormentors, especially the Department of Justice, in much the same manner as earlier articles. But in the January piece, titled "Haywood of the I.W.W.," there was a new theme. Bill Haywood was now said to be similar to the Civil War era's John Brown. Brown had dreamed of freeing the chattel slaves, Haywood of freeing the wage slaves. Haywood's prosecution was just like the prosecution of the martyred John Brown after his Harpers Ferry raid on a government arsenal. John Brown was remembered in the famous marching song, and so too, Phillips predicted, would Haywood be remembered (*ISR* 49, 50). Here, through the use of a broad historical analogy, was a new way of understanding what was happening. It could obviously not be explored further in the pages of the *Review* or in the *Daily News*. In some important respects, though, this new way of understanding events became a central subject of *Cornhuskers*, the second volume of poetry Sandburg was working on through late 1917 and early 1918 as he went through the turmoil of the first several months of American engagement in the Great War.

Sometime during that period he wrote "Chicago Poet," a short poem that, without dealing with specific events, wryly contemplated questions of self-identity and authenticity. "Chicago Poet" had the speaker looking into a mirror, discovering his image, saying, "Hello, I know you," and immediately realizing that "I was a liar to say so." The poem went on to characterize the man in the mirror and his relationship to the speaker:

> Ah, this looking-glass man!
> Liar, fool, dreamer, play-actor,
> Soldier, dusty drinker of dust—
> Ah! he will go with me
> Down the dark stairway
> When nobody else is looking,
> When everybody else is gone.

Such a self-appraisal, especially the line "Liar, fool, dreamer, play-actor," might very well have yielded self-disgust, or a resolution to discover an authentic self, or even, perhaps, a statement about a need for rest and therapy. But Sandburg had none of those conventional responses. Rather, in its last few lines "Chicago Poet" became conventionally Whitmanesque. The speaker and the double in the mirror joined together in a line echoing a moment of manly comradeship in Whitman's "Song of Myself," the Sandburg version reading "He locks his elbow in mine / I lose all but not him" (*Poems* 101). Like Whitman, whose spirit loomed and occasionally danced behind much of *Cornhuskers,* this verse seemed to say that the Chicago poet would live in his multiple identities and travel on.

# V

# *Heartland Poet, Overseas Correspondent, Suspect*

I n 1917 and early 1918, while he zigged and zagged through his multiple identities as patriotic supporter of the war, opportunistic supporter, anti-Socialist party hatchet man for the American Alliance and *Daily News,* well-behaved poet, apologist for the Wobblies, and *Review* propagandist, Sandburg was conducting relationships with literary figures such as Amy Lowell, Robert Frost, Ezra Pound, Alice Corbin Henderson, Sherwood Anderson, and Louis Untermeyer and was also putting together a second volume of poetry. Not surprisingly, *Cornhuskers,* sent off to Alfred Harcourt in May 1918, was of a piece with his varied political work of the period, that is, full of contradictory though somewhat more subtle positions and desires. Thematically, it contained poems about the urban masses and poems expressing faith in the "people," but then its clearest center of interest, expressed in the title section, "Cornhuskers," was the rural, harmonious, wholesome, and apolitical folk culture of the American prairies. In its other main topic, the Great War, the book was similarly conflicted, containing poems expressing absolute support for American engagement and others expressing far less enthusiasm. There were, however, unifying elements in *Cornhuskers.* It was written in an assertive, clear, mature voice. It was replete with Sandburg's proclamations that as a Whitmanesque poet he was multiple, omniscient, and able to reconcile opposites and contradictions. It was full of mainstream viewpoints that reflected wartime (and, as they would develop, postwar) political and social realities.

Sandburg as the poet of the urban working class was not entirely absent from *Cornhuskers,* however, for approximately a quarter of the one hundred or so poems in the book could have fit into the title section of *Chicago and Other Poems.* "Always the Mob," "Cartoon," and "Testament" essentially recapitulated earlier statements of faith in the masses. Wide-angle views of smoky urban landscapes were provided in "Slants at Buffalo, New York" and "Joliet." Two poems, "Leather Leggings" and "Prayers of Steel," explored the power of new technologies. The rich came in for Sandburg's usual treatment in "Legends," "Lawyer," "Southern Pacific," and "Ashurnatsirpal III." "Cool Tombs" restated the theme of death the leveler. Workers and working-class culture were portrayed in "Washerwoman," "Portrait of a Motorman," "Girls in a Cage," "Singing Nigger," "Psalm," "Horses in Rain," "Near Keokuk," "Summer Shirt Sale," and "Bricklayer Love."

Many if not all of these poems, it can be surmised, were of *Chicago* vintage. When Alfred Harcourt accepted that book, he had told Sandburg that cuts would have to be made but that "very likely most of these we would suggest omitting from the volume could find a place in the later volumes which, with the public favor, we would both want to do." Other letters also indicate that just before the publication of *Chicago*, Sandburg was trying to include poems that Harcourt had not seen before; at one point, Sandburg sent him three but Harcourt said, "I think I should save them for the next collection." A few days later Harcourt acknowledged receiving "Lawyer," and several weeks later, after *Chicago* was published, Harcourt said he had received another Sandburg manuscript (CS Coll: Holt folder 1, March 14 and June 8, 1916). The insights that arise from a knowledge of this correspondence go beyond explaining the appearance of urban working class poems in a volume of poetry such as *Cornhuskers*. The correspondence also suggests that at least some of the redundancy that characterizes Sandburg's poetry as a whole may have been the result of his apparently having written so much poetry in his extremely productive 1914–17 period and an editorial decision to save the redundant poems for later issue. Furthermore, a recent collection of previously unpublished Sandburg poems, *Billy Sunday and Other Poems,* indicates that not everything he sent to Harcourt in the *Chicago* manuscript was later used in collections like *Cornhuskers.* Many of the poems included in the new volume—for example, "God's Children," another poem about Billy Sunday, "The Eastland," in which Sandburg took up the sinking of that ship in much the same manner as he had in his 1915 *Review* article, three antiwar poems, and four poems about African Americans—could also have easily found a place in one of the early collections. At least two others were written in the 1920s.

In any case, though there were thematic connections between some poems in *Cornhuskers* and some in *Chicago,* there were also details that indicated Sandburg's growth, especially his development of a degree of ironic distance and reservation, wryness and bemusement, if not downright skepticism about these subjects. "Cartoon," for instance, written in an uncharacteristic epigrammatic style and containing surreal elements, introduced a sense of complexity about the masses as well as some parody of himself as a cartoonist (*Poems* 112). Poems such as "Washerwoman" and "Portrait of a Motorcar," the former a portrait of a woman who sings of Jesus washing her sins away, the latter a portrait of a trolley motorman who conflates his "gray-ghost eagle car" with his dreams of "women in red skirts and red sox" (*Poems* 106), surely one of the earliest instances of male confusions of motorcars and sex in American literature, registered psychological ironies and complexities of a new sort. The most significant development in these poems about urban workers and the masses, though, was Sandburg's relative silence on the ideology of social change. No proponents of revolutionary direct action raised their voices, no Promethean working-class hero promised or implied revolution.

In the thematically related poems of *Chicago* there had been a general tone of expectancy. Here, however, the tone alternated between ironic bemusement and flat hopelessness. One of the most accomplished poems in the volume, "Memoir of a Proud Boy," demonstrated this point almost too well. The elegiac "Memoir" was about one of Sandburg's friends, Don MacGregor.[1] It recounted MacGregor's exploits during the class warfare that had erupted in Ludlow, Colorado in 1913 and how as a result of the publicity ("As a home war / It held the nation a week," Sandburg commented sardonically) there had been a near uprising of "one or two million men" (another sardonic comment if read as the arithmetic of real power in the class war), it told of his devotion to the working class and of his only mother being Mother Jones, and it ended its consideration of MacGregor's labor experience with a remark on how he had been indicted for murder by a grand jury playing out the infamous Colorado brand of justice, his flight to Mexico, and his participation in the revolution in that country. Then the "Memoir" became despairing. MacGregor had been shot and killed in a nameless Mexican town by three Carranzistas. A local boy had tried to keep the pigs away from his body, and then, further dishonoring him, "The Villa men buried him in a pit / With twenty Carranzistas." With unrelieved despondency, Sandburg commented on how MacGregor's death could be exploited by the sentimentalizing mass media, made, for instance into a Griffith "movie to fetch sobs" or a couple of melodramatic lines by a hack for the Hearst papers. Sandburg provided no reassurance of the meaningfulness of MacGregor's death such as could be found in traditional elegies. Rather, the poem ended on still another note of loss. MacGregor had been a writer of promise as well as a revolutionary, but he had left nothing of his creative work. "Somewhere in Chihuahua or Colorado," Sandburg said, "Is a leather bag of poems and short stories" (*Poems* 103–4).

Though some of its details were drawn from a slightly earlier period, "Proud Boy" accurately reflected Sandburg's despondency regarding the wartime misfortunes of the left. In its outlook, its sense of possibilities for social change in the United States, if not in Russia, it was of a piece with his Jack Phillips articles in the final issues of the *International Socialist Review.* As he was putting together the manuscript of *Cornhuskers* in the spring of 1918, no more hopeful events unfolded to modify this outlook. Indeed, the most prominent political and labor event of that spring, the trial of the IWW leaders in Chicago, could have yielded only deeper gloom. In February, Sandburg had written one *Daily News* article about the impending trial in which he reported on the defense's effort to picture the government's case as "stupid" because the IWW really supported the war effort and, furthermore, that the organization should be left alone because it was opposed to military autocracy in any form and because "no American organization is more in sympathy with the bolsheviki in Russia and European labor organizations in particular" (*DN* 13). This article was reprinted in the Wobbly press ("Prosecution Stupid"). He also apparently covered the trial for the *Daily News,* though none of the newspaper's many stories carried his byline. Political and labor events hardly improved in the months after *Cornhuskers* was sent off. Violent attacks by citizens' councils on war dissenters and others continued, and he reported on a spate of these in Minnesota (*DN* 18, 19). One of the major symbolic events of the period occurred on June 30, when Eugene Debs was arrested for an anticonscription speech he had given in Canton, Ohio. Debs's trial began on September 9 and ended with his conviction for violating the Espionage Act and the imposition of a long jail term. A couple of months after Debs's arrest, Judge Kenesaw Mountain Landis handed down his decisions in the IWW trial. Few had doubted that the Wobblies would be convicted, but the long jail terms that Landis imposed were surprising to most commentators. Under these circumstances, despondency was a reasonable emotional outlook, perhaps the *only* reasonable outlook.

But as the opening section from which the book's title was taken, and as its closing section of war poems called "Shenandoah" suggested, *Cornhuskers,* which Sandburg said he had tried to make "very American" (Niven 305), was not primarily engaged with labor issues. This could be seen dramatically in its first pages. Like *Chicago and Other Poems, Cornhuskers* began with an overview. Here, though, it was not the meaning and value of the brawling, lusty workers' city that concerned Sandburg but the meaning and value of the heartland, the other America, which he emptied of its contemporary and past radicalism. "Prairie," like "Chicago," was an attempt at capturing the spirit of place. It was at times geological, with references to how the land was formed, at times anthropological, with references to history before white settlement. The prairie was said to be timeless, preexisting the cities and bound to exist long after the cities decayed. It was history's ultimate witness, speaking (for Sandburg let the land mass speak as a person) of what it had seen across time. It was the great philosopher of war, removed from human pain, able grandly to transform the ugly into the beautiful:

> I last while old wars are fought, while peace broods
> mother-like,
> While new wars arise and the fresh killings of young men.
> I fed the boys who went to France in great dark days.
> Appomattox is a beautiful word to me and so is Valley
> Forge and the Marne and Verdun.
> I who have seen the red births and the red deaths
> Of sons and daughters, I take peace or war, I say
> nothing and wait.

And when it wasn't talking philosophy and history, it was providing beautiful sunrises, sunsets, sweet days, natural abundance, settled ways, familiar sights, and people who did not ask a great deal from life:

> A wagonload of radishes on a summer morning.
> Sprinkles of dew on the crimson-purple balls.
> The farmer on the seat dangles the reins on the rumps
> of dapple-gray horses.
> The farmer's daughter with a basket of eggs dreams of
> a new hat to wear to the county fair.
>
> On the left- and right-hand side of the road,
> Marching corn—
> I saw it knee high weeks ago—now it is head high—
> tassels of red silk creep at the ends of ears.

It was, in short, everything.

Over the years, Sandburg had consistently alluded to Walt Whitman as a great poet and a great democrat and, on occasion, Whitman's long lines and other devices obviously influenced his own verse. In this respect, he was not unusual. Early twentieth-century left culture in the United States and Europe discovered in Whitman a sympathetic predecessor at the least (some, including Horace Traubel, claimed more, that is, that Whitman had indeed been a true socialist). Allusions to Whitman's broad humanity, hopefulness, empathy with the downtrodden, and so forth, were constant in left discourse, and Whitman's influence on left poets such as Arturo Giovannitti, James Oppenheim, and Vachel Lindsay was transparent. Writing in 1915, Floyd Dell put the point succinctly, remarking that Whitman "seems to have been accepted by Socialists as peculiarly their poet. In the library of the ordinary 'local' he stands on the shelf not far from Karl Marx." Dell's claim, though, was that in his emphasis on the emotions rather than intellect and passion rather than reason, Whitman was in reality an antisocialist. But, Dell said, he was still worth reading and was an "honorary member of the party" because his work fulfilled basic human needs.

"Prairie" was Sandburg's most Whitmanesque poem to date, though the Whitman involved was, as in *Cornhuskers* generally, more like Dell's "antisocialist" Whitman than the one celebrated in traditional left culture. Throughout "Prairie," as in Whitman, there were lengthy catalogs of scenes and people. It was laced with echoes of some of Whitman's most famous motifs and phrasings, so much so that at times it seemed more a pastiche than an original. The lines about Appomattox and the other battle names being "beautiful" words echoed one of the refrains of "Song of Myself," in which Whitman announced again and again for the beautiful in the ugly, the wondrous in the mundane, the equality of the unequal. Lines addressing the reader with "Have you seen" or "Have you heard" exactly echoed Whitman's phrasings as he introduced his readers to his catalogs of American scenes. A stanza of "Prairie" began "Out of prairie-brown grass crossed with a streamer of wigwam smoke— out of a smoke pillar, a blue promise—out of wild ducks woven in greens and purples," and used the identical "Out of" in its last line. This pattern duplicated both the rhythm and the refrain of Whitman's elegy for Lincoln: "Out of the cradle endlessly rocking, out of the mocking bird's throat, the musical shuttle." A Sandburg line began "A thousand red men cried and went away to new places for corn and women," echoing another Whitman passage. Near the end of "Song of Myself" Whitman shook hands with men of the distant future; Sandburg said, "To a man across a thousand years I offer a handshake." Whitman was son and brother to everything. Near the close of "Prairie," using one of Whitman's favorite "folk" words, "hanker," Sandburg proclaimed:

> O, prairie mother, I am one of your boys.
> I have loved the prairie as a man with a heart shot
>   full of pain with love.
> Here I know I will hanker after nothing so much as
>   one more sunrise or a sky moon of fire doubled to a
>   river moon of water

and followed it up with "I speak of new cities and new people" (*Poems* 79–85).

None of the other twenty-one poems in the title section was as cosmic as "Prairie." Rather, these shorter poems focused on the vernacular landscape of the Midwest, emphasizing the local, the particular. Here Sandburg celebrated the beauty of the natural life of the heartland and the traditional, settled lives of the human inhabitants in some of the most imagistically subtle, fluid pieces he had written to date. "River Roads" enumerated the qualities of passing crow, woodpecker, and redwinged blackbird, leading to a conclusion in which a human being's presence, "a woman's shawl on lazy shoulders," was impressionistically caught (*Poems* 85–86). "Prairie Waters by Night" struck a counterpoint with the "shoulders of the running water" flowing across russet stones while willows "drowse" to the accompanying "low laughter of a red moon" (*Poems* 86). In "Early Moon," the lunar imagery was carried forward to conjure the Native American past. Here, what Sandburg called "The baby moon, a canoe, a silver papoose canoe" led to conventional images of the Indian past (*Poems* 86). "Laughing Corn" pictured the winds rustling the yellow corn and concluded with a down-home image of prairie life, a white farmhouse in which "The farmer and his wife talk things over" (*Poems* 87). In "Autumn Movement" and "Falltime" there were images of sweet abundance, yellow cornflowers metaphorically "a scarf at the neck of the copper sunburned woman," the golds of straw and moon, the blues of thistle and larkspur, and "Tomatoes shining in the October sun with red hearts" (*Poems* 87–88). "Illinois Farmer" noted how a man was laid to rest in the soil he worked, under the winds he had listened to during his life (*Poems* 88). "Hits and Runs" recorded the memory of watching a small-town baseball game that went on for sixteen innings, "Village in Late Summer" caught the torpor of dog days, "Still Life" had the speaker recording bits of Americana—hayfields, horses hitched in front of a village post office, a barnyard full of Holsteins—from the observation car of a train. It opened up other dimensions of prairie life in its last line: "A signalman in a tower, the outpost of Kansas City, keeps his place at a window with the serenity of a bronze statue on a dark night when lovers pass whispering" (*Poems* 90). "Band Concert" recorded a small town evening filled with gigglers, girls in white dresses, and "crushed strawberries of ice cream soda places" (*Poems* 90–91). "Alix" recorded a horse race with "the grand stand jammed with prairie people yelling themselves hoarse. Almost the grand stand and the crowd of thousands are one pair of legs and one voice standing up and yelling hurrah" (*Poems* 94–95).

Although the poems in the title section of *Cornhuskers* sometimes seemed like the result of a self-conscious vacation, a home-front rest and relaxation period, there were, especially near its end, intrusions of the more conflicted world beyond the heartland. In "Sunset from Omaha Hotel Window," the speaker noted in passing that the dusk of that city was "bitter" as was Kenosha's and Chicago's (*Poems* 89–90). At the end of "Localities" there was a quick comment on people the speaker knew, including some who "are not on payrolls anywhere," whose "mothers are through waiting for them to come home." In "Three Pieces on the Smoke of Autumn" the meditation of the speaker was interrupted by a parenthetical comment on the war in Europe: ("A newspaper in my pocket says the Germans pierce the Italian line; I have letters from poets and sculpters in Greenwich Village; I have letters from an ambulance man in France and an I.W.W. man in Vladivostok") (*Poems* 93–94). In "Manitoba Childe Roland" there was a brutal metaphor remembering the war: "And as the shuttling automatic memory of man clicks off its results willy-nilly and inevitable as the snick of a mouse-trap or the trajectory of a 42-centimeter projectile" (*Poems* 98–100). But in their contexts these were only passing remarks, oblique reminders of hardship and death. As if to reassure himself and his readers of the steadfastness of the folk culture, Sandburg had a fellow traveler provide an apparent summation of the attitude toward the world's evil. In "Caboose Thoughts," an ordinary man who nonetheless knew things of importance spoke with the wisdom and faith of the ages: "It's going to come out all right—do you know? / The sun, the birds, the grass—

they know. / They get along—and we'll get along" (*Poems* 93–94). In the broadest sense, this was what could be learned in the heartland.

Were the sentiments of the "Cornhuskers" section the result of Sandburg's recent transformation into a patriot, was he here reinventing himself as kin to Whitman's "good grey poet," was he duplicating the spirit and content of the representation of the wholesome American folk in a good many Liberty Bond posters? To some extent, each of these elements was probably involved. But there was a larger context as well. As two recent historical studies suggest, none of the sentiments found in "Cornhuskers" should be seen as peculiar to Sandburg. Both Michael Kammen's *Mystic Chords of Memory: The Transformation of Tradition in American Culture* and John Bodnar's *Remaking America: Public Memory, Commemoration, and Patriotism in the Twentieth Century* argue convincingly that in the later decades of the nineteenth century and the earlier decades of the twentieth century, cresting after the Great War, the American "memory" of history was thoroughly metamorphosed. Read in this context, "Cornhuskers" becomes far clearer than it would be otherwise. Bodnar's analysis of the development in the Midwest as in other regions of a history celebrating local people and the natural landscape of "prairies, woodlands, cornfields, and small towns" as part of an effort to assert the uniqueness of the region and to foment regional pride (Bodnar cites Sandburg as a primary illustration) applies to the poems directly (121–22). Shortly after *Cornhuskers* was finished, Sandburg commented on this agenda for American literature, writing in a *Daily News* review of a collection of plays produced by Zona Gale and Laura Sherry of the Wisconsin Players of Milwaukee, "In the soil and people of America is the material out of which plays can be made as true to this country as are the 'Noh' plays to Japan and certain heavy inarticulate dramas to Russia" (*DN* 17). Kammen's discussion of the multiple means by which "tradition" and "memory" were transformed in the years after World War I is equally applicable. The period's fascination with "folk" culture was, beginning with "Cornhuskers," reflected throughout Sandburg's later work. The manner in which "Americana" was collected by antiquers and curators was reflected in Sandburg's own collecting of songs for *The American Songbag* and in his deep interest in Lincolniana. The period's interest in "tourism" and "seeing America first" was mirrored in what became a characteristic narrative strategy of Sandburg's poetry, as in "Cornhuskers," *Slabs of the Sunburnt West, Good Morning, America,* and parts of *The People, Yes.* And as Kammen himself recognizes, Sandburg ultimately played a central role in the period's invention of Abraham Lincoln as perhaps the major American folk hero (417).

Sandburg did not begin his books on the great president until the early 1920s, but Lincoln and, more so, the Civil War were sometimes part of the "memory" of *Cornhuskers,* its way of understanding the present through the past. In one poem, Sandburg used Lincoln to comment on violence. "Knucks," the poem that had been announced in the table of contents of one of the last issues of the *International Socialist Review* and been replaced by the gallows humor of the mock playbill of the "Hold the Fort" entertainment to be held in the Cook County jail by the IWW class warfare prisoners, commented on the destruction of the legacy of Abraham Lincoln and the ubiquitousness of violence in American life. It began with a description of Springfield, "Abraham Lincoln's city," and then presented a short narrative about the speaker going into a local store whose owner, Mister Fischman, sells a "carload" of cast-iron knucks every month. The speaker tries on a pair, thinks, "Mister Fischman is for Abe and the 'malice to none' stuff," and goes on to enumerate how everybody on all sides of the current issues is "for Abe and the 'malice to none' stuff" (*Poems* 121–22).[2] "Knucks" was restricted to ironic commentary on rhetorical gestures about Lincoln as opposed to social realities. In "Shenandoah," the final section of *Cornhuskers,* the Civil War experience was used more expansively, for broader purposes.

The sixteen poems in "Shenandoah" had a clear ultimate direction— to glorify the Great War. Despite this purpose, however, or perhaps in support of it, because they documented Sandburg's awareness of the agonies and stupidities of the Great War and war in general and so made it seem as though he had not come to his patriotism easily, many poems commented on war as a vainglorious or inglorious exercise.

That was the upshot of the four brief poems that opened the section, the title poem "Shenandoah," "New Feet," "Old Osawatomie," and "Grass," the first and third of which were about the Civil War. Each of the four stated similar themes—the meaninglessness of old battles, the old heroes and ordinary soldiers turning to dust or, at best, "phantoms," the vegetation covering battlefields, the absence of historical memory, as in "Shenandoah," whose blue and gray battlefield riders "nobody re-members" (*Poems* 135–36). "Flanders," the fifth poem in the sequence, commented on events of the Great War by noting ironically that no one knows where the region is and that before its fame it was simply a place like other country places. With a few adjustments for geography, the image used—cows, radishes, "raw-boned plowmen"—could have appeared in one of the prairie poems of "Cornhuskers" (*Poems* 136–37). How war broke the rhythms and traditions of ordinary people, thrust them into the iron jaws of the death gods (one poem, "Gargoyle," was a horrifying dream of such a violent monster), was also the theme of "Old Timers" and "House." In the first, a series of historical voices speak of how they were conscripted into armies they had no wish to serve. In the second, a Civil War veteran, Uncle Joe, tells two Swedish boys living in the same building with him about battles he witnessed and inspires in them a lust for a war of their own. Two other brief poems were also about motivations. "Remembered Women" presented a standard motive developed in the propaganda of all the Great War combatants. Men fight on through mud and charge into the murderous storm "for the women they hate and the women they love—for the women they left behind, they fight on" (*Poems* 140). In "A Million Young Workmen, 1915," in contrast, the motivation of soldiers was neither the lust for adventure nor the need to do honor to women hated or loved. Rather, it was the desire for freedom from autocracy, or so the poet dreamed: "I dreamed a million ghosts of the young workmen rose in their shirts all soaked in crimson . . . and yelled: / God damn the grinning kings, God damn the kaiser and the czar." One interesting feature of this poem was how it shifted meanings with shifting publication contexts. Sandburg had originally published the poem in the November 1915 issue of the *International Socialist Review,* among his articles on the indictment of American capitalism in the "Walsh Report." Juxtaposed against his call for direct action against American industrial autocrats, it had suggested the possibility of revolution. Here in *Cornhuskers* it signified young workers fighting to save democracy.

After due regard for the pain, terror, meaninglessness, and foolishness of war, Sandburg turned in the last half of "Shenandoah" to glorify it. "Remembered Women" and "A Million Young Workmen" were parts of that effort, but four other poems were more direct, more oratorically developed, and more patriotic. "Memoir" did honor to the French hero of the Marne, General Joseph Joffre. Opening with "Papa Joffre, the shoulders of him wide as the land of France," and later remarking that Joffre's voice was "a voice of the long firing line that runs from the salt sea dunes of Flanders to the white spear crags of the Swiss mountains," associating him with Lincoln and Washington, Sandburg, fusing the imagery of Joffre and France, blue sea, salt, and stony Flanders beaches, ended "Memoir" in pure melodrama: "This is the hero of the Marne, massive, irreckonable; he lets tears roll down his cheek; they trickle a wet salt off his chin onto the blue coat. / There is a play of American hands and voices equal to sea-breakers and a lift of white sun on a stony beach" (*Poems* 140–41). "A Tall Man" used similarly mythic terms, asserting the existence of an indwelling spirit of America, a wise, monumental force who was "the head of the people." It was silent about the real-life name of the subject, but a reader could easily have imagined that it was a mythicized Woodrow Wilson (*Poems* 142–43). "John Ericsson Day Memorial, 1918" (Ericsson was the Swedish-born inventor of the ironclad man-of-war used so decisively by the North in the Civil War), set side by side with the poem about the Swedish boys learning about the Civil War from Uncle Joe, so perhaps Sandburg was underscoring the patriotism of Swedish-Americans like himself, was in the tone of a full-blown oration memorializing fallen heroes, complete with a civics lesson about the stars and stripes including "For the soldier who gives all, for the workshop man who gives all, for these the red bar is on the flag—the red bar is the heart's blood of the mother who gave him, the land that gave him" (*Poems* 139).

While "John Ericsson Day Memorial, 1918" sounded like an orthodox oration on the war dead, "The Four Brothers: *Notes for War Songs* (November 1917)," which appeared as the lead poem in the November 1917 issue of *Poetry* and then, according to Sandburg, went through several reprintings (CS Coll: Cornhuskers file, autobiographical sketch), befitting its composition just after Sandburg had written about and joined the American Alliance, sounded like a speech by a rhetorically gifted Liberty Bond salesman who had spent a good deal of time contemplating the imagery and devices of war poster illustrators. In patriotic effusions, Sandburg here outdid himself, though it should be remembered that he was always a propagandist and that many of his earlier poems, "Chicago," for example, and a number of poems about the masses, were equally patriotic, at least in the narrower sense of pledging complete allegiance to the "nation" of the working class of the world. Of the poetry printed at the time the war was taking place— and judging by the number of newspaper advertisements printed from 1917 to 1919, there were dozens of anthologies glorifying the war in verse (for example, Gibbons and *War Poems*) and, so far as I know, not a single poem damning it in the familiar manner of postwar literature— Sandburg's "The Four Brothers" was easily the most distinguished.

Nearly every image used by the United States government to accomplish its war propaganda was used by Sandburg. The kaiser, always presented as part crackpot, part bloodthirsty madman, was depicted by Sandburg as "the one-armed mastoid kaiser," the "half-cracked one-armed child of the German kings," "the child born with his head wrong-shaped, / The blood of rotted kings in his veins," "the last of the gibbering Hohenzollerns," a piece of "trash." The Allied soldiers, always presented as clean-scrubbed, clear-eyed, peaceful, were now eager for battle and self-sacrifice, ready, as he heard them saying as they marched by, to be killed. Killing, the object of the war, was as enthusiastically endorsed in the poem as it was in the best of the stories George Creel's bureaucracy was able to place in American newspapers. In one stanza, where the cornhuskers and the other plain folk were transformed into "toothed and tusked man-killers," Sandburg wrote:

> Eating to kill,
> Sleeping to kill,
> Asked by their mothers to kill,
> Wished by four-fifths of the world to kill—
> To cut the kaiser's throat,
> To hack the kaiser's head,
> To hang the kaiser on a high-horizon gibbet.

What could justify such blood lust? That humanist question was answered by Sandburg with as much aplomb as Woodrow Wilson ever mustered. At first, he said, he had been brought by pure anger to his conclusion that killing was the order of the day, but then he had meditated "among the mountains, by the sea-combers in storm," in portentously philosophical places, in other words, and now, he said, he knew that the killing was to "save the world." What world? a skeptical reader might have asked. Sandburg's answer duplicated government propaganda. Saving the world first of all meant saving the Western tradition, keeping "alive the names of those who left red prints of bleeding feet at Valley Forge in Christmas snow." He swore to the truth of this "On the cross of Jesus, the sword of Napoleon, the skull of Shakespeare, the pen of Jefferson, the ashes of Abraham Lincoln," as well as the "mothers of the world" and "By the God of morning glories climbing blue the doors of quiet homes, by the God of tall hollyhocks laughing glad to children in peaceful valleys, by the God of new mothers wishing peace to sit at windows nursing babies." God, incidentally, was not used by Sandburg only to swear on. Increasingly and repetitively as the poem neared its conclusive promise that the children and mothers of the world would someday "sing new songs," God, "a God of the People," the "God of the Four Brothers," became the Great Endorser of the allied cause if not exactly a signatory to the alliance (*Poems* 143–47).

As a patriotic tour de force, as a sonorous orchestration of the Wilson administration's line on the Great War, "The Four Brothers" could not have been more mainstream, at least in the fall of 1917. But then, wartime politics, like politics always, could change dramatically. When it was written and for a few months afterward, the poem properly reflected the fact that there were indeed four allied brothers, England, the United States, France, and Russia. A couple of months before the manuscript of *Cornhuskers* was sent to Alfred Harcourt, however, there were only three brothers, Russia under Lenin and Trotsky having settled a "separate peace" with Germany. Sandburg's poem thus befell a fate not uncommon to topical, engaged literature written in highly dynamic situations. It was soon irrelevant. Far worse, from the point of view of the mainstream, it was "incorrect" in that it provided aid and comfort not to the "gibbering Hohenzollerns" certainly but to those who had killed the real Russia, the murderers of the czar (Sandburg, paralleling him with the kaiser, referred to him as the "last of the gibbering Romanoffs" in the poem), the likes of Lenin and Trotsky.

Three book reviews Sandburg published in the *Daily News* between November 1917 and April 1918 made it clear that he was far more sensitive to a number of issues involved in thinking and writing about the war than "The Four Brothers" and the other patriotic poems of "Shenandoah" suggested. In the first of these, on Karl Liebknecht's *Militarism* and Henri Barbusse's *Under Fire*, in which he noted that he had "read three or four dozen books on the war the past year, and bales of newspaper and magazine articles," he highly recommended both books, Liebknecht's because it indicated that there was a democratic Germany which also hated kaiserism, Barbusse's mainly because it told its story from within the ranks, where a sense of responsibility to defend one's country rather than a search for glory or a love of war was the prevailing motivation. In the second, another review of *Under Fire*, he praised Barbusse's reporting skills, his honesty in viewing the war as a chaotic blur, a dizzying spectacle impossible to see vividly, and his sense of proportion. In the third, a review of an anonymously authored book called *Men in War* published by Boni and Liveright, which he said had "mostly gibberings" compared to *Under Fire*, there were two highly suggestive remarks. The first was that "no form of human anguish but is intensified and widened by war. These are all the more reasons why we should keep our heads cool and our heartbeats even in some measure of decent health while the war lasts." The second, stated at the end, was that what he wanted was war books "showing how the impulses that underlie 'the patriotic and pugnacious' motives of men can be directed toward the achievement of a democratized earth" (*DN* 12, 15, 16). None of these absolutely valid recognitions, however, caused Sandburg to modify, qualify, or tone down his patriotic "Shenandoah" poems.

Sandburg's literary persona was seemingly transformed in major ways in *Cornhuskers*. No longer the tough-guy poet of the working class, which was the image most readers, pro or con, carried away from *Chicago and Other Poems*, now, especially because of the opening "Cornhuskers" section and the closing "Shenandoah" section, he was to be seen as a 100 percent American poet, the singer of the greatness and grandeur of the country's rolling heartland, the thoughtful patriot who knew how its ordinary folk would sacrifice themselves to save the world for democracy, the Whitman-like poet of multiple selves.

In July, two months after the manuscript of *Cornhuskers* was sent off to Alfred Harcourt, the Newspaper Enterprise Association (NEA), the Scripps wire service, offered Sandburg a high-paying job in Stockholm, Sweden, one of the centers for reporting the war and the Bolshevik Revolution. The job promised to give him his first international reporting experience and, because the NEA served several hundred papers, a large audience. There were, as could be expected, family issues to be faced (his wife was then pregnant with their third child), but Sandburg jumped at the offer and quickly started to make travel plans.

During this time, all American travelers to Europe, but especially newspaper correspondents, faced enormous difficulties in getting passports and visas and booking passage on one of the few ships still allowed to venture into contested seas. So it was not surprising that soon after making his initial efforts and running into a thicket of red tape, Sandburg wrote to Samuel T. Hughes, his editor at the NEA, "They want to know every mole and scar on a guy's frame. And he has to go get mugged and hand in three pictures of what kind of a pickpocket he looks like." Understanding that "100 percent Americanism" was now demanded of all citizens, he asked Hughes to send a testimonial to the passport authorities and suggested the appropriate biographical details to stress:

> Recite for them that I am 40 years of age, was born at Galesburg, Ill., and have lived all my life in the United States, except the time for an expedition to Puerto Rico in 1898 as an enlisted soldier with the Sixth Illinois Volunteers, that I am a newspaper man and for the past six years have been continuously in active newspaper work in Chicago: that I am leaving a position as editorial writer on the *Chicago Daily News*, the world's largest afternoon newspaper, to go to Stockholm for the Newspaper Enterprise Association, which serves 320 newspapers with news stories and descriptive articles and has a circulation going to 4,500,000 subscribers, being the most extensive service of its kind in the world. Tell them I have co-operated actively with the American Alliance for Labor and Democracy, which is the loyalty legion of the American Federation of Labor, and that the Alliance gave wide circulation to my war poem "The Four Brothers." Make me important as hell. Make bands and girls in white dresses strewing flowers on my pathway to the steamboat slip. (*Letters* 130–31)

As events over the next few months would demonstrate, Sandburg seriously miscalculated if he truly believed that this sort of all-American fluff would convince the people with whom he was now dealing that he was a fine, upstanding citizen.

Shortly after the declaration of war, the Wilson administration unleashed a network of operatives of the Bureau of Investigation and the army's Military Intelligence Division to ferret out foreign agents and to aid, and sometimes lead, the assault on dissenters. "Surveillance" was the polite way of describing efforts that, when they did not actually cross the line into blatantly illegal activity, were at least questionable. The tactics used were crude: infiltrating targeted groups, intercepting mail addressed to suspects, attending public meetings and recording what was said (or inventing what *could* have been said), interviewing employers, collecting incriminating statements by writers, seeing to it that violent attacks against radicals were not vigorously pursued, and so forth. They were nonetheless effective.

Dramatic results of surveillance could be seen in some of the espionage and sedition cases and in the IWW trials, a significant element of which, according to the huge case file, was the infiltration of the Wobbly legal staff by government agents and the resulting ease with which the prosecution parried all of the defense strategies (*U.S. Military Intelligence*, reels 5 and 6, file 10110–235, parts 1–4). But the sensational show trials reflected only a small part of the government's efforts. As the archives of both the Military Intelligence Division and the Bureau of Investigation indicate, thousands of citizens were investigated or otherwise ensnared in the surveillance net, bureaucratically convicted of radicalism—or pacifism, or being less than 100 percent American—without ever having the opportunity to face their accusers or, in many cases, without even knowing they were accused of anything.

Over the next couple of years, Sandburg was a subject of great interest to the Military Intelligence Division, first with regard to his passport and visa applications, then about what he did when he finally got to Stockholm, then about what he brought back with him, and, finally, about some of his newspaper writing and other activities in 1919. He, too, was bureaucratically convicted and was fortunate that matters did not go further.

Five days before writing the letter about his all-American credentials to Hughes, he had his first contact, or at least the first contact in which he knew to whom he was talking, with a division agent. His own situation was not, however, the subject of the interview. Rather, the Military Intelligence agent was asking about Victor Berger, his old nemesis and more recently one of the antiwar socialists he had been denouncing in the *Daily News*. The government was preparing an Espionage Act case against Berger, and the agent was apparently seeking background information. He found in Sandburg an enthusiastic source. Sandburg, the agent wrote,

> stated that he has known Victor Berger for about twelve years; that in his estimation [he] is very pro-German and that since the war he has bought a $7500 home in Milwaukee and has recently spent approximately $5000 on the improvement of same and according to the salary which he is drawing states this hardly seems possible. Sanburg [*sic*] also stated that Berger is one of the largest shareholders in the *Milwaukee Leader* and that since the war, the *Leader* seems to get all the financial backing necessary and states that Berger himself is a very conceited egotistical man.

At the end of his report the agent indicated that Sandburg had suggested further Military Intelligence interviews with A. M. Simons, Chester M. Wright, Elizabeth Thomas, Winfield R. Taylor, and J. E. Moriarity, some of whom were active with him in the American Alliance. But as the Berger case file indicates, this was not fresh information. Simons, his wife, Wright, and several other of Berger's old allies had already been interviewed by the division and had equaled or surpassed Sandburg's performance (*U.S. Military Intelligence,* reel 3, file 10110–120). Back-stabbing had for years been as dominant a feature of radical politics as it was of mainstream politics, but now a new stage seems to have been entered, one in which the capitalist enemy was used as the executioner of a fellow radical with whom one disagreed. This may seem tragic, and Sandburg's denunciation of Berger may seem especially poignant. But in fact his service as a government informant was more pathetic and darkly comic than anything else, for shortly after his meeting with the agent, the Military Intelligence Division began to turn its considerable powers against him. His savaging of Berger was the last time for many years that he would ally himself with the government and that the government would look upon him as anything other than an enemy.

When its agent interviewed Sandburg about Berger, the division was involved in several other investigations in Chicago. One of these had to do with Charles H. Kerr and Company, the former publisher of the *International Socialist Review* and still the publisher of other radical books and pamphlets. The justification for the investigation was straightforward: "The intimate connection of this company with the IWW, it is believed, justifies the expenditure of time and energy required in the investigation." On July 19, the investigation began when one Lloyd Canby, working as a member of the American Protective League, the government-supported citizens' network of spies, informers, and toughs, visited Kerr's offices on behalf of the division.

Something of the simple-mindedness and clumsiness of the less professional of these investigations is preserved in the reports filed by Canby. Shocked by what he found at the Kerr offices, Canby breathlessly reported to his superiors that "the premises . . . have I.W.W. banners on the wall and a large printed sheet signed by Wm. D. Haywood calling upon the steel workers to strike for better wages. The whole place reeks of Socialism and I.W.Wism." A couple of weeks later he returned to the Kerr offices, made inquiries, found out that the *International Socialist Review* was no longer published (hardly a startling revelation), and tried to purchase some of the books that Kerr continued to mail. Apparently the office help smelled a fish, for they refused to sell him anything.

Canby, a true-blue sleuth, was not easily deterred. That evening he broke into the offices and liberated a number of books. Unfortunately, though, there was no incriminating evidence to be found in those he looked at after leaving: he reported that books written by Karl Marx, Friedrich Engels, Jack London, and Karl Kautsky "rarely mentioned" the war. This blatant ignorance that dead men did not write about contemporary events was too much even for the Military Intelligence officer in charge of the investigation. After reading Canby's report, he wrote a memo in which he suggested that "further investigation of C. H. Kerr & Co. be called off or that an investigator be selected who has some discriminating knowledge of Socialism." A new agent was assigned to the case, but the investigation did not proceed much further. The last entry in the file concluded that there was no real case against Kerr; the company was no longer printing "seditious or questionable articles for the I.W.W. or Socialist leaders" (*U.S. Military Intelligence*, reel 5, file IOIIO–219: 309, 270, 333, 327, 323, 320, 319, 358, 102).

The Kerr investigation suggests much about how the division sometimes operated, and it can serve as a cautionary story about how its investigations were sometimes tainted by illegal methods, incompetent agents, and bureaucratic confusion. It also should indicate just how lucky Sandburg was, for had the investigation been started a few months earlier, when he was active as Jack Phillips, or had the investigation gone deeper to expose his past connection to the *Review*, events would have taken a sharply more dangerous turn for him. As it turned out, the division never found out anything about Sandburg's ultra-radical writing in the magazine, and this was of tremendous advantage to him over the next several months.

He was not so fortunate in the outcome of another Chicago investigation then being pursued by the division, that of the *Daily News*. In August, Colonel Carl Reichmann of the Chicago office sent to the chief of Military Intelligence a clipping from the paper, which showed, he said, "Bolshevik influence upon the editorial opinion of this periodical. . . . You will note that the 'Chicago Daily News' is expressly in favor and sympathy of recognition of Bolshevik or Soviet government in Russia. Recently, the whole tenor of this paper has changed editorially, and it now may be classified as Chicago's most radical sheet." This sounds particularly rabid. Given the logic of antiradicalism, though, it had a perverse accuracy. Like other cities, Chicago had been cleansed of radical publications, but, assuming that a left always existed, which surveillance agencies were in the business of assuming, some paper or magazine had to be found which was the "most radical." By this logic, the *News* was it.

Self-fulfilling paranoia aside, the *News* had in fact published an editorial endorsement of Bolshevism. The editorial recognized the essential differences between the Bolsheviks and the U.S. populace, but it argued that democracy was developing in Russia through workers' councils, that is, soviets, which were depicted as grass-roots associations of free men ("Bolshevism").[3] This, from the government's perspective, was tantamount to treason, for over the previous six months or so, the Wilson administration, like other Western governments, had become deeply anti-Bolshevik. This was so first because of the threat Bolshevism's doctrines represented to capitalism, second because of Lenin's stated intention to make the Russian Revolution the first step toward a worldwide revolution of the working classes, and, finally, after the Bolsheviks saw the risks involved in continuing to fight with the Allies while fighting a civil war against counterrevolutionaries at home, because of the separate peace it signed in March 1918 with Germany. By August, as the *News* investigation suggested, Bolshevism was replacing homegrown radicalism as the country's number one enemy. Ironically, when he wrote to Sam Hughes emphasizing his support of the war, Sandburg was behind the times and his great claim to patriotic fame, "The Four Brothers" was now a politically suspect document because there were, according to the government, only three.

For an explanation of why the paper had begun to "support" Bolshevism, the division turned to Henry Justin Smith, its news editor. It apparently did not occur to Smith to assert the right of a newspaper to take a position different from the government's, to assert free press principles, or simply to tell the investigating agent that its editorial policies were none of his business. But he did have one—thoroughly unprincipled—hesitation: he agreed to speak only "on the assurance that his employers would know nothing of his conversation with an agent of this department." That assurance was received, and lest a reader of his report think that the editor was holding something back, the agent wrote that he believed Smith was "100% American." Then Smith gave his explanation. The publishers of the *News* had given the editorial staff no direction on what to say about Bolshevism. The editorial stance was totally the fault of Louis Edgar Browne, who was corresponding for the paper from Russia: "The News editorially endorsed the Soviet form of Russian government emphatically after Browne had returned to Chicago recently for a brief conference," was how Agent Westcott summarized Smith's explanation of his correspondent's amazing control over the *News*'s editorial staff.

On the surface, Sandburg, who was also discussed in this interview, probably because of his passport and visa application, fared better than

Browne. Smith, who had a professional reputation as an editor who was extremely supportive of his writers, especially those among them, like Sandburg and Ben Hecht, who were also artists (Niven 292, 332, 454–56), seems to have tried to help his friend and recent employee. But his portrait of Sandburg could not have been comforting:

> Mr. Smith also discussed Carl Sandburg to some extent stating that in recent conversations with Sandburg the last named had been so vehement in his bitterness toward Germany that he felt inclined to cease any writings that would tend to be construed as I.W.W. utterances in substance. Smith states that in his opinion Sandburg is really in sympathy with the I.W.W. but that those feelings are prompted by a desire to assist those whom he would believe to be "underdogs."
>
> Smith advised that Sandburg is a misguided genius who would not knowingly to [sic] anything to help the cause of Germany nor accept money for his I.W.W. utterances but that he would work day and night to further the cause of those whom he believed are not getting that which they deserve out of life. A "harmless socialist" was the strongest term Smith cared to use regarding Sandburg ( U.S. *Military Intelligence* reel 10, file 10110–853: 0302).

To the division, of course, there was no such thing as a "harmless" socialist, and the idea that Sandburg was a "misguided genius" with a predilection for the IWW and other underdogs probably did not help his cause either.

Sandburg was aware that he was under investigation, and in one letter to his wife he turned philosophical about his destiny, seeing it as relatively unimportant in the context of the times. If he were the government, he told her, he "would refuse passports to any and all for Stockholm, permitting no one to go there except in a military intelligence connection. The whole war machine is tightening up. Such tremendous destinies hang in the balance that I can't have a distinct personal reaction about being turned down" (CS Coll: NEA and earlier Chicago letters 1918–19 folder). In a letter to Sam Hughes, he again waxed philosophical, saying that, if it turned out that way, he could understand that "no man of ex-socialist connections and with known bolshevist friends, should be permitted at this time to go to Stockholm" (*Letters* 135). Other comments in letters to his wife captured his mood as he awaited word on whether he would pass muster and be allowed to sail to Europe. In one he remarked, "Sometimes I wonder if I'm alive or a lizard on a high rock watching a smoky salty misty stupendous drama. Take care of John [the child his wife was carrying, who turned out to be Helga Sandburg]: he may see great days never known to our eyes" (*Letters* 138). A few days later he meditated on the new lesson he was learning, this time underscoring his separateness from his wife as well as from events: "I'm sure you have little idea of what I have been learning in New York, the resignation and humility and obedience of the infinitesimal human unit in the world storm" (*Letters* 139–40). Meanwhile, at about the same time that he was being so philosophical about destiny, he wrote a long statement about his politics to the French intellectual Romain Rolland. Sounding cosmic once again, he described his independence from parties, said that he was "with all rebels everywhere all the time as against all people who are satisfied," and ended with a remark about his eclecticism that, had it been known to government agents, would probably have ended his chances: "I am for reason and satire, religion and propaganda, violence and assassination, or force and syndicalism, any of them, in the extent and degree to which it will serve a purpose of the people at a given time toward the establishment eventually of the control of the means of life by the people" (*Letters* 169–72).

At the same time, he did what he could to help himself. He got more testimonials from associates in the American Alliance as well as George Creel, Alfred Harcourt, and a friend of Harcourt's who worked in the State Department (CS Coll: NEA and earlier Chicago letters 1918–19). He tried to stay away from socialists and Wobblies, he told his new employer. If he happened to be "thrown" into their company, he said, as he had been twice with Louise Bryant and John Reed in New York, he limited the conversation to things nonpolitical, a task of some difficulty given Reed's pro-Bolshevik zealotry (he was then writing *Ten Days That Shook the World*) and probably beside the point because mere contact with Reed, one of the most spied-upon of radicals, was enough to establish guilt in the eyes of agents (CS Coll: NEA file, Sandburg to Hughes, September 12, 1918).

The Military Intelligence Division's investigation of Kerr and Company yielded nothing incriminating about the publisher or, as might have happened, about Sandburg. Its *Daily News* investigation yielded only his former editor's picture of him as a harmless do-gooder. Finally, however, neither of these spying efforts, nor any of Sandburg's efforts to portray himself as a hundred percenter, mattered at all. Several months later, in March 1919, after the Sandburg case had become far broader, Colonel

John M. Dunn, the acting director of Military Intelligence, summarized the division's understanding of Sandburg in a memorandum to the chief of staff. Included as part of the summary was a biography of Sandburg that told a very different story from the one Sandburg told Sam Hughes or, for that matter, any of his future readers and biographers. Dunn wrote:

> Carl Sandberg [*sic*], a poet and newspaper writer of Chicago, is of Swedish descent, highly educated, and speaks several languages fluently. He is known as a radical and is one of the original members of "The Dill Pickle," a club composed of intellectual anarchists, radicals, freelovers and revolutionists. He has been connected with the Lithuanian radicals, the stockyards I.W.W., and in 1918 was elected by the Lithuanian branch of the Stockyards I.W.W. to represent it in Russia on the proposed American Economic Mission. He was born in the United States and served as a private in the 6th Illinois Volunteer Infantry in Porto Rico in 1898. He was recently a special writer for the Daily News. The name "Carl" is of recent adoption. Prior to the outbreak of the European War he was known as Charles Sandburg. (*U.S. Military Intelligence*, reel 9, file 10110–749: 0532, item 16)

That high-level assessment and nothing else was what mattered.

Not an unusual instance of how the division smeared its victims, Dunn's summary suggested the degree to which paranoia shaped government "information" and, as well, the ease with which even top officers used innuendo as a basic descriptive technique. Rationally structured and seemingly matter-of-fact, the characterization depended for its effect on an understanding of its code language. Sandburg's "Swedish descent" meant that he was not 100 percent American and was therefore untrustworthy. The fact that he changed his name "prior to the outbreak of the European War" (true, but Carl was his birth name) meant that he was a German sympathizer. The fact that he was "highly educated" (that is, he went to college for a few years) and "speaks several languages fluently" (that is, English and some Swedish) meant, again, that he was not 100 percent American and, furthermore, that he had the ability to manipulate ordinary folk. His low moral character was indicated by his membership (as if it were a real organization) in the Dill Pickle, a more or less avant-garde discussion group that served as one of Chicago's intellectual centers.

The division, of course, took the position that Sandburg should not be allowed to go to Stockholm, and that should have ended Sandburg's career as an international correspondent. But then, in one of the many ironic twists that characterized the case, the division was overruled. Dunn described this aspect of the case in his summary: "Protests were made at this time [that is, in early October 1918] against the sailing of Sandberg [*sic*], and the English authorities stated that he could not enter England, but in the absence of positive evidence of any act of disloyalty and upon the strong recommendation of his loyalty by Mr. Hughes, he was permitted to depart" (*U.S. Military Intelligence* reel 9, file 10110–749: 0532, item 17).

Some part of this statement was probably motivated by a need for the division to cover its bureaucratic rear. By the time it was written the following March, Sandburg had already returned from his trip abroad, where he had done vital service for the Bolsheviks, according to the division, and this might have been Dunn's way of saying that those who had believed Hughes, not the intelligence professionals, were to blame for the results. Part of it might also have been motivated by an attempt to discredit those who had listened to anything said by the NEA because the division had its own, far less generous, appraisal of the wire service. In a case file on *Daily News* and *Masses* cartoonist Robert Minor, an agent made what sounded to be an authoritative generalization about the NEA, saying that a "great many of the writers for this syndicate are either suspects or known, pro-German and Bolshevik sympathizers" (*U.S. Military Intelligence* reel 7, file 10110–546). Part of it might also have been aimed at contrasting the correct disposition of the Sandburg matter by the British authorities, who, as opposed to the Americans, followed the advice of their intelligence experts. But whatever his attempt at bureaucratic positioning, Dunn's statement registered correctly the division's final opinion on Sandburg's venture. He should not have been allowed to go. He was clearly not to be trusted.

It is impossible to say what, aside from hearsay and plain animus, Dunn and his subordinates used in arriving at their conclusions. The division's files on Sandburg are fragmentary; there are no IWW records indicating that Sandburg was connected to the Chicago Stockyards' IWW local; whatever the British secret service said has not been released. But they were right.

# VI

## *Sandburg in 1919*

T he revolution in Russia in October 1917 led to a civil war between counterrevolutionary "whites" and the Bolsheviks, some efforts by the Bolsheviks to spread their revolution across Europe, and, in early 1918, the declaration of the separate peace. Stockholm, where Sandburg's ship docked on October 25, 1918, almost exactly one year after the revolution, was relatively unaffected by the events in Russia, at least directly. But Finland, its close neighbor, on which Sandburg was to concentrate much of his attention as a correspondent, was as deeply affected by Bolshevism as any northern European country.

Shortly after the Bolsheviks seized power in Russia, a revolution took place in Finland and a new state, the Socialist Workers Republic of Finland, was declared. Civil war had erupted as in Russia, pitting the revolutionary Red Guards, supported by forty thousand Russian Bolshevik troops, against the counterrevolutionary White Guards. It continued into the spring of 1918, when, just after the separate peace, which included a provision calling for the withdrawal of Bolshevik troops from Finland, a White Guard-German treaty was signed. Germany agreed to press for international recognition of Finland as an independent country (it had for several decades been part of czarist Russia); in return, Finland promised not to cede territory to a foreign power without German permission (C. Smith 61–62; Hamalainen; Paasivirta). After the civil war ended with the defeat of the Red Guards, there were debts to be repaid. The "White Terror" launched against the losers and the few revolutionaries who continued fighting was, by all accounts, especially vicious. By November 1, nearly twelve thousand of the seventy-three thousand prisoners taken by the victorious government had died of disease or starvation (C. Smith 88). Representatives of the revolutionary government in exile, working through Finnish Socialist Workers

Republic information bureaus set up in the Allied nations, claimed those figures were just the tip of the iceberg.

By the fall of 1918, fourteen Allied nations had been engaged for more than six months in fighting with the counterrevolutionary White Russians against the Bolsheviks. The United States had between seven thousand and ten thousand troops in Russia, a significantly smaller number than the British, who were the most active force. Little news reached the United States about the war in Russia (or Britain, or, for that matter, any of the other nations that had invaded to stop Bolshevism in its tracks). That was because the administration, through its wartime ability to censor cables and to pressure news organs (as it did to the *Daily News*, for example), did not allow information to be published unless it served its purposes. Among its purposes was not journalistic fairness or balanced reporting. The "secret war" of the Allies was rarely mentioned. The administration line was that Russian "patriots" were fighting bravely against the Bolshevik beasts and were winning (the imminent collapse of Bolshevism was predicted with stunning regularity in the *New York Times* and other mainstream bulwarks) (Knightly). The line about reporting on events in other countries, like the White Terror in Finland, was simpler. They did not happen; they were not to be reported.

One of the first cables Sandburg sent from Stockholm to the NEA was about an event in Russia, the successful attack on the White Russian stronghold of Jaruslav by the Bolshevik Red Guards. The city, Sandburg reported, had been destroyed, and the victors had proclaimed the event "a perfect example of what would happen to any nest of royalist counterrevolutionists." The source of this news, he said, was "Mitchell Berg, a former Chicago school teacher" who had just come to Stockholm from Russia. Other travelers he had talked to also indicated that the Bolsheviks were killing (without trial) suspects thought to be involved in royalist conspiracies. The article was published in the *Cleveland Press*, the NEA's flagship paper, on November 4 (*CP* 1).

With this one article, which stressed the power of the Red Guards and used "royalists" and "counterrevolutionists" instead of "patriots" or "fighters for freedom," Sandburg violated all the administration's basic rules on reporting the situation in Russia. By using Mitchell Berg as a source for the Jaruslav story, he committed an even more serious breach. For Berg, also then known as Michael Gruzenberg, was of great interest to U.S. Military Intelligence agents, who were as much a presence in Stockholm as they were in Chicago or New York.

Why Sandburg's cable was allowed to go through to the NEA is a mystery. Why the *Press* published it, even with some heavy-duty editing and spinning (the subtitle read "Terrorists Shoot Down Hundreds Without Trial," a standard *Press* treatment of the Bolsheviks), is also a mystery. The results, though, were clear. Sandburg continued writing long cables and letters back to the NEA, some about events in Russia, some about the White Terror in Finland, all of them revealing his sympathy with the Bolsheviks and the failed revolutionaries of Finland. The missives were received in Cleveland. None of them were published in the *Press* or distributed to the other NEA outlets, at least until late December, when a trickle of very short articles—short because severe editorial surgery had been performed on them—began to appear (*CP* 2–9).[1] Sandburg, in brief, was fundamentally through as an effective correspondent after one performance. Little more than a month later, he was back on board a ship headed to New York.

What Sandburg did from early November to early December aside from writing unpublishable cables and, more important, why he did it, became a major subject of dispute between himself, various U.S. government agencies, and his employer. Military Intelligence had a well-formed opinion of his activities. It had, to begin with, a jaundiced view of his character, and it had opposed approval of his passport and visa. Sandburg's main contact with the Bolsheviks, according to division agents, was Berg-Gruzenberg, who was a member of the Russian commission in Sweden, the group that was also the contact between the Bolsheviks and German revolutionaries. During his stay in Stockholm, division agents apparently kept close track of his activities. Another document spoke of several letters having been sent to the acting director of Military Intelligence about Sandburg (*U.S. Military Intelligence* reel 2, file 10110–92).

Although the division understood something of Berg-Gruzenberg's importance, it did not yet know precisely how important he was to the efforts of the Bolsheviks to spread their revolution across the world. As Sandburg had said in his early November article in the *Cleveland Press*, Mitchell Berg had been a Chicago teacher (of Russian immigrants in a school he and his wife ran), having come to the city following the abortive 1905 revolution in Russia in which he had been active. In Chicago, he also published a radical magazine or newspaper, or so later scholars said (though none have been able to produce a single copy). After the Bolshevik Revolution, he left the United States and rejoined his revolutionary colleagues in Russia. For a while, working as Lenin's trusted agent, he assumed his birth name, Gruzenberg, which is how the division knew him, and worked as an agent in northern Europe and then, for a short period, back in the United States. A few years later he emerged as Stalin's primary agent in attempting to bring communism to China. Then he used the name by which he became known in the history and mythology of the world revolution, Mikhail Borodin (Holubnychy; Jacobs; Spence 184–204).

He was, at least until labyrinthine Chinese politics destroyed him (Chiang Kai-shek sent him scurrying back to the Soviet Union after the Shanghai massacre of the communists in 1927), one of the best of the Bolshevik agents, if not the very best, in his ability as a strategist and his capacity for ruthlessness. Sandburg would, without a doubt, whether as Charles, Carl, Live Wire, Jack Phillips, or Militant (these were meetings of men with multiple identities), have had immense trouble keeping up with him, keeping the agenda straight, and separating the facts from revolutionary fictions in Borodin's information and requests for help.

When he learned that Sandburg was soon to return home, Borodin asked Sandburg to bring information about the Bolsheviks back with him, to deliver $10,000 in bank drafts to Santeri Nuroteva, the head of the Finnish Socialist Workers information office in New York, so that the government in exile could tell its story to American workers, and to bring a few hundred dollars to his wife, who was still living in Chicago. Sandburg agreed.

Then, amazingly, he went to the American legation in Stockholm to tell officers what he was doing and to ask them to forward four packages of Bolshevik propaganda films to him in the United States. Was he trying to throw the intelligence agents off the track by appearing to be forthcoming, was he naive, was he being honest? The officers at the legation probed. They wanted, of course, to know from whom he had gotten the $10,000 for Nuroteva. Sandburg refused to tell them, and, as if nothing were troubling him, he sailed for home on December 14. Two days later, the local Stockholm agents cabled their stateside superiors about their interview with him. Two days after that, Colonel Dunn in Washington cabled a Captain Whytock in New York that Sandburg "refused to divulge the source of the funds which he has, likewise his connections, yet he had ostensibly been conferring with the Legation" (*U.S. Military Intelligence* reel 2, file 10110–92).

Sandburg could not have picked a worse time to come back to the United States with Bolshevik money in his pocket, money intended to spread "true" and "proper" information about the situation in Finland.

First, the Wilson administration had already moved close to recognizing the Finnish "White" government, had isolated the New York information office of the Finnish "Reds," and with World War I ended (the armistice had been declared in mid-November) had along with the other invaders stepped up the armed campaign against Bolshevism in Russia. Second, there was growing fear that the Bolsheviks were about to launch a major campaign to foment a revolution among American workers. In December, as Sandburg sailed across the Atlantic, the proto-communist *Class Struggle,* edited by Louis Fraina and Ludwig Lore, published Lenin's "Letter to American Workingmen" as its lead article. This was a piece discussing, among other things, the abject circumstances of American workers, the obscene concentration of wealth in the country, and the "inevitability" of a world revolution. Lenin stopped short of calling for revolt in America, but not by much. To add to this fear, three days before Sandburg's ship docked in New York, the *New York Times* published a front-page article in which it was reported that the Bolsheviks were sending great sums of money to the United States to foment revolution ("Bolsheviki at Work").

Not surprisingly, when Sandburg landed on Christmas Day, he was greeted by agents representing Military Intelligence, the Department of Justice, the Bureau of Investigation, United States Customs, and the New York State attorney general. They were interested in the $10,000 Sandburg was bringing to the Red Finns, and, in a continuation of the efforts begun at the legation in Stockholm, they immediately demanded to know the source of the money. They also discovered that Sandburg was carrying two suitcases packed with Bolshevik propaganda. This, they thought, was a bonanza, and they began to examine the documents.

Sandburg was not arrested but was detained at a New York hotel and, though free to move about (but no doubt surveilled all the way), grilled by the agents over several days about why he carried Bolshevik propaganda back with him, what his attitudes toward the Bolsheviks were, and who gave him the money for the Finnish information office. Sandburg maintained that he was a newsman and that he intended to write about the events in Russia using the two suitcases of documents as his sources. On the question of who gave him the $10,000, he was resolutely silent, as he had been at the legation in Sweden.

None of his responses impressed the agents. His silence about who gave him the money, of course, was interpreted to mean not that he was claiming an arguable journalist's right to protect sources but that he was protecting the Bolsheviks. In the case summary written three months later, the same summary in which he assessed Sandburg's background and character, Colonel John M. Dunn laid out the division's assessment of Sandburg's sympathies, motives, and goals. During the New York questioning, Dunn wrote, Sandburg had "admitted his entire sympathy with the Russian Soviet and that he had been on intimate terms with the Bolshevist representatives during his entire stay in Stockholm." Regarding Sandburg's journalistic purposes, Dunn said, "In fact his mission abroad appears to have been to confer with the Russian and Finnish revolutionaries in Sweden and to obtain their propaganda" ( *U.S. Military Intelligence* reel 9, file 10110–749: 0532, items 18, 22).

During January, government agents made a serious effort to assess the importance of the documents Sandburg brought back with him, translating and indexing them, and, finally, concluding that there were "some items of the greatest interest as indicating the policy of the Russian Soviet Government toward the allied powers." Of special interest was a document which indicated that the Bolsheviks had set aside some two million rubles to be spent on propaganda efforts in foreign countries; Sandburg's mission, the assessment concluded, was a result of that policy ( *U.S. Military Intelligence* reel 9, file 10110–749, synopsis).

Fortunately for Sandburg, prosecution was not a possibility because Russia still enjoyed diplomatic recognition by the United States, not having been declared an enemy nation despite the secret war. Under these circumstances, the agents presented Sandburg with a legal document to sign, giving the government the right to retain the materials but also providing that some items could be returned to him if it turned out that publishing them would not be a violation of the Espionage Act. Sandburg signed on January 28 ( *Letters* 149). So far as the division files indicate, nothing was ever returned to him. The division used its bonanza find on later occasions in spying on radicals and trying to understand the connections between American events and Bolshevik foreign policy (for example, *U.S. Military Intelligence* reel 10, file 10110–747, April 15 and 24, 1919).

Sandburg went to see Santeri Nuroteva at the Finnish Socialist Workers information bureau in early January, which spurred Nuroteva to write two letters, one to the U.S. attorney, the other to Military Intelligence. In the first, Nuroteva professed not to know the source of the money because Sandburg had refused to divulge it. The second spoke of his having urged Sandburg to reveal the name to the U.S. attorney and of

Sandburg, discharged from his obligation to be silent, having followed his advice. Nuroteva said that ended the case, and so he asked for his money. He did not get it, then or later. But it was, as he said, the end of the case, at least in terms of what the government agents wanted to know when they greeted Sandburg on Christmas Day. They now had a complete picture, they thought, of his character, his political allegiances, his motives, and the name Berg-Gruzenberg, the Bolshevik agent he served.

Sandburg, of course, presented his own version of events to his employer and his wife. In letters he wrote in December and January he emphasized his journalistic righteousness, his personal history of patriotism from his army service in 1898 to his pro-war stance, his interest in balanced reporting of the situation in Finland, and his belief that not he but the government was anti-American (*Letters* 145–49). Formally, his employers at the Newspaper Enterprise Association defended him, writing letters of protest to Washington and enlisting friends within the Hearst organization to do the same (*U.S. Military Intelligence* reel 9, file 10110–749: 0532). Privately, though, they were considerably less supportive. A December 30 letter from Sam Hughes to Frederick M. Kerby, head of the NEA's New York bureau, declared that had Sandburg not compromised himself by bringing in money for propaganda purposes he, Hughes, would have "raised all kinds of hell" and that if the wire service made a public issue of the matter it could expect that "Washington would immediately follow our first blast by charging quite truthfully that Sandburg had made himself an agent of the Finnish Bolsheviki by taking charge of the money they wished to send to their compatriots in the United States" (CS Coll: NEA S. T. Hughes 1918 file, December 30, 1918). A letter from Hughes to Sandburg, while telling him that the NEA would pursue the matter with the government, said plainly that Hughes did not blame the government for censoring Bolshevik propaganda (CS Coll: NEA file, December 31, 1918). In later years, long after the events, Sandburg was joined in his defense by scholars who, basing their opinions on his words alone and on later FBI documents but not on Military Intelligence documents or the contemporary American political context, saw him as a victim of government stupidity and excess (*Letters* vi; Mitgang 87–92; Niven 303–30; Robins 43–46, 456–57).

Was Sandburg a dupe of Berg-Gruzenberg-Borodin, a good journalist who was just doing his job, or was he a victim of hysterical government anti-Bolshevism? Considering the players, those are not great choices.

On the one hand, Berg-Gruzenberg-Borodin was a master plotter, a conspirator of mythic fame, and he apparently never said anything about the affair. Agents of the Military Intelligence Division, on the other hand, were not hesitant about cooking information when it suited their purposes, committing illegal acts, crafting facts to serve their theories, or, even at that early point in the history of U.S.-Soviet relations, discovering Bolsheviks everywhere they looked. For his part, Sandburg had at times shown himself to be a political opportunist, a journalist who was anything but objective and balanced, a far left radical even when he portrayed himself as a patriot, a man who wrote under several disguises, a man who on occasion lied to advance or save his career.

What really happened perhaps became somewhat clearer in 1956, when at the top of his mid-century fame Sandburg returned to the subject in a letter to Theodore Draper, who was collecting material for *The Roots of American Communism*. His memory of the events did not vary greatly from what he said earlier. But he added one detail: "My person was not searched," Sandburg wrote, "and I voluntarily handed over the draft for $10,000.00. In the same pocket with the draft was a pamphlet, 'A Letter to American Working Men' by Nikolai Lenin which I handed over to Nuortava [*sic*] and it was published and circulated." He added that the account he was providing to Draper was "scanty," that there were many more particulars to the affair, and that in his *Ever the Winds of Chance* there would be a chapter on it (CS Coll: Draper file, February 25, 1956). Unfortunately, the chapter was apparently never written.

In a bemused tone, Draper recorded the admission about the Lenin pamphlet, commenting on the strangeness of this revolutionary document, in some formal senses the foundation stone of American communism, having been transported by the future biographer of Lincoln (Draper 236–38). In fact, as Draper should have known, the "Letter" had already been published in the *Class Struggle* when Sandburg was still transporting it—to be sure it got to the United States, Borodin probably had several smugglers set up[2]—but this should not blunt the significance of Sandburg's statement. With it, he seems to have admitted that he was doing service above and beyond the call of journalism, that he was trying to serve the international revolutionary cause.

This should not be taken as a revelation. Nothing in his political behavior of recent years suggests that he would have done other than attempt to support and serve the Bolsheviks. His words as Jack Phillips in the summer of 1917 about the first revolution as an event that "fairly trembles, glitters, and coruscates with the chaos" and the "incalculable magic of suggestion" of the revolutionary news from Europe made his position abundantly clear.

For several months after his return to the United States, Sandburg continued with the Newspaper Enterprise Association. Then in May he was fired. In his letter giving Sandburg notice of his termination, Samuel T. Hughes made his decision sound as if it were based on purely professional reasons, a matter of an imperfect "fit" between employer and employee (CS Coll: NEA file, May 16, 1919; an imperfect version is in *Letters* 163). There was some truth to this, as indicated by the number of pieces written and proposed by Sandburg in early 1919 and never used by the wire service (CS Coll: NEA files; *Letters* 158–59). But another letter to Sandburg, this one from acting editor Leon Starmont, to inform him that he was being taken off the payroll, contained a remark suggesting that there were other causes involved. "Perhaps our methods can't coincide," Starmont wrote. "But I don't believe you're as dangerous as some people would have us imagine, and I know we are not as stodgy as some folks would have you think" (CS Coll: NEA file, June 6, 1919).

At almost precisely the same moment in June that he was being fired by the NEA, Sandburg was gathering laurels from other observers, receiving a half-share of the annual prize for a volume of poetry given by the Poetry Society of America (a prize said to be the predecessor of the Pulitzer for poetry). When *Cornhuskers* was issued the previous fall, while he awaited clearance to sail to Europe, it had not made nearly as much of a splash as *Chicago and Other Poems*. There was virtually no radical press left to boom the new volume as revolutionary poetry to be enjoyed by all with red blood running in their veins or, as would have been more likely, to condemn a substantial part of it as patriotic drivel. Reviews in the mainstream press were at best restrained. O. W. Firkins, writing in the *Nation,* for example, allowed that Sandburg had his "good moments" but accused him of writing "half-cooked free verse." William Stanley Braithewaite, as he had when he reviewed *Chicago,* condemned Sandburg's lack of artistry. The reviewer for the *Outlook* said he would pray that Sandburg would learn the lesson that art takes time to make ("Untitled"). The reviewer for the *New York Times* approved the toning down of Sandburg's socialist preachings, but he discovered that *Cornhuskers* was melancholy (he attributed this not to the current world situation but, in part, to "the racial soberness of the Scandinavian"), and, emphasizing the line in "Prairie" regarding the past as a "bucket of ashes," which he took as a central message, concluded that Sandburg needed to get a "firmer intellectual grip on the past" ("Mr. Sandburg's Poems"). Three reviews in smaller organs were enthusiastic. Louis Untermeyer wrote in the *Dial* about Sandburg's vitality and energy as he had in his review of *Chicago* for the *Masses;* he, too, explained Sandburg in "racial" terms, claiming that in *Cornhuskers* "the rude practical voice of the American speaks through a strain of ruder Swedish symbolism." John L. Hervey praised Sandburg's contemporaneity and nonintellectual power in *Reedy's Mirror.* And though he did not like the propagandistic element in "Shenandoah" or the longer poems in the book, Alfred Kreymborg, writing in *Poetry,* admired the short lyrics without qualification and argued vigorously that Sandburg's art should be taken for the vernacular, democratic art that it was, not judged by extraneous standards.

Although *Cornhuskers* did not seem like a great or even a good book to most reviewers, it won a share of the coveted Poetry Society prize, and Sandburg no doubt saw it as a wonderful turn of events, a stroke of good fortune following an especially difficult, gloomy period. If he had any thought that his difficulties were over or that gloom would give way to sunlight, he was wrong. Indeed, in the longest notice of the Poetry Society award, there was a clear indication that however much he tried to tone down his political inclinations, in the contemporary atmosphere his work would be subjected to careful examination for signs of Bolshevism. Thus Carolyn Hall, writing in the *Evening Post Magazine,* seemed to go out of her way to inform her readers that *Cornhuskers* contained elements of the "ranting Socialist" alongside the "pure poet." She went further, quoting the assessment of Sandburg by war novelist Major Rupert Hughes, who had set a Sandburg poem to music: "I can only say that I admire Mr. Sandburg's poetry as much as I abominate his politics. I share with him his intense sympathy for the poor, the shabby, and all the victims of life, but I think that the Bolshevik remedies which he seems to advocate are like all other patent cure-alls, a criminal waste of hope and money, and certain to increase misery."

At least as important to Sandburg as either his firing by the NEA or his award of the half-share of the Poetry Society prize was his rehiring in June by the *Chicago Daily News* as its "labor and industrial reporter," which brought him full circle back to where he had been before he began his venture as an international correspondent. His new stint at the *News* settled the financial problem he faced by being out of work. More significantly, it placed him in a central position to participate as a journalist in the watershed political and social events that were then unfolding dramatically and very rapidly.

Befitting the end of a decade as troubled as any the modern world had seen, the first postwar year of 1919 was surreal and violent. Though politicians and other opinion makers sometimes spoke of a coming new world order, signs were everywhere of what seemed to be the collapse of moral centers, the loss of civil restraint, continuing threats to all the old publicly celebrated virtues and verities. Throughout the year, strikes occurred with startling frequency in nearly every economic sector, setting new records for workdays lost and involving, in the end, more than four million workers, about 22 percent of the work force. Both for the realpolitik of labor-management relations and their contemporary and lasting symbolic content, the most notable included the general strike in Seattle, the strike by policemen in Boston, quelled by future president Calvin Coolidge, and the great steel strike that began in late September, pitting 365,000 steelworkers against the fiercely antiunion industry. In July, race riots occurred in Washington, D.C., and Chicago, where before the violence was quelled by the military some thirty-eight people were killed and more than five hundred reported injured. In addition to labor-management and racial strife, nearly every day saw newspapers printing front-page stories about Bolshevik gains in Russia, or, alternatively, the impending death of Bolshevism, anarchist bombs and bomb threats in American cities, and discoveries of "reds" in public institutions such as schools and offices of local governments. In early September, at the Socialist party convention in Chicago, the communist movement in the United States was begun with the formation of two contending communist parties while old-line socialists summoned Chicago police to restore order to the meeting hall. In early October, while news of President Wilson's dire illness along with steel strike reports dominated the news, following rumors of the involvement of gamblers in the "game of democracy," baseball, the World Series was fixed in the famous Black Sox scandal. On Armistice Day in November, another "massacre" of IWW members occurred, this one in Centralia, Washington. In December, after the steel strike had been crushed, there was a major national coal strike, more news of the impending defeat of

Russian Bolshevism, more on its gains, and, finally, reports of the sailing of the SS *Buford,* the ship on which some 240 alien anarchists, including Emma Goldman and Alexander Berkman, were deported to northern Europe.

Sandburg's first assignment in his new stint at the *News* was to cover the June convention of the American Federation of Labor. He filed several articles on daily convention proceedings. Clearly recognizing what seemed fundamental, seminal changes in labor-management relations, the most important of these articles, titled "Labor Gives Minimum to Avert Bolshevism," reported the increasing radicalization of the AFL, its seeming openness to new methods of organizing and to winning its demands through direct action (*DN* 20). His second assignment, a series of articles on the social conditions that had evolved in Chicago's Black Belt as a result of the Great Migration north of blacks, was on a subject that also seemed pivotal.

Most of Sandburg's articles on conditions in the Black Belt, shortly afterward collected in a pamphlet titled *The Chicago Race Riots, July 1919,* were done two to three weeks before the riots began. Writing in an uncharacteristically dispassionate manner, Sandburg gave due recognition to the overcrowded situations in which new black migrants lived, the high rents they paid, the fears of whites that real estate values dropped when blacks moved in, and the existence of criminal elements in the black community. But he stressed black progress and clear signs of white acceptance. Blacks were said to have participated enthusiastically in the recent war effort and expected to be treated like other Americans. They were clean. They were in the process of developing their own strong social and economic institutions. They had educated leaders who counseled racial pride. Their goals were reasonable and just: they sought equal treatment under the law, access to education, and, most of all, equality of economic opportunity. When economic opportunity came, when blacks got decent jobs, racial discrimination by the great majority of whites ended: "Most of this thing we call a race question is down at rock bottom a labor question," a black official with an M.A. from Yale and a Ph.D. from Harvard was quoted as saying (25). The packinghouses were said to employ some fifteen thousand black workers, and packing unions were playing key roles in assimilating blacks. A black official of one local celebrated the brotherhood he had found with whites, and though he emphasized that sexual mixing was not occurring—at a recent union ball blacks had danced with blacks and whites with whites—he predicted that racial fighting would not happen: " 'Here they are learning that it pays for white and colored men to call each other brother' " (54). A white union organizer's recent speech was quoted: " 'You notice there ain't no Jim Crow cars here to-day. That's what organization does. The truth is there ain't no negro problem any more than there's a Irish problem or a Russian or a Polish or a Jewish or any other problem. There is only a human problem, that's all. All we demand is the open door. You give us that, and we won't ask nothin' more of you' " (56).

While these almost sanguine accounts of black progress in Chicago were being published in the *News,* race riots broke out in Washington, D.C., and then in Chicago following the killing of a black child who was swimming on a white beach on Lake Michigan. No riot coverage with bylines by Sandburg appeared in the *News,* but in the introduction to *The Chicago Race Riots, July 1919* he tried to account for them. Essentially, he said, there were two major causes. First, there was the policeman who, summoned to the place where the black child had been killed, had refused to make arrests. This, he concluded in a flourish that indicated he continued thinking of Lincoln and Civil War analogies to explain current events, was an instance of "blind lawless government failing to function through policemen ignorant of Lincoln, the Emancipation Proclamation, and a theory sanctioned and baptized in a storm of red blood." Second, there were the social conditions of Packingtown, the district from which most of the white rioters came. Conditions in that impoverished district, he said, created hoodlums, the perpetrators of the riots. But Sandburg suggested near the end of his introduction, stressing the positive again, thousands of white and colored men had not rioted. Instead, they had stood up in brotherhood, proclaiming that as union men they were opposed to race violence (4–6).

In one of the three chapters at the end of the pamphlet written after the riots, Sandburg returned again to the role of the unions. This time, the riots were "not a race question but a labor union question" because, according to the "prominent official of one of the packing companies" he used as his only source, "The trouble is that the negro is not naturally a good union man. He doesn't like to pay union dues" (74). In contrast to his comments earlier in the pamphlet, this sounded as if the riots were perpetrated by union men against freeloaders who happened to be black. Perhaps Sandburg was simply representing management's point of view in this chapter and had not lost his faith that unions as social institutions could pave the way for a revolution in race relations. But when after ten days of riots black workers finally returned to their stockyards jobs, they were met with significant protests by white workers ("5,000 White Men").

Over the next several months, Sandburg wrote a number of miscellaneous *News* articles dealing with race relations in and around Chicago, none of which returned to the topic of union solidarity as the cure for racial conflict or hoodlums and miscreant police as the cause (*DN* 21–23, 25, 26, 34, 38, 41, 42). Over the next several months, he also wrote a few articles that dealt directly with some of the major events that made 1919 such a watershed year.

In mid-August he filed a story on the Socialist party convention that was to be held in Chicago in which he reported on party fractiousness; a great number of members were seceding and forming Bolshevik organizations and the old party was tremendously weakened (*DN* 24). When the convention took place, the *News* ran two stories reporting on the breakup of the party, the first titled "Socialists in Uproar; Left Wing Biffs Right," the second titled "Haul Down Red Banners." Though both were unsigned, stylistically they were clearly Sandburg's. The second opened with a description of how "Jack Reed, left wing publicist, endeavored to punch Julius Gerber, member of the right wing, somewhere in the face" before the right wing leaders summoned the Chicago police. It ended with a touch of vaudeville comedy, Sandburg showing his bemusement about the utter fractiousness of the movement: "The fight between the left and right wings of the socialist party will undoubtedly be repeated—but this time between the left and right wings of the left wing" (*DN* 27, 28). In mid-September he reviewed Arthur Ransome's *Russia in 1919,* which he called "the best book on Russia." This was an extremely enthusiastic celebration of Ransome, who was known, Sandburg said, in the "hysterical fashion of imperialist propagandists as a 'bolshevik'" but who, he said, was no such thing. Using one of his standard formulas, he described Ransome, who he said he met in Europe, as a man who looked "like a sea captain, a deep-chested, deep-voiced British seadog . . . [who] smokes a black pipe, which he fills and refills from dry plug tobacco that he chips loose with his pocket knife." Ransome's book, in any case, was honest, objective, a warts-and-all account of the new Russia. And, Sandburg said in his lead, though Russia was being made to look like a ridiculous joke by the agencies that controlled communication, transport, and censorship, it might turn out that "the years 1917–1919 were to the nation of Russia what Valley Forge days were to the thirteen colonies" (*DN* 29). In mid-September, shortly after the beginning of the great steel strike, Sandburg published an article in which he analyzed the internal politics of the American Federation of Labor, the differences between its emergent left and right wings, and, most significantly, the possibility that the left, if the strike were successful, could launch a new radical labor party. Quoting at length from the potential platform of the possible new party, Sandburg used about half his article to describe in warm terms the two left leaders, Chicago's John Fitzpatrick and William Z. Foster who, despite his background in the syndicalist movement and the IWW, was still an acceptable man in the eyes of the federation's left wing (Foster went on to become a key leader of the Communist Party-USA) (*DN* 31).

Sandburg was the *News*'s chief labor and industrial reporter, and he should have been assigned to write the paper's reports on the progress of the steel strike in South Chicago and Gary, Indiana. But he was not. Instead, through the most intense weeks of the strike, he wrote articles that had nothing to do with it. Shortly after it began, he was sent to Williams Bay, Wisconsin, from where he reported on observations of the sun being made through a telescope (*DN* 30). Though in the first week of October he visited the South Chicago strike zone with William Allen White and cited White's melancholy reactions (*DN* 32), the articles he wrote in the weeks when the strike crested were on the moving of the Field Museum in Chicago, the passing through the city of cooperative food buyers from England, and the risks that certain businesses were undergoing in Germany (*DN* 33, 35, 36). The *News*, of course, covered the strike, but through Associated Press dispatches and a few articles by Ben Hecht. Only near the very end of the strike in Chicago and Gary did another Sandburg article appear. Written in an appropriately funereal tone, for it was clear that the steelworkers had lost in a grand way, it reported on the efforts of the union to secure the release from jail of several wrongfully charged workers (*DN* 37).

Why had Sandburg not been assigned to cover the steel strike, or, as it would turn out, why was he not assigned to cover any of the other major labor and left political events that unfolded in the ensuing months? He never tried to explain it, nor was there any indication in the pages of the newspaper. But fragmentary evidence in Military Intelligence case files indicates that the agency kept careful tabs on him in the months after he rejoined the *News*. After he published his article on the split within the American Federation of Labor that emerged at the annual convention, John B. Campbell of the agency's Chicago office wrote to the director: "1. Reference is made to our letter of December 20th, 1918. 2. Inclosed for your information is a clipping from the Chicago Daily News dated June 16, 1919, containing an article by Carl Sandburg, entitled " 'Labor Gives Minimum to Avert Bolshevism' " ( *U.S. Military Intelligence* reel 10, file 10110–853: June 25, 1919). After he published his article on the hopes of AFL radicals that the steel strike would lead to a labor party, a copy was sent to Washington and filed, accompanied by the notation, "This article shows the nature of Sandburg's writings recently. A part of M.I.D. History." A few pages earlier in that file there was the marginal notation that "Sandberg [*sic*] has a long M.I.D. history" ( *U.S. Military Intelligence,* reel 9, file 10110–749: 15). Elsewhere was a report on the founding of the Communist Labor party in September, shortly after the Socialist party convention, including a document called "Report of the Committee on Class War Prisoners" calling for a vast educational campaign and a general strike of American workers to commence on October 8 to force the release of political prisoners and withdrawal of American forces from Russia and Hungary, signed by three people, including Carl Sandburg. This was a different Carl Sandburg, a Chicago dentist, but that was not noticed by the agent who conducted the surveillance. Saddling the author with the ideological sins of the communist doctor, he commented, "It will be remembered Carl Sandburg, who carried drafts to America for delivery to [Santeri Nuroteva], was interested in Conditions in Finland, and opposed to the White Guard—he signs this Report, with other noted Communists" ( *U.S. Military Intelligence,* reel 9, file 10013: 574), thus beginning a confusion of the two Sandburgs that would persist in later government surveillance files (Niven 367). Given the beliefs recorded and implied in this surveillance record, it is not much of a leap to conclude that Military Intelligence agents, who were very active in Chicago during the steel strike (Talbert 190ff.), let their distrust of Sandburg be known to the *Daily News* editors, as they had to those same editors a little more than a year earlier and as they probably had to the editors at the NEA (it will be remembered that in his termination letter, Leon Starmont had referred to people who called Sandburg "dangerous"). Although there is no smoking gun, given the record of the press during this period, it is also not much of a leap to conclude that they bowed to the pressure and assigned Sandburg to do stories in which he did not pose a danger, real or imagined. There is, however, no proof for this interpretation of events, and it may be possible that, quite independently, the editors simply reassigned him to write editorials and miscellaneous stories.

Sandburg also wrote a few other prose pieces in addition to those he published in the *News* in 1919 and early 1920 (*DN* 39, 40, 43–46). In April 1919, he published "Baltic Fogs" in *Reedy's Mirror.* The first section of this piece was a graphic description of murders and other atrocities committed against captured Finnish Red Guards by counterrevolutionists and their German supporters, as told by a prison survivor. The second section provided a clear counterpoint. It narrated the circumstances of Sandburg's meeting and interview with Constantine Greaves, the former chamberlain to the czar's court in Petrograd, focusing on Greaves's relatively abject current circumstances in Christiana and his hope for the ultimate victory of the White Guards over the Bolsheviks in Russia. Sandburg concluded the section on Greaves by responding to his question about the possibility of American commitment. He first quoted a speech by Woodrow Wilson in which the president said that liberty and prosperity could not be imposed on any country by an outside force; then he told "the Romanoff henchman I couldn't see where he would get what he wants until an outright imperialist government is running America" (*RM* 2). Eight months after the *Reedy's* essay appeared, he again demonstrated how deeply he had been affected by his European experience. This time the occasion was an interview with him published in the *Chicago Socialist,* a weekly newspaper, titled "Sandburg Tells Story of How the U.S. Stole $10,000." According to the interviewer, he said that "he was not a Bolshevik or a Socialist, but he had an element of fair play in his make-up and he challenged the right of the government 'to discriminate against a democratic government of Finland and favor an imperialistic government.'" His disavowal of radical politics notwithstanding, this piece was picked up and digested by Military Intelligence operatives as part of their investigation of Finnish socialists in the United States (*U.S. Military Intelligence,* reel 10, file 10110: 61).

Repression of ideas and of people was the subject of two other pieces from this period. In his contribution to a volume of tributes called *Debs and the Poets,* he wrote, "The holding of Debs, caged, barred, effectually shackled in our national hoosegow in Georgia draws commentary not so much on the plight of Debs—he can stand it— as on the nation. To a nation that speaks in a Christ vocabulary, we might almost say, 'If the light that is in thee be darkness, then how great is that darkness'" (LePrade 39–40). At the end of January 1920, just after Attorney General A. Mitchell Palmer had conducted his "Red Raids" and just after the ship loaded with deported anarchists had crossed the Atlantic, he published "Propaganda" in *Reedy's Mirror*. This essay recorded his understanding of the broad repression under way and, quoting Frank I. Cobb, a *New York World* editorialist and noted speaker, warned of its dangers. No one, Cobb was quoted as saying, "will ever remove the cause of unrest and discontent by trying to suppress their manifestations." Furthermore, the repression was anti-American. Cobb was again quoted: "What I am pleading for is a restoration of the traditions of the republic, for the restoration of the proved safeguards of human liberty, for the restoration of the free play of public opinion, without which democracy is stifled and cannot exist. God forbid that our supreme achievement in this war should be the Prussianizing of ourselves!" Sandburg went on to note how U.S. authorities were propagandizing by allowing the Mannerheim government of Finland to present itself freely to Americans; with an oblique reference to his own experience as a courier of money for Borodin, he remarked that the Mannerheim government's "documents and funds are admitted to the United States without question or bother." At the end of the essay, he predicted that the repressed "propagandists" would turn out to be heroes. Once again, as he had in one of his last *Review* pieces where he had compared Bill Haywood to him, Sandburg used the analogy of John Brown, saying that a few years after he was hanged Brown had become a great American inspiration, speaking from his grave his message of freedom (*RM* 3).

Despite his absorption in his journalism, most of Sandburg's energy in 1919 and 1920 apparently went into the writing of *Smoke and Steel*, his third book of poetry. Working on it for a year beginning in the spring of 1919 and producing in the end a book that was nearly twice the size of *Chicago and Other Poems* and *Cornhuskers* put together, at about the time he sent his manuscript to Alfred Harcourt he defiantly told Alice Corbin Henderson, "Those who holler propaganda will holler louder than ever at this" (*Letters* 187). This comment overstated the propagandistic elements in the book, but his point can be seen throughout. For though *Smoke and Steel* also contained nature lyrics, domestic poems, and the like—numerically, these were the vast majority—it addressed all the social policy issues he had taken up over the past few years:

the butchery of the Great War; the beauty, creativity and potential power of the people; their harsh working and living conditions; the violence of the race riots; the rapacity of the wealthy; Bolshevism and the counterrevolutions. Together with two poems in *Slabs of the Sunburnt West,* the volume he published in 1922, the poems he wrote on these subjects provided a clear summary of his positions as his radical phase came to an end. Moreover, at least two, the title poem "Smoke and Steel" and the lead poem in *Slabs,* "The Windy City," were among his most powerful, most compelling work.

"Passages," the seventh section of *Smoke and Steel,* was another take on his European experience, and two angry poems in particular read like poetic versions of prose such as "Baltic Fogs" and "Propaganda." Concerning his attempt to interview a White Russian (probably Constantine Greaves, but he was here unnamed), Sandburg wrote in "High Conspiratorial Persons," datelined Christiana in December 1918: "From such a rag that has wiped the secret sores of kings and overlords across the milleniums of human marches and babblings, / From such a rag perhaps I shall ring one reluctant desperate drop of blood, one honest-to-God spot of red speaking a mother heart." "Mohammed Bek Hadjetlache" told the story of a former czarist colonel who now wished to go to Hollywood to ride horses in the movies. Sandburg reported this "bull-roarer's" press conference speech, his description of his possessions and connections (he was, among other things, "an old family friend of Clemenceau"). Then, in a neat editorial summary, he added details that demonstrated the colonel's pure murderousness. "These hands," he wrote, "strangled three fellow workers for the czarist restoration, took their money, sent them in sacks to a river bottom . . . and scandalized Stockholm with his gang of strangler women" (*Poems* 239–40).

Invective of this predictable sort was not, however, the main thrust of "Passages." Rather, several linked poems in the section recorded Sandburg's experience while he awaited clearance to sail to Stockholm and while he was actually en route and concerned his doubt and ambivalence, his sense of aloneness, and his questions about self-identity.

During his wait in the late summer of 1918, he had gone to Washington, where he wrote "Smoke Rose Gold" and "Tangibles." The two were set in view of the Capitol dome, a setting which in *Cornhuskers* would likely have produced a discourse on national commitment. "Smoke Rose Gold" and "Tangibles," though, were meditations on the meaning of the dome which said that the great public symbol of

American purpose was now open to interpretation. Both poems created the impression that Sandburg had spent hours staring at the dome and noticing how it changed when day became night, how its meaning shifted with its atmospheric context. In "Smoke Rose Gold," a star appeared above the dome in the evening. In *Cornhuskers* there would have been no doubt about the relationship of star and dome, national monument and heavenly body: the two would have been fused to underscore the relationship between the American mission and God's will, but this poem ended by noting the long distance between the star and the dome. Similarly, "Tangibles" asked whether a national monument could express the purposes of "living men." The dome itself provided a sort of answer. Like a woman, Sandburg said, the answer was really a postponement, a way of saying keep hoping and keep asking. The dome spoke in "a croon of a hope," a "dream whisper." "Not today, child," she said, "not today, lover; maybe tomorrow, child, maybe tomorrow, lover." What did the lover do when he heard this? Did he go away in the pain of unrequited love or did he continue trying to win his lady? "Tangibles" ended with Sandburg still asking his question and with something of a renewed commitment to the dome goddess conveyed in an elliptical closing line: "There is . . . something . . . here . . . men die for" (*Poems* 232).

In his September 1918 letters to his wife, Sandburg had spoken of his lizardlike disconnection from the "smoky salty misty stupendous drama" that the world was witnessing and about "the resignation and humility and obedience of the infinitesimal human unit in the world storm." The same feelings suffuse the three poems he wrote while en route to his assignment in Stockholm. These were not, however, poems about the "world storm," never once mentioning the Great War or other events. Rather, they were about a man confronting the endless sea—a prairie, so to speak, devoid of human life and historical associations—and as a result, in almost Melvillean fashion, confronting his own significance. The poems came to similar conclusions about identity and meaning as "Chicago Poet," finally resting on the assertion of multiple identities, a self whose chief quality was its proclivity to change.

Of the poems in the sequence written about the trip to Stockholm, "North Atlantic" went the farthest in creating an identification between the sea's essential mutability and the speaker's. The sea was always the same, and "yet the sea always changes," the sea was the mother and father of us all, the sea was timeless. Against its vastness, man was nothing and man's works were mere vanities and playthings. This logic, of course, could lead in devastating directions—if I am nothing, then what?—but Sandburg gave it a different twist. Rather than devastation, the poem ended by glorifying the speaker. He was not quite the sea itself but was the next best thing, the "kin of the changer," the son of the sea and wind. "Fog Portrait," the next poem in the sequence, made no such proclamation as its speaker confronted endless fog on the high seas. But "Flying Fish" carried forward the idea of the forever changing self. Here self-identity was discovered by watching the fish gracefully moving between water and air, seemingly living in neither, and recognizing the analogy to his own life: "Child of water, child of air, fin thing and wing thing . . . I have lived in many half-worlds myself . . . and so I know you" (*Poems* 232–36).

Although "Passages" was finally less about the conflicts over Bolshevism and more about shifting self-identities, the several poems in *Smoke and Steel* which dealt with the Great War recorded Sandburg's solid, clear, and altogether bitter postwar assessments. Short lyrics like "Long Guns" and "A.E.F.," the first a comment on the awful dominance of guns in recent times, the second a brief forecast of what would happen to a gun (it would rust away and become home to a spider), made the meaninglessness of the events as transparent as any of Sandburg's pre-*Cornhuskers* poems on the subject (*Poems* 187, 194). But "The Liars" was easily the clearest summation in the book. Written in March 1919 and called by Sandburg a "sequel" to "The Four Brothers," its nine unalloyed stanzas, its drumbeat of the words "liar" and "lies" and "lie," its stripped vocabulary, and its sledgehammer directness left nothing to a reader's imagination. With no effort to restrain his white-hot anger, Sandburg wrote about how the liars of the nations had conspired to lie to their citizens and to drink their blood "with a laugh and a lie," how they had met behind closed doors to conspire, how their guns produced seven million people "shoving up the daisies." At war's end, the argument continued, there was nothing more than a return to the old way, the liars telling each other, "Let us run the world again, us, us. / Where the doors are locked the liars say: Wait and we'll cash in again." That, and only that, was what the Great War meant. And what of the future, what of the time to come when the liars invented the next war? Sandburg was as direct as could be, saying that he heard "The People" telling each other to "Take things in your own hands" when the liars told them to go to war again (*Poems* 192–93). It sounded as if the old left dream of the masses repudiating their rulers and refusing war was alive once again.

The brutal bitterness of "The Liars" was not repeated elsewhere in *Smoke and Steel*, but Sandburg returned to something close to it in a long poem published in *Slabs of the Sunburnt West*. "And So Today" was about the burial of the Unknown Soldier in his tomb on November 21, 1921, an occasion intended to solemnify and glorify the sacrifices of the war. But as Sandburg presented it, the parade that preceded the internment was a macabre march of skeletons and the oratory of the day a mockery. Down Pennsylvania Avenue in Washington came

> Skeleton men and boys riding skeleton horses,
> the ribs shine, the rib bones curve,
> shine with savage, elegant curves—
> a jawbone runs with a long white slant,
> a skull dome runs with a long white arch,
> bone triangles click and rattle,
> elbows, ankles, white line slants—
> shining in the sun, past the White House,
> past the Treasury Building, Army and Navy Buildings,
> on to the mystic white Capitol Dome.

Government officials—"they are all for the Boy" and "they are all for the Republic," Sandburg said, dismissing their sincerity—spoke rotund nonsense. He wondered, "Do they ever gag with hot ashes in their mouths? / Do their tongues ever shrivel with a pain of fire / Across those simple syllables 'sac-ri-fice' "? Meanwhile, hard-boiled journalists commented on the ceremonies with "Moonshine" and "Feed it to 'em, / they lap it up, / bull . . . bull . . . bull," while in the distance another orator, Death himself, spoke what could be written on a "postage stamp," that ten million men had died. Sandburg concluded, "He said it and quit and faded away, / A gunnysack shirt on his bones" (*Poems* 283–88). Unrelenting, wickedly surreal, complete in its denunciation of the ceremony, "And So Today" anticipated a good many of the attitudes that characterized later American writing about the Great War and its celebrants. In it, as in "The Liars," Sandburg came full circle back to his pre-1917 beliefs.

*Smoke and Steel* also contained more than two dozen poems in which Sandburg returned to his core subject, workers and working class culture. These poems were similar to ones in *Chicago* and *Cornhuskers*. There were panoramas of gritty, smoky industrial landscapes, as in "Five Towns on the B. and O.," "Omaha," "Real Estate News," "Pennsylvania," and "The Sins of Kalamazoo." There were close-ups of working-class street scenes, groups of workers, and individual portraits, as in "Work Gangs," "Eleventh Avenue Racket," "Home Fires," "Crabapple," "Manual System," "Hoodlums," "Killers," "Alley Rats," "Cahoots," and "Man, the Man-Hunter." But while the subjects were the same, there were significant differences in tone and outlook in *Smoke and Steel*. Here there was no heroic working class about to rise up to take its just due, no models of proper working-class behavior, no noble immigrant workers, and no happy, autonomous, humanistic workers who danced and sang in spite of their lowness. There was still said to be a great deal of energy and picturesqueness present. But to a large extent, the explicit, overt ideological framework into which Sandburg had fit his earlier working class portraits, street scenes, and landscapes was missing.

Perhaps the most noticeable feature of the *Smoke and Steel* poems about the working class was the degree to which violence was present. Not in any way similar to the heroic (or at least admirable) violence of various forms of direct action, as in the earlier "Dynamiter" and "Ice Handler," or to the patriotic killing of the Great War, as in "The Four Brothers," having no strategic or tactical goal, the violence depicted in some of these poems was purely gratuitous. This, of course, reflected recent urban history, specifically the violence characteristic of 1919 generally and the race riots of that summer. Indeed, the original typescript of one poem, "Hoodlums," made it clear that Sandburg was thinking of the race riots when he wrote it. It contained as an epigraph a statement by A. K. Foote, a "negro secretary of a stockyards labor union." Foote, who Sandburg had quoted in the *Chicago Race Riots,* here said, "It's working people killing each other, that's all there is to these race riots" (CS Coll: Smoke and Steel file). The poem itself, a monologue depicting a man with unrelieved blood-lust, began with the speaker talking about his blood-lust and hatred, his passion for the death of others, and ended with a wish: "Let us do this now . . . for our mothers . . . for our sisters and wives . . . let us kill, kill, kill—for the torsos of the women are tireless and the loins of the men are strong" (*Poems* 201). Other short poems in *Smoke and Steel* also emphasized violence. "Man, the Man-Hunter" had its speaker overhearing the murderous cries of a lynching mob and the next morning seeing the results: "Two butts of something, a smoking rump / And a warning in charred wood" (*Poems* 171–72). "Alley Rats," which began as a typical Sandburg portrayal of the charm of working-class boys, including their capacity to create metaphorical language, turned into a sardonic statement about their murderousness and the deaths of two of them at the hands of the state's executioner: "And two of them croaked on the same day at a 'necktie party' . . . if we employ the metaphors of their lips" (*Poems* 159). "Killers" was a monologue by an executioner, the "high honorable killer" assigned to kill a young man who had "stood at an intersection of five sewers and there pumped the bullets of an automatic pistol into another man, a fellow citizen" (*Poems* 197).

Reflecting recent events, these *Smoke and Steel* poems about workers and working-class culture differed fundamentally from earlier ones. But the book's title poem made it clear that, whatever the flaws to be found in theories of class solidarity, whatever the disappointments Sandburg, like other radicals, had experienced over the past few years, his faith continued unabated. "Smoke and Steel" was the longest poem in the volume and it was also the most complex. Obviously written in the context of the steel dispute of 1919, it never mentioned the great strike. Obviously an occasion on which Sandburg could have written as angrily as he had in "The Liars," denouncing the exploiters and the awful conditions that prevailed in the industry, it was instead quietly (for Sandburg, at least) philosophical, elegantly meditative. From beginning to end, it contained some of the most intense, suggestive language he ever wrote.

The worker-as-creator was, once again, Sandburg's theme. Suffused in the smoke of the mills, the smoke of the mills mixing with the smoke of the fields and the smoke of burning autumn leaves, the steel the workers created, Sandburg argued, *was* them. In one stanza, he described what became of the workers in the mills, how the hot blast fires metamorphosed men. In one remarkable passage he described how the steel was something more than the result of high heat applied to iron ore. In one place, the steel was "smoke and the blood of a man," in another "Smoke into blood and blood into steel" and "they make the steel with men."

This argument was developed in two ways. It was humanized by Sandburg directly addressing a steelworker—Whitman-like once again, he said "I hook my arm in cinder sleeves; we go down the street together,"—commenting on his workaday life and assuring him, come their ends in heaven or hell, that they were brothers. This was a relatively brief passage. It was followed by the central conceit of the poem, the

*hoc est corpus* made manifest. Prefaced by "Luck moons come and go,"
five men fell into a pot of molten steel and

> Their bones are kneaded into the bread of steel:
> Their bones are knocked into coils and anvils
> And the sucking plungers of sea-fighting turbines.
> Look for them in the woven frame of a wireless station.
> So ghosts hide in steel like heavy-armed men in mirrors.
> Peepers, skulkers—they shadow-dance in laughing tombs.
> They are always there and they never answer.

A catalog of illustrations of the uses of steel, the presence of steel across
the world, the wonder of steel, followed. Then, nearing the end, a
hot blast, really an epiphany of flame and smoke, was celebrated as the
wonder of creation:

> Ears and noses of fire, gibbering gorilla arms of fire,
>     gold mud-pies, gold bird-wings, red jackets riding purple
>     mules, scarlet autocrats tumbling from the humps of
>     camels, assassinated czars straddling vermilion balloons;
> I saw then the fires flash one by one: good-by: then smoke,
>     smoke;
> And in the screens the great sisters of night and cool
>     stars, sitting women arranging their hair,
> Waiting in the sky, waiting with slow easy eyes, waiting
>     and half-murmuring:
>         "Since you know all
>         and I know nothing,
>         tell me what I dreamed last night." (*Poems* 151–56)

Visionary, mystic, and thoroughly uncharacteristic, the passage, like the
poem generally, showed Sandburg working at a different level, thinking
beyond the sociology of conflict and despair.

Very different in tone and manner, though in its own way as passionate, "The Windy City," the lead poem in *Slabs of the Sunburnt West*,
also showed that Sandburg had not lost his faith. Thematically similar
to the earlier "Chicago" and "Skyscraper," it was far more specific,
arraying long catalogs of illustrations, metaphors, and leitmotifs and, as
well, ranging across its subjects with the polemical vigor that Sandburg
was able to marshal in a considerable body of his best writing. "The
Windy City" also directly owed something to Sandburg's earlier radical
prose. At a central point, where he said, "Put the city up; tear the city
down; / put it up again; let us find a city," he seemed to echo his

phrasing in a 1916 *International Socialist Review,* when, as Jack Phillips, he had looked at the "human Niagara" of a preparedness parade and remarked, "Look at 'em. They can tear the town down and build it again. These moving masses of mechanics and day laborers, they can pull the skyscrapers to pieces and stick up new skyscrapers any time they want to" (*ISR* 28: 9).

Aside from any wish he may have had to extend or amplify his earlier work, judging by the number of echoes and parallels, part of the original motive for "The Windy City" could have been an Edmund Wilson essay that appeared in *Vanity Fair* in late 1920. Titled "The Anarchists of Taste," this was a comically thin attempt to explain why American poets wrote free verse. Using Sandburg as his primary example, Wilson claimed that the cause was environmental. French poets wrote majestic verse in set forms because France (all of it, he seemed to say) was harmonious, sweet, picturesque, and so forth, while Americans like Sandburg wrote tasteless verse because tastelessness was all they knew. Wilson described Chicago, where he said Sandburg was born, in language dripping with snobbish superiority. The "he" and "him" referred to was the disadvantaged Sandburg:

> There is nothing in Chicago to encourage a sensitive lover of life. There is no suggestion of harmony in anything about him: the language which he hears spoken is the harsh patois of the city; the streets through which he walks are drab and unspeakably ugly, drab gulches with barren walls built of department stores and offices. Instead of the swift little rivers of France, lined with grey-green poplars, he sees only the dull sprawling Lake, lined with sooty railroad tracks. The harsh commercial landscape of Chicago is about him from his earliest days; his life is full of blank buildings and slaughter-houses and factories, of Claxon-blowing motor-cars and typewriters cracking like machine-guns, taxicabs, jazz-bands, trick electric signs, enormous hotels plastered heavily with garish magnificence, streets and street-cars swarming with tackily dressed people, the crash and grinding of the traffic, the sour befoulment of the air, the whole confused and metallic junk-heap of the modern American city, which is built not for people to live in, but for making and spending money. And whatever aesthetic impulse he may have against such a background as this,—in a newspaper office full of typewriters, or a street-car crowded with people,—does not naturally lend itself to the music of majestic verse. (65)

None of these perceptions were new—it had all been said about Chicago and other American cities countless times before—but, arguably,

Sandburg took Wilson's outrageous remarks as his point of departure for "The Windy City." After the first two sections, in which he placed Chicago in its geographical and historical setting and commented on a few kinds of respectable bourgeois, some "dead from the neck up," who stood above the lifebeat of the city, it was almost as if he were answering Wilson's remarks point by point.

Wilson's comment about Chicago's "harsh patois" became in the third section an invitation or demand to

> Lash yourself to the bastion of a bridge
> and listen while the black cataracts of people go by,
> baggage, bundles, balloons,
> listen while they jazz the classics.

There followed nine snippets of the innovative vernacular bound to make any schoolmarm shudder, ending

> "Hush baby!
> Shoot it,
> Shoot it all!
> Coo coo, coo coo"—
> This is one song of Chicago.

Wilson's revulsion at the ugliness of Chicago's streets and architecture was answered in a long series of sentences, each of which began with an ironic "Forgive us." One said,

> Forgive us if the lumber porches and doorsteps
> Snarl at each other—
> And the brick chimneys cough in a close up of
> Each other's faces—
> And the ramshackle stairways watch each other
>
> As thieves watch—
> And dooryard lilacs near a malleable iron works
> Long ago languished
> In a short whispering purple.

Others recorded children being murdered, cripples sitting in the streets on their stumps, and further indelicacies. Along the way, Sandburg asked that Chicagoans be forgiven

> If these bother respectable people
>   with the right crimp in their napkins
>   reading breakfast menu cards—

Wilson's dismissal of the "dull sprawling Lake, lined with sooty railroad tracks" was answered in Sandburg's ninth section with a lyrical description of the lake's lights and colors and then an inspired description of how the coming of nighttime on the lake transformed the city:

> The canyons swarm with red sand lights of the sunset.
> The atoms drop and sift, blues cross over, yellows plunge.
> Mixed light shafts stack their bayonets, pledge with
>     crossed handles.

Wilson's disgust at Chicago's sordid commercialism and its gruesome noise was answered with an image of crowds that "only the blind get by without acknowledgements." Know them by their day's work, Sandburg demanded:

> Mention proud things, catalogue them.
> The jack-knife bridge opening, the ore boats,
>     the wheat barges passing through.
> Three overland trains arriving the same hour,
>     one from Memphis and the cotton belt,
>     one from Omaha and the corn belt,
>     one from Duluth, the lumberjack and the iron range.
> Mention a carload of shorthorns taken off the valleys of
>     Wyoming last week, arriving yesterday, knocked in the
>     head, stripped, quartered, hung in ice boxes today,
>     mention the daily melodrama of this humdrum, rhythms of
>     heads, hides, heels, hoofs hung up. (*Poems* 271–82)

More broadly and more sharply than he had in either "Chicago" or "Skyscraper," Sandburg here endorsed a particular view of cities. An aesthetic approach to cities, the approach that Wilson and other critics used, was limiting because it failed to recognize the functional basis of living, for example, adaption to circumstances, the creation of language, work, the commercial connections with the hinterlands. And failing that, it failed to understand that all of these things, the entire culture of urban life, was the product of people. Chicago had a special character, it was different from Vienna and Paris and London. It was largely a working-class city, a city that had existed only since industrialism. Its housing and public buildings were impermanent and sometimes ephemeral, its dialect derived from a variety of sources, and, though Sandburg never used the word in "The Windy City," its artfulness could be understood and appreciated only if a viewer put tradition aside. This, of course, was a way of saying that the people of the city—the working class of the city—could be understood and appreciated only if, similarly, predispositions about human behavior were put aside. Seen in their context for what they were, as Sandburg had been saying all along, the people of Chicago, the people anywhere, were the great creators.

# EPILOGUE

As the 1920s began, American radicalism as it had been known over the past two decades had been totally defeated. The Socialist Party of America and the IWW were shattered, anarchist groups were defunct or underground. The recently radicalized AFL, defeated in the great steel strike and other adventures, was reeling, swiftly deradicalizing, and beginning a long period of virtual dormancy. Many activists kept a low profile. Others languished in jail. Ralph Chaplin, Sandburg's *Review* colleague, wrote to him from Leavenworth, reporting that eight IWW prisoners had died of disease, seven had committed suicide, and five had been driven to insanity. Saying that many writers and intellectuals were interested in getting amnesty for the prisoners, he asked, "Couldn't Carl Sandburg do something too?" (CS Coll: Ralph Chaplin file, November 30, 1921). Left leaders were also gone. Emma Goldman was in exile, Eugene Debs was in prison, John Reed died in Russia in 1920, and that same year Bill Haywood jumped bail and went to Russia after the Supreme Court refused to hear his appeal of his conviction. With the notable exception of the *Liberator,* the heir to the *Masses,* and a few other struggling periodicals, the left press that had been so vital a few years before was gone. Only the newly formed communist movement existed with any vitality, but in a short time and for many years afterward it would become a clandestine organization, small in number, deeply surveilled by the government, and ineffectual.

If Sandburg wished to continue writing radical prose after 1920, and there is no evidence that he did, he, like others, would have found publication possibilities severely limited. If he wished to continue to cover labor for the *Daily News,* his reporter's life would have been as an eyewitness to defeat and unending despondency. The fruitlessness of continuing to publish socially engaged poetry must have become clear to him when he read the reviews of *Smoke and Steel* that began appearing in late 1920. The nascent communist press, most notably the *New Majority,* had earlier picked up a few poems from the book that were part of a prepublication offering by Harcourt, but that was all the attention it received in those quarters (CS Coll: Smoke and Steel file). The mainstream press and literary press were interested, but reviewers concentrated mostly on technical matters. The reviewer for the *Nation,* for instance, while noting that Sandburg seemed to be repeating himself, remarked, "Technically, Mr. Sandburg is as interesting as any poet alive." He was especially curious about the form of Sandburg's long line: "That line, easy as it is to read, is anything but easy to write. It is fluid, impetuous, a veritable tidal wave of wrathful or ecstatic recitative; but it is not the utterance of a drunken, heedless man. It is regularly controlled, and the means of its control would be worth knowing" ("Somersaults"). Emanuel Carnevali, writing in *Poetry,* stressed what he said was Sandburg's gift for writing "A purely and originally American language . . . a language of today." Louis Untermeyer was just as positive about Sandburg's technical accomplishments as the reviewer for the *Nation* and Carnevali. Reviews which were negative about *Smoke and Steel,* however, such as those in the *Dial* and the London *Times Literary Supplement,* stressed Sandburg's technical ineptness (A. Wilson; "Smoke and Steel"). By far the most important of the reviews in its potential impact, Amy Lowell's in the *New York Times,* argued that there were signs of great technical mastery in Sandburg but, she said, her earlier fear that Sandburg the poet would be overtaken by Sandburg the propagandist was coming true. Sandburg had become obsessive about sociology and terribly limited because of his contact with people she said were "unfit": "His experience with people is limited to a few types, and it is a pity that these types should so often be the kind of persons whom only the morbidly sensitive, unhealthily developed, modern mind has ever thought it necessary to single out for prominence—prominence of an engulfing sort, that is." Oddly, Lowell allowed at the end of her review that posterity might very well discover in Sandburg a first-rate poet. This review, incidentally, like earlier Lowell commentaries, did not produce a rupture in their relationship. Sandburg wrote a letter profusely thanking Lowell for it (*Letters* 194). And when Lowell later read "The Windy City" and "And So Today," two poems she could have been expected to dislike strongly, she wrote to him, saying, "I am not sure that I don't like 'The Windy City' as well as 'Slabs' [the title poem of the volume], they are both beautiful, and I had the advantage of hearing you read 'The Windy City.' 'And so, Today' is one of the finest things I have read in years" (CS Coll: Lowell file, October 22, 1922).

The couching of commentary on *Smoke and Steel* in largely formalistic terms reflected the fact that by 1920 "social poetry" of the sort that had been popular in politically radical and progressive circles for two decades and more had become old-fashioned and suspicious as art precisely because of its clearly proclaimed attitudes. The cultural debate about the purposes of literature, in other words, had been won by the arguers for "apolitical" art. And no one responded with defenses of "social poetry," attacks on aestheticism, or proclamations about "manliness." Under these circumstances, Sandburg, like other poets and novelists who subscribed to the now outmoded political aesthetic, faced either outright condemnation of their work as "propaganda," neglect, or, at best, assessments that refused to consider "content" as anything more than ancillary to technique.

Sandburg, who Penelope Niven describes in 1920 as ready to "travel new roads" because he was psychologically "battered" by the "pain and seeming futility of" the fray, "scarred" and "sick of the struggle" (362), was then forty-two years old, married, with all the responsibilities that went along with having three young daughters. From 1922 on, according to Niven, his need to earn money, "his concern for his family's long-term security motivated every professional decision he made" (386), especially after ten-year-old Margaret was diagnosed with epilepsy in 1921 (a few years later, it became clear that the youngest of the three daughters, Janet, was learning disabled).

In September 1920, Sandburg underwent a major change in his career as a journalist when the *Daily News* assigned him to write movie reviews and provided him with a very flexible work schedule. But he needed to supplement his newspaper income because of his family situation. How? Over the past several years he had developed an interest and something of a following in "high" literary circles, but he knew that publishing poetry and essays in the little magazines and bringing out an occasional collection was not the way. An exchange he had with Paul Lyman Benjamin, who had published two articles in the *Survey,* the social work journal, one of which included Sandburg and one of which was devoted to him, made his understanding clear. Admiring, perceptive, and bright about Sandburg's social intent, Benjamin had told Sandburg before publishing his second article that "less time for journalism and more for creative work" would be good. Sandburg responded by telling Benjamin that he was right but that "I can earn a decent bricklayer wage the year round with newspaper work while three years sale of poetry would not keep my family for six months" (*Letters* 189). He was not exaggerating. Over the first quarter of 1921, *Smoke and Steel* sold five hundred copies, which probably gave Sandburg a bit less that $100 in royalties (CS Coll: Holt file 1). He might have added that those successful poets who retained a commitment to avant-garde literature, Pound, Lowell, Stevens, William Carlos Williams, and a few others, could afford to; they either had independent means, or no families to worry about, or lucrative professional careers.

How to make the necessary money for his family and have a wide audience for his writing was, apparently, soon clear to him. Ever resourceful and with what seemed to be stunning ease, Sandburg soon brought about other career changes. Using his flexible *Daily News* work schedule to advantage, within the space of a very few years he became a successful performer and personality on the country's lecture and recital circuit, an accomplished writer of children's stories, and a budding Lincoln biographer. And that was just the opening chapter in what over the next three decades would become the story of Carl Sandburg, the popular culture icon and legend. Would he have made these career decisions if a viable left continued to exist? The question is hypothetical, but my guess is that, given his family responsibilities, he would have moved in these new directions no matter the situation of American radicalism. Furthermore, he may have simply been written out—how many times could he have returned to the same themes, how many more poems could he have written about the working class? The subjects were by no means inexhaustible. In addition, as far back as his days in Milwaukee he had had an interest in Lincoln and in his postcollegiate years an interest in becoming a platform performer. Indeed, the return of his interest in platform work came in 1919, when radical possibilities had seemed great. That year, with Lew Sarett, an outdoor writer, he signed on with the J. B. Pond Lyceum Bureau to do joint lectures and recitals. In the brochure Sandburg and Sarett put together, Sarett was advertised as a poet who wrote about "tough, picturesque, laughing and singing people who live on the outposts and the borderlines of our accumulated culture," Sandburg as a man in the tradition of Whitman, O. Henry, and Lincoln who "uses the speech of the common people of America, with its colloquialisms and its slang." The performance given by the two was a celebration, the brochure said, of "Americans all in an All American Program" (CS Coll: Sarett-Sandburg). That there was already an audience with no sense of his radicalism is suggested in a letter from Holt and Company telling him that a businessmen's club wanted to reprint "Chicago" (CS Coll: Holt file 1, October 24, 1919).

Did Sandburg look back to his radical phase? Judging by what is in print or available in the Carl Sandburg Collection, he did so infrequently. He and Eugene Debs had a warm relationship after Debs's release from jail along with twenty-three other political prisoners on Christmas Day

1921. Sandburg visited Debs while he was in a sanitarium, Debs visited the Sandburg home, and the two corresponded (Debs 3: 359, 410, 438–39, 452; *Letters* 219–20, 227). When Debs died in late 1926, Sandburg wrote a beautiful elegy in which he summarized the great and gentle leader as "an orator, a jailbird, a presidential candidate, an / enemy of war, a convict, a philosopher, storyteller, friend / of man." At about the same time that Debs was dying, from May 1926 to January 1927, Sandburg was listed on the masthead of the *New Masses* as a contributing editor, but none of his writing appeared in that magazine. The deaths of Sacco and Vanzetti in 1927 (the two had been arrested during the Red Scare) caused him to write a description of the execution scene as chilling and moving as any others written at the time. But like the Debs poem, the Sacco and Vanzetti poem was not published until 1993, when it was released by the Sandburg estate (*Billy Sunday* 97, 105–6). That Sandburg was reluctant to publish or recite the Sacco and Vanzetti poem seems clear from a letter he wrote to Alfred Harcourt shortly after the executions: "I have accepted an invitation to deliver the Poem before the Phi Beta Kappa Chapter of Harvard University next June. They pay $100 and board you for two days. Somehow, I have to laugh about it rather than take it solemnly. There is something Rootabaga about it. Please don't say anything about it; let any announcement come from Harvard. The only thing certain is that I will not read the Sacco Vanzetti poem now in manuscript. Yours patriotic as hell" (*Letters* 254).

That same reluctance to look back—or, perhaps, to have his radical past impinge on his fame and good fortune—emerged in 1941, when he took great care to get some comments on his labor sympathies made in an appreciative study of his work "corrected." He asked his editor to get the author, working under the same editor, to tone them down, saying, "For the writing of the Lincoln I knew the Abolitionists better for having known the I.W.W. I knew Garrison better for having known Debs" (*Letters* 406–7). This worked very nicely, for the author deleted the offending remarks and incorporated exactly, but without quotation marks, what Sandburg had written to the editor (Detzer 119).

# NOTES

## Chapter II

1. *Lead* 54 was a fairly full paraphrase of the charges against the IWW leveled by the local craft union president and Bill Haywood's response. Preserved in the *Leader* files in the University of Illinois Sandburg Collection is the source for his comments on Haywood's response, "What J. Golden Has Done." More interesting is that another article in the same issue of *Solidarity*, the main IWW newspaper, titled "Automobile Workers" and signed by "An Automobile Worker," was bracketed by Sandburg in the same manner he used to indicate other unsigned appearances throughout his career as a journalist. Stylistically, it was similar to other pieces he wrote at the time. If indeed the article was his, it would place his IWW connection a good deal earlier than I have argued.

2. Sandburg had written about the commission's work earlier, in "The Voices" for *Reedy's Mirror*. Stylistically and substantively, the article was far closer to his earlier work than to his *Review* writing. The testimony he cited in it was based on Industrial Relations Commission hearings held in Chicago from July 21 to 23, 1914, as indicated in Manly 4: 3173–3457.

## Chapter III

1. For a discussion of Wobbly poetry, see Salerno and Winters. An interesting and useful discussion of left poets such as H. H. Lewis, Ralph Chaplin, Arturo Giovannitti, and Covington Hall is in Nelson 39–70. Nelson argues that such poetry was repressed as the result of the formulation of a literary canon in the American academy.

2. Sandburg told Norman Corwin, the creator of *The World of Carl Sandburg*, that "Chicago" was written when he worked for *System*, a magazine whose every page took the position that capitalists, business managers, inventors, and entrepreneurs—the "Players in the Great Game," as the magazine's profile series called them—were the sources of wealth, the great creators, the artists supreme. Sandburg's contributions to *System* usually maintained this overriding theme. Assuming his memory was correct and that he did indeed write "Chicago" while working in his office there, a delicious irony was involved. See Corwin 32.

3. Aside from the title, a few changes were made in the poem for its book publication. Most were slight grammatical changes, but one short stanza was deleted, perhaps because it was uncharacteristically stilted: "Sometimes I wonder what sort of pups born from mongrel bitches there are in the world less heroic, less typic of historic greatness than you" (*ISR* 9).

At about the same time, Sandburg used the same poison-pen letter form in a *Day Book* poem, "Sandburg to Loeb." The poem is an attack on

Jacob M. Loeb for his antiunionism. Its flavor can be discerned from its closing line: "You belong with the trash of history, the oppressors and the killjoys."

4. In *Ever the Winds of Chance*, Sandburg said he had first heard Johannsen speak in Chicago in 1907, remarking that "he had a rolling, flowing voice, eloquence, and humor" (160). Their friendship continued into the 1940s, when Johannsen was working as the circulation and business manager of the Chicago Federation of Labor *Federation News*. See CS Coll: Anton Johannsen folder.

5. For discussions of other writers who transformed fact into creative work, see Fishkin and Sims. Both books are useful, though with the exception of Fishkin's chapter on Whitman, poetry is hardly touched.

6. Given his political beliefs, Sandburg was always interested in the type, the representative man or woman or child who was the end result of socioeconomic determinants, as opposed to the individuated person. This was commonplace in left culture of the period but is nonetheless a feature of his work which has been distressing to ahistorical literary critics. An interesting discussion of this, including a persuasive justification of Sandburg's position, can be found in Nelson 68–69. Sandburg's depiction of African Americans is discussed in Aldon Lynn Nielsen, *Reading Race: White American Poets and the Racial Discourse in the Twentieth Century*. Nielsen says that, like Robert Frost, Sandburg spoke the "vocabulary of white racism" with "fluency and with few signs of self-consciousness" (29). He attributes Sandburg's alleged racism to his roots as a child of Scandinavian and Irish [*sic*] immigrants, his belonging to "a social class that sometimes resented deeply the later massive influx of Mediterranean people and southern blacks" (34). Nielsen, of course, does not refer to Sandburg's political position, his poems about Italians, his Milwaukee journalism containing extremely sympathetic treatment of African Americans, the entirely sympathetic tone and substance of *The Chicago Race Riots*, and so forth. The issue of how Sandburg and others depicted African Americans is further complicated when it is understood that turn-of-the-century left movements usually reflected mainstream racial beliefs: for example, the American Railway Union of the 1890s was for whites only, the AFL rarely attempted to organize blacks, and the SPA leadership typically saw racial oppression as a result of class oppression. The IWW proclaimed itself color-blind, but this did not prevent speakers like Bill Haywood from using racist appeals. See, for example, his comment in his Cooper Union speech of the dreadful black soldiers who not only served the ruling class but spent their time "insulting, outraging, ravishing their wives, mothers, sisters and sweethearts" while workers were in jail ("Socialism the Hope" 467). For a discussion of how one socialist movement debated the race question, see Green 94–115.

7. The myth of Sandburg as a rough-and-tumble character which informed this review and later comments in the left press started earlier than

*Chicago*. Shortly after his first appearance in *Poetry*, the *Western Comrade*, where some of his associates from his Milwaukee days worked, published a short commentary praising Sandburg's work and noting with heavy irony how he had presented himself to newspaper reporters: "When representatives of the newspapers sought Sandburg, after the publication of his verses, he submerged all the intellectual side of his life and concealed the story of his college training, and the writers drew a tolerably faithful picture of the poet as a rugged brickyard toiler and a railroad construction worker" ("Revolt").

8. Sandburg and Alfred Harcourt were attentive about getting *Chicago* to radical readers. At one point shortly after the book was published, Harcourt express mailed another twenty-five copies to Chicago's Radical Book Shop. Among the very few individuals receiving complimentary copies of the book under Sandburg's instructions were Bill Haywood and Matthew Schmidt, one of the dynamiters in the *Los Angeles Times* case. See letters of May 9 and July 16, 1916, to Sandburg from Alfred Harcourt in CS Coll: Holt folder 1.

## CHAPTER IV

1. See, for example, the discussion of the oration Schmidt gave when he was sentenced to life imprisonment in *ISR* 22 and the comments on Joe Thomas and Pulvio Pettinello in *ISR* 30: 139. Among other things, Schmidt claimed he had been offered his freedom if he agreed to testify against Anton Johannsen and another famous dynamiter. Sandburg maintained his friendship with Schmidt through 1926 at least, sending him his books when they were published (Schmidt had also been on the list for a complimentary copy of *Chicago and Other Poems*). His letters to Schmidt when he was in prison are apparently not extant; there are three letters from Schmidt to Sandburg in CS Coll: Matthew Schmidt, one of which, written on August 6, 1916, includes his approving comments on Sandburg's "Dynamiter" and "Iceman": "I recognize the 'Dynamiter', he is one of the salt of the Earth; and that Iceman, it was his type that made Chicago the city of spirit which it now is. I see him now, looking at the knuckles of his hand and saying, 'the damned bastard wont [*sic*] have teeth enough to bite anybody else for a while.'"

## CHAPTER V

1. Sandburg knew MacGregor from the time both had worked on the *Chicago Day Book*. MacGregor was in Ludlow as a journalist, and it is clear that he became involved in the action there. In the CS Coll: Don MacGregor folder, there are two letters from MacGregor to Sandburg, dated March 15 and April 12, 1914, detailing his difficulties in Colorado and describing how his fellow journalists were serving ruling-class interests.

2. "Knucks" was very possibly inspired by a trip to Springfield and Joliet that Sandburg made in October 1917 to cover a coal strike (*DN* 10, 11). The first article was unsigned but was plainly his. The second ends with a treatment of Nathan Lee, a black coal miner who was a strong union man. Another poem he wrote at the time, not published for several decades, was apparently based on his interview with Lee or with other black miners. See "Sayings of Henry Stephens" (*Springfield, Illinois, 1917*) in *Poems* 691–94.

3. In the letter in which he had told Sam Hughes what to say to the government about his credentials and on a few other occasions, Sandburg said that he had been an editorial writer for the *News*. The CS Coll: *Daily News* files contain several dozen editorial clips, most of them concerning the IWW prosecution, the Great War, and Bolshevism, that presumably were saved by Sandburg because he had written them. Unfortunately, these pieces do not carry any of Sandburg's telltale stylistic signs but comport with other editorials they appear among. I assume they were indeed written by him, but I have not drawn upon them in this study. The key editorial on Bolshevism that drew the attention of Military Intelligence is not among the preserved editorial clips.

The *News* had serially published a translation of Leon Trotsky's book *The Bolsheviki and World Peace* beginning on January 15, 1918, which may have given surveillance agents further cause to suspect the editors. Sandburg, incidentally, published a very positive review of Trotsky's essays *Our Revolution*. See *DN* 14.

## Chapter VI

1. Judging by the number of reprints filed in the CS Coll: NEA folder, only *CP 9* received attention in other newspapers serviced by the NEA. A few other short articles appeared in papers other than the *Press,* but, unfortunately, bibliographical information has not been preserved with the clippings. In addition to clippings, there are stored a few typescripts in which Sandburg dealt at length with subjects pertaining to revolutionary events in northern Europe. These were apparently not published in any form.

2. Sandburg thus entered the sweepstakes of who brought Lenin's sacred document to America. John Reed was one possibility because of his close association with both Lenin and the editors of the *Class Struggle.* Pyotor Travin, another Bolshevik, later put in his own claim.

A further complication having to do with Sandburg's claim is that another Lenin letter, *A New Letter to the Workers of Europe and America,* was published by the Socialist Publication Society of Brooklyn (which also published the *Class Struggle*) in early 1919. A copy of it was retained by Sandburg, and on its cover he wrote, "I brot the text of this from Stockholm, gave it to Nuorteva, who had this printed from it—C.S." (CS Coll: NEA file). There is no indication of when Sandburg wrote the note, but, because the *New Letter* was datelined by Lenin January 12, 1919, a month after Sandburg left Stockholm, I have concluded that he was misremembering what he brought in with him.

# WORKS CITED

## I. Books by Carl Sandburg

*Abraham Lincoln: The Prairie Years.* 2 vols. New York: Harcourt, Brace, 1926.

*Abraham Lincoln: The War Years.* 4 vols. New York: Harcourt, Brace, 1939.

*Always the Young Strangers.* New York: Harcourt, Brace, 1953.

*The American Songbag.* New York: Harcourt, Brace, 1927.

*Billy Sunday and Other Poems.* Ed. George and Willene Hendrick. San Diego: Harcourt, Brace, 1993.

*The Chicago Race Riots, July 1919.* Intro. Walter Lippmann. Preface Ralph McGill. 1920. New York: Harcourt, Brace and World, 1969.

*Complete Poems of Carl Sandburg.* San Diego: Harcourt Brace Jovanovich, 1970.

*Ever the Winds of Chance.* Ed. Margaret Sandburg and George Hendrick. Urbana: U of Illinois P, 1983.

*Home Front Memo.* New York: Harcourt, Brace, 1943.

[Charles Sandburg]. *In Reckless Ecstasy.* Foreword Philip Green Wright. Galesburg: Asgard P, 1904.

*The Letters of Carl Sandburg.* Ed. Herbert Mitgang. 1968. San Diego: Harcourt Brace Jovanovich, 1988.

*The Poet and the Dream Girl: The Love Letters of Lilian Steichen and Carl Sandburg.* Ed. Margaret Sandburg. Urbana: U of Illinois P, 1987.

## II. Archives

Carl Sandburg Collection, Rare Book and Special Collections Library, University of Illinois at Urbana-Champaign.

## III. Periodical Appearances by Carl Sandburg, Arranged Chronologically Under the Titles of Magazines and Newspapers

*La Follette's Weekly Magazine*

All except number *LA* 7 were printed under the byline of Charles Sandburg.

*LA* 1 "Letters to Bill." 22 May 1909: 14–15.
*LA* 2 "Letters to Bill." 29 May 1909: 9.
*LA* 3 "Letters to Bill." 31 July 1909: 12–13.
*LA* 4 "Letters to Bill." 14 Aug. 1909: 12.
*LA* 5 "Letters to Bill." 18 Sept. 1909: 12.
*LA* 6 "Fighting the White Plague: How the People are Being Educated to Stamp Out Tuberculosis." 16 Oct. 1909: 7–8.

*LA* 7 "The 'Municipal Dance': How Milwaukee Is Trying to Eliminate Evil from Social Recreation." 24 Dec. 1910: 9+.

## *Milwaukee Social-Democratic Herald: A Journal of the Coming Civilization*

Numbers *SDH* 1–4 were printed under the byline of Charles Sandburg, number *SDH* 5 under the name Charles Sandland.

*SDH* 1 "Child Labor—With Special Reference to Wisconsin." 11 Dec. 1909: 2.
*SDH* 2 "Child Labor—With Special Reference to Wisconsin." 18 Dec. 1909: 3.
*SDH* 3 "Child Labor—With Special Reference to Wisconsin." 25 Dec. 1909: 2.
*SDH* 4 "Child Labor—With Special Reference to Wisconsin." 1 Jan. 1910: 2.
*SDH* 5 "Child Labor—With Special Reference to Wisconsin." 8 Jan. 1910: 3.
*SDH* 6 "The Muck Rakers." 23 July 1910: 3.
*SDH* 7 "A Labor Day Talk." 3 Sept. 1910: 3.
*SDH* 8 "Why Is High Meat [Meat High?]." 24 Dec. 1910: 2.
*SDH* 9 "Robbery, Up-to-Date." 7 Jan. 1911: 8.
*SDH* 10 "Lincoln's Birthday." 11 Feb. 1911: 3.
*SDH* 11 "Lying About Milwaukee." 11 Feb. 1911: 6.
*SDH* 12 "Lake Seamen Grappling the Steel Trust." 6 May 1911: 4.
*SDH* 13 "A Letter to Bill." 24 June 1911: 3.
*SDH* 14 "Milwaukee's Tammany." 7 Oct. 1911: 6.
*SDH* 15 "Otis' Fakes About Milwaukee." 6 Jan. 1912: 2.
*SDH* 16 "Labor." 17 Feb. 1912: 2.
*SDH* 17 "The Poor Strikebreaker." 30 Mar. 1912: 5.

## *Milwaukee Leader*

*Lead* 1 "Work and Workers." 12 Dec. 1911: 8.
*Lead* 2 "God's Taken' Care o' Me Says Mammy Johnson at 106." 15 Dec. 1911: 1.
*Lead* 3 "Work and Workers." 22 Dec. 1911: [10].
*Lead* 4 "Work and Workers." 26 Dec. 1911: [10].
*Lead* 5 "Says Capital Has Committed Same Kind of Crimes as the M'Namaras." 2 Jan. 1912: [8].
*Lead* 6 "Railroads Have Killed 23 Since M'Namaras Confessed." 10 Jan. 1912: 4.
*Lead* 7 "Work and Workers." 10 Jan. 1912: 5.
*Lead* 8 "Here Are the Hours No. 739 Is Compelled to Work on Street Car." 11 Jan. 1912: 4.
*Lead* 9 "Work and Workers." 11 Jan. 1912: [10].

*Lead* 10 "Work and Workers." 15 Jan. 1912: 4.

*Lead* 11 "Jane Addams, Social Center Originator, to Speak in Milwaukee." 17 Jan. 1912: 4.

*Lead* 12 "Work and Workers." 19 Jan. 1912: 5.

*Lead* 13 "Work and Workers." 22 Jan. 1912: [5].

*Lead* 14 "Dr. Woods Hutchinson Possesses Art of Saying What He Thinks." 31 Jan. 1912: 4.

*Lead* 15 "Work and Workers." 31 Jan. 1912: 5.

*Lead* 16 "Work and Workers." 3 Feb. 1912: 3.

*Lead* 17 "Non-Partisanship Has Been Tried and Has Failed." 8 Feb. 1912: 10.

*Lead* 18 "Work and Workers." 9 Feb. 1912: 5.

*Lead* 19 "Work and Workers." 10 Feb. 1912: 12.

*Lead* 20 "They Confess Milwaukee Is Making Good." 14 Feb. 1912: 8.

*Lead* 21 "Notorious Labor Spotter Heads Crew Brought Here to Wreck Car Men's Union." 20 Feb. 1912: 1.

*Lead* 22 "Trainmen's Card, Operative's Report, Welfare Membership, Car Men's Application and Expense Account of Labor." 20 Feb. 1912: 8.

*Lead* 23 "Kraft Heads City Life Saving Crew That Is Helping Workers." 28 Feb. 1912: 10.

*Lead* 24 "Carney and Bading Address Quiet Meeting; Statement Is Challenged." 29 Feb. 1912: [12].

*Lead* 25 "Burglars in the House." 5 Mar. 1912: [8].

*Lead* 26 "Entire Labor World Crackles with Unrest as Living Cost Soars." 8 Mar. 1912: [10].

*Lead* 27 " 'Red' McGlory Finds Milwaukee Unhealthy Town for Union Workers." 11 Mar. 1912: 4.

*Lead* 28 "Is This an Explanation?" 16 Mar. 1912: [10].

*Lead* 29 "Milwaukee Bag Co. Exploits Girls, Says 'Hands Off' to Health Police." 18 Mar. 1912: 10.

*Lead* 30 "Two Political Knockouts." 22 Mar. 1912: 4.

*Lead* 31 "Joe Carney, Why Don't You Tell People About $600,000 Graft in Asphalt Pavement?" 1 Apr. 1912: 4.

*Lead* 32 "River Street and Polite Society." 9 Apr. 1912: 10.

*Lead* 33 "Snowing Them Under: A Short Farce." 10 Apr. 1912: 8.

*Lead* 34 "Lessons from Lawrence." 13 Apr. 1912: 10.

*Lead* 35 "They Feel Queer About the New Rebellion." 16 Apr. 1912: 10.

*Lead* 36 "How to Help the Red Storm." 22 Apr. 1912: 8.

*Lead* 37 "How They Look at It." 25 Apr. 1912: 12.

*Lead* 38 "J. B. Lennon in Tribute to Seidel." 4 May 1912: 1.

*Lead* 39 "No Scabbing May Soon Be Slogan of the Metal Trades." 9 May 1912: 1.

*Lead* 40 "Work and Workers." 22 May 1912: 5.

*Lead* 41 "Workingman's Struggle Against Hard Luck Brings Out Shameful Conditions in County Institution." 24 May 1912: 14.

*Lead* 42 "Nothing to Lose But Chains." 31 May 1912: 10.

*Lead* 43 "Here's How Your Vote at the Grocery Helps Bakery Workers." 6 June 1912: 10.

*Lead* 44 "Husky City Firemen Delight in Watching Ferret Kill Rat in Pit; Like Game of Modern Business." 12 June 1912: 3.

*Lead* 45 Untitled review of Caro Lloyd's *Henry Demarest Lloyd*. 15 June 1912: 10.

*Lead* 46 "State Labor May Ask Change in Recent Compensation Law." 20 June 1912: 12.

*Lead* 47 "Party Is Busy on State Issues." 26 June 1912: 1.

*Lead* 48 "Legien, Our A.F. of L. Guest." 27 June 1912: [10].

*Lead* 49 "Work and Workers." 10 July 1912: 3.

*Lead* 50 "Labor World Is Sizzling with Action Proclaiming Class Struggle." 11 July 1912: 4.

*Lead* 51 "Work and Workers." 11 July 1912: 4.

*Lead* 52 "Democratic Legal Lights Battling with Eyes on Chances for Jobs." 12 July 1912: 2.

*Lead* 53 "Economic Injustices Cause Denunciation of Old Parties." 20 July 1912: 2.

*Lead* 54 "Work and Workers." 22 July 1912: 3.

*Lead* 55 "Work and Workers." 23 July 1912: 3.

*Lead* 56 "Work and Workers." 24 July 1912: 5.

*Lead* 57 "Work and Workers." 29 July 1912: 5.

*Lead* 58 "Labor News." 2 Aug. 1912: 5.

*Lead* 59 "Work and Workers." 5 Aug. 1912: 5.

*Lead* 60 "Work and Workers." 6 Aug. 1912: 5.

*System*

*Sys* 1–3 and 6–7 were printed under the pseudonym R. E. Coulson.

*Sys* 1 "Are $300,000,000 Worth Saving?" 23 (Apr. 1913): 363–71.

*Sys* 2 "The High Cost of Government." 23 (May 1913): 481–89.

*Sys* 3 "Planning the Nation's Spending." 23 (June 1913): 612–19.

*Sys* 4 "Muzzling Factory Machines." 24 (July 1913): 11–17.

*Sys* 5 "Training Workers to Be Careful." 24 (Aug. 1913): 124–32.

*Sys* 6 "How I Buy for My Customers." 24 (Sept. 1913): 248–54.

*Sys* 7 "How I Hold My Customers." 24 (Oct. 1913): 367–71.

*Western Comrade*

"What Happened March Fourth." 1 (1913): 20–21.

*Chicago Day Book*

"Sandburg to Loeb." 8 Sept 1915: [3].

*International Socialist Review*

Sandburg acknowledged his pseudonyms of "Militant" and "Jack Phillips." Two unsigned articles were part of signed series. Other unsigned articles and one by "Live Wire" were attributed to him for two reasons. First, each repeats themes and concerns, most usually in similar phrasing and sometimes in duplicated phrasing, stated in signed and acknowledged articles. Second, each is written in the distinctive "workingman's" language developed by Sandburg in early 1915 *Review* articles. In some cases, the attribution was reinforced by the author's use of titles the same as those used in signed pieces. One piece, *ISR* 48, was assigned to Sandburg because it was printed in his telltale handwriting. Finally, Sandburg kept most of his *Review* articles. They are in CS: Coll: International Socialist Review file. Missing from the file are *ISR* 12, 21, 22, 28, 29, 32, and 47.

*ISR* 1 "The Wops of Kenosha." 13 (Aug. 1912): 133–35.

*ISR* 2 "Fixing the Pay of Railroad Men." 15 (Apr. 1915): 589–93.

*ISR* 3 [Unsigned]. "Fixing the Pay of Railroad Men." 15 (May 1915): 656–58.

*ISR* 4 "Ashes and Dreams." 15 (May 1915): 671.

*ISR* 5 "Fixing the Pay of Railroad Men." 15 (June 1915): 709–13.

*ISR* 6 "The Two Mr. Rockefellers—and Mr. Walsh." 16 (July 1915): 18–25.

*ISR* 7 "Looking 'Em Over." 16 (Aug. 1915): 68–72.

*ISR* 8 "Looking 'Em Over." 16 (Sept. 1915): 132–37.

*ISR* 9 "Billy Sunday." 16 (Sept. 1915): 152–53.

*ISR* 10 [Unsigned]. "You Slobs of Politicians Sitting Around Washington." 16 (Oct. 1915): 197.

*ISR* 11 "That Walsh Report." 16 (Oct. 1915): 198–201.

*ISR* 12 [Unsigned]. "The Garment Workers Strike." 16 (Nov. 1915): 260–64.

*ISR* 13 [Unsigned]. "That Walsh Report." 16 (Nov. 1915): 265–68.

*ISR* 14 [C.S.] "A Million Young Workmen." 16 (Nov. 1915): 268.

*ISR* 15 [Unsigned]. "Joe Hill." 16 (Dec. 1915): 329–30.

*ISR* 16 [Unsigned]. "Just a Minute." 16 (Dec. 1915): 335.

*ISR* 17 [Unsigned]. "Bunk Mills Open Again in Washington." 16 (Jan. 1916): 387–89.

*ISR* 18 [Unsigned]. "Railroad General Strike. Will Warren Stone Put the Brakes On?" 16 (Jan. 1916): 390–93.

*ISR* 19 [C.S.]. "Child of the Romans." 16 (Jan. 1916): 393.

*ISR* 20 [Live Wire]. "Looking 'Em Over." 16 (Feb. 1916): 465–67.

*ISR* 21 [Unsigned]. "Flashes from the Rails." 16 (Mar. 1916): 520–22.

*ISR* 22 [Unsigned]. "Labor Notes." 16 (Apr. 1916): 621–22.

*ISR* 23 "Government." 16 (May 1916): 643.

*ISR* 24 [Jack Phillips]. "Will the Rail Strike Be Side-tracked?" 16 (May 1916): 657–61.

*ISR* 25 "Ready to Kill." 16 (June 1916): 710.

*ISR* 26 [Jack Phillips]. "Jolts and Jabs." 16 (June 1916): 733–37.

*ISR* 27 "Wars." 17 (July 1916): [4].

*ISR* 28 [Jack Phillips]. "Doings of the Month." 17 (July 1916): 5–10.

*ISR* 29 [Unsigned]. "Doings of the Month." 17 (Aug. 1916): 69–73.

*ISR* 30 [Militant]. "Flashes Along the Battle-Line." 17 (Sept. 1916): 137–40.

*ISR* 31 [Militant]. "Why the Rails Won." 17 (Oct. 1916): 199–202.

*ISR* 32 [Unsigned]. "Politics and People." 17 (Oct. 1916): 206–7.

*ISR* 33 [Militant]. "Politics and People." 17 (Nov. 1916): 265–68.

*ISR* 34 [Militant]. "Nine Short Ones." 17 (Dec. 1916): 338–39.

*ISR* 35 [Militant]. "Flashes Along the Battle-Line." 17 (Jan. 1917): 402–5.

*ISR* 36 [Militant]. "Looking 'Em Over." 17 (Feb. 1917): 476–79.

*ISR* 37 [Militant]. "The Once Over." 17 (Mar. 1917): 547–49.

*ISR* 38 [Jack Phillips]. "The 8-Hour Rail Drive." 17 (Apr. 1917): 603–4.

*ISR* 39 [Jack Phillips]. "The Drift of the War." 17 (May 1917): 658–59.

*ISR* 40 "Will Marshall Field III. Enlist?" 17 (May 1917): 660.

*ISR* 41 [Unsigned]. "The Russian Revolution." 17 (June 1917): 709–14.

*ISR* 42 [Jack Phillips]. "Along the Line." 17 (June 1917): 740–43.

*ISR* 43 [Jack Phillips]. "As We Go Along." 17 (July 1917): 30–32.

*ISR* 44 "Grass." 17 (Sept. 1917): 141.

*ISR* 45 [Jack Phillips]. "Look at It!" 17 (Sept. 1917): 149–50.

*ISR* 46 "Government." 17 (Oct. 1917): 203.

*ISR* 47 "Haywood Longs for 'Other Boys' in Jail." 18 (Nov.-Dec. 1917): 277–78.

*ISR* 48 [Unsigned]. "Hold the Fort Grand Entertainment." 18 (Jan. 1918): 279.

*ISR* 49 [Jack Phillips]. "Haywood of the I.W.W." 18 (Jan. 1918): 343.

*ISR* 50 [Jack Phillips]. "Speaking of the Department of Justice." 18 (Feb. 1918): 406–7.

*Chicago Daily News*

*DN* 1 "Loyal Labor Men to Join Unique Meeting." 3 Sept. 1917: 3.

*DN* 2 "Red, White and Blue as Colors for Labor." 4 Sept 1917: 4.

*DN* 3 "Labor and Radicals Join to Support U.S." 5 Sept. 1917: 1.

*DN* 4 "Platform of Labor to Be Used in Europe." 7 Sept. 1917: 3.

*DN* 5 "Varied Forces Unite in Labor War League." 8 Sept. 1917: 5.

*DN* 6 "Less 'Free Speech' for Aids of Kaiser." 12 Sept. 1917: 6.

*DN* 7 "Urge Socialists to Get in and Win War." 13 Sept, 1917: 13.

*DN* 8 "Haywood Longs for 'Other Boys' in Jail." 2 Oct. 1917: 2.

*DN* 9 "Sabotage 'Knockout Drops' for Industry." 11 Oct. 1917: 19.

*DN* 10 "Sees End of Strike in Coal Mines Soon." 18 Oct. 1917: 5.

*DN* 11 "Here's Miners' Side of Illinois Coal Strike." 20 Oct. 1917: 3.

*DN* 12 "Because of This Book." 7 Nov. 1917: 13.

*DN* 13 "I.W.W. Prosecution Called Stupid Move." 19 Feb. 1918: 5.

*DN* 14 "Trotzky, the Jailbird." 3 Apr. 1918: 13.

*DN* 15 "Men in War." 10 Apr. 1918: 12.

*DN* 16 "As a Reporter Views It." 17 Apr. 1918: 8.

*DN* 17 "Wisconsin Plays and Players." 5 June 1918: 13.

*DN* 18 "Labor Host Stirred by Chicago Woman." 13 June 1918: 12.

*DN* 19 "Tar and Feathers in Minnesota's Primary." 19 June 1918: 6.

*DN* 20 "Labor Gives Minimum to Avert Bolshevism." 16 June 1919: 2.

*DN* 21 "Yards Race Clashes Seen as Labor Mixup." 5 Aug. 1919: 4.

*DN* 22 "Negroes Not Leaving Chicago for South." 7 Aug. 1919: 4.

*DN* 23 "Race Commission Faces Huge Task." 8 Aug. 1919: 4.

*DN* 24 "Socialist Factions Will Convene Here." 13 Aug. 1919: 4.

*DN* 25 "Names Commission on Race Problems." 20 Aug. 1919: 1.

*DN* 26 "Race Commission Unique in Character." 26 Aug. 1919: 6.

*DN* 27 [Unsigned]. "Socialists in Uproar: Left Wing Biffs Right." 30 Aug. 1919: 3.

*DN* 28 [Unsigned]. "Haul Down Red Banners." 1 Sept. 1919: 1.

*DN* 29 "The Best Book on Russia." 17 Sept. 1919: 12.

*DN* 30 "Tiny Wisp of Flame Is 200,000 Miles Long." 23 Sept. 1919: 5.

*DN* 31 "Radicals Eye Strike with Intense Hope." 27 Sept. 1919: 5.

*DN* 32 "William Allen White Visits Strike Zone." 4 Oct. 1919: 3.

*DN* 33 "Packing Up to Move Elephants and Bugs." 6 Oct. 1919: 15.

*DN* 34 "A.M.E. Bishops Ask Race War Inquiry." 13 Oct. 1919: 4.

*DN* 35 "Five Big Tracts Feed British Co-Operators." 15 Oct. 1919: 6.

*DN* 36 "U.S. Business Risks Millions in Germany." 17 Oct. 1919: 17.

*DN* 37 "Strikers to Demand Release of 7 Held." 20 Oct. 1919: 1.

*DN* 38 "Colored Folk Rule Cook County Town." 6 Nov. 1919: 15.

*DN* 39 "W. B. Lloyd Attacks Former Comrades." 18 Nov. 1919: 20.

*DN* 40 "Darrow's Book." 19 Nov. 1919: 12.

*DN* 41 "469 More Negroes in Business Than in 1916." 4 Dec. 1919: 12.

*DN* 42 "Chicago Is Second in Negro Population." 17 Dec. 1919: 17.

*DN* 43 "Clothing Workers Get Wage Increase." 24 Dec. 1919: 5

*DN* 44 "Garment Shops Run Without Shutdown." 26 Dec. 1919: 7.

*DN* 45 "Garment Workers Abide by Contract." 27 Dec. 1919: 7.

*DN* 46 "Mutual Trust Need in Shop Conciliation." 6 Jan. 1920: 15.

*Cleveland Press*

*CP* 1 "Carl Sandburg on Red Reign." 4 Nov. 1918: 2.

*CP* 2 "Food Thieves Fill Jails." 21 Dec. 1918: 1.

*CP* 3 "Bolshevik Fear of America." 24 Dec. 1918: 7.

*CP* 4 "Crooks Swell Red Army." 30 Dec. 1918: 8.

*CP* 5 "Russ Tales Out of School." 2 Jan. 1919: 14.

*CP* 6 "Iron Crosses Torn Off." 3 Jan. 1919: 13.

*CP* 7 "Berlin's View of Kaiser." 9 Jan. 1919: 12.

*CP* 8 "Finnish Guards Spurn Foe." 11 Jan. 1919: 14.

*CP* 9 "The Ex-Czarina's Last Love Letter Written to the Late Czar." 4 Feb. 1919: 3.


## *Reedy's Mirror*

*RM* 1 "The Voices." 22 Aug. 1914: 8.

*RM* 2 "Baltic Fogs." 11 Apr. 1919: 207–8.

*RM* 3 "Propaganda." 29 Jan. 1920: 74.


### IV. SECONDARY SOURCES

Aiken, Conrad. "Poetic Realism." *Poetry Journal* 6 (1917): 117–21.

An Automobile Worker. "Automobile Workers." *Solidarity* 20 Apr. 1912: [3].

Ashleigh, Charles. "A Momentous Document." *Solidarity* 13 May 1916: [2].

———. *Rambling Kid*. London: Faber and Faber, 1930.

Baritz, Loren, ed. *The American Left: Radical Political Thought in the Twentieth Century*. New York: Basic Books, 1971.

Basinet, Victor J. " 'Chicago Poems': Echoes of the Revolt in Verse." *Solidarity* 7 Aug. 1916: [3].

Benjamin, Paul Lyman. "A Poet of the Commonplace." *Survey* 2 Oct. 1920: 77–78.

———. "The Poetry of Existence: Some Recent Social Poetry." *Survey* 29 Nov. 1919: 188–89.

"Billy Sunday Has Hard Row in Paterson." *Solidarity* 24 Apr. 1915: [4].

Bodnar, John. *Remaking America: Public Memory, Commemoration, and Patriotism in the Twentieth Century*. Princeton: Princeton UP, 1992.

"Bolsheviki at Work in Berlin and Here . . . Propaganda Fund Sent to New York Said to Exceed Outlay in Germany." *New York Times* 22 Dec. 1918: 1+.

"Bolshevism." *Chicago Daily News* 8 June 1918: 6.

Boris, Eileen. *Art and Labor: Ruskin, Morris, and the Craftsman Ideal in America*. Philadelphia: Temple UP, 1986.

Bradley, William A. "Four American Poets." *Dial* 14 Dec. 1916: 528–29.

Braithewaite, William Stanley. "Carl Sandburg's 'Chicago' Poems." *Boston Transcript* 13 May 1916: 6.

———. "Carl Sandburg's *Cornhuskers*." *Boston Transcript* 11 January 1919: 9.

Calkins, Earnest Elmo. "Education of an American Poet." *Saturday Review* 17 Jan. 1953: 9–10.

Carnevali, Emanuel. "Our Great Carl Sandburg." *Poetry* 17 (1921): 266–72.

Chaplin, Ralph. "Joe Hill's Funeral." *International Socialist Review* 16 (1916): 400–404.

———. *Wobbly: The Rough-and-Tumble Story of an American Radical.* Chicago: U of Chicago P, 1948.

Comyn, Stella. "The Futility of Investigations." *Mother Earth* 9 (Feb. 1915): 376–79.

Corwin, Norman. *The World of Carl Sandburg: A Stage Presentation.* New York: Harcourt, Brace & World, 1961.

Debs, Eugene V. *Letters of Eugene Debs.* 3 vols. Ed. J. Robert Constantine. Champaign: U of Illinois P, 1990.

———. "Sound Socialist Tactics." *International Socialist Review* 12 (1912): 481–86.

"Defining Sabotage." *Chicago Daily News* 20 Oct. 1917: 6.

Dell, Floyd. "Walt Whitman, Anti-Socialist." *New Review* 15 June 1915: 85–86.

Detzer, Karl. *Carl Sandburg: A Study in Personality and Background.* New York: Harcourt, Brace, 1941.

Draper, Theodore. *The Roots of American Communism.* 1957. New York: Octagon, 1977.

Firkins, O. W. "Pathfinders in America." *Nation* 4 Jan. 1919: 20–21.

Fishkin, Shelley Fisher. *From Fact to Fiction: Journalism and Imaginative Writing in America.* Baltimore: Johns Hopkins UP, 1985.

"5,000 White Men Quit Yards; Negroes Back: Walkout in Protest of Non-Union Colored Workers and Presence of Guard." *Chicago Daily News* 7 Aug. 1919: 1.

Fraina, Louis. "Four New American Poets." *New Review* 15 July 1915: 143–44.

Gibbons, Herbert Adams, ed. *Songs from the Trenches: The Soul of the A.E.F.* New York: Harper, 1918.

Giffin, Frederick C. *Six Who Protested: Radical Opposition to the First World War.* Port Washington: Kennicat, 1977.

Golden, Harry. *Carl Sandburg.* New York: World, 1961.

"The Great Issue." *International Socialist Review* 18 (Aug. 1917): 114.

Green, James R. *Grass-Roots Socialism: Radical Movements in the Southwest, 1895–1943.* Baton Rouge: Louisiana State UP, 1978.

Grubbs, Frank L., Jr. *The Struggle for Labor Loyalty: Gompers, the A. F. of L., and the Pacifists, 1917–1920.* Durham: Duke UP, 1968.

Hall, Carolyn. "Two Poets Who Share a Prize." *Evening Post Magazine* 28 June 1919: 4, 11.

Hamalainen, Pekka Kalevi. *In Time of Storm: Revolution, Civil War, and the Ethnolinguistic Issue in Finland.* Albany: State U of New York P, 1979.

Harcourt, Alfred. "Forty Years of Friendship." *Journal of the Illinois State Historical Society* 45 (1952): 395–99.

Haywood, William D. "Murderous Fire Is Turned on Workers by Lumber Barons." *Milwaukee Leader* 9 July 1912: 1.

———. "Socialism the Hope of the Working Class." *International Socialist Review* 12 (1912): 461–71.

———. "What J. Golden Has Done." *Solidarity* 20 Apr. 1912: [2].

Hendrickson, Kenneth E., Jr. "The Pro-War Socialists, the Social Democratic League and the Ill-Fated Drive for Industrial Democracy in America." *Labor History* 11 (1970): 304–22.

Hervey, John L. "Carl Sandburg's 'Cornhuskers'." *Reedy's Mirror* 22 November 1918: 596–98.

Holubnychy, Lydia. *Michael Borodin and the Chinese Revolution, 1923–1925.* New York: University Microfilms International, 1979.

Hunter, Robert. "Comrade Hunter Makes Reply to Comrade Kerr." *Milwaukee Leader* 27 Dec. 1911: [9].

———. "Lincoln the Emancipator." *Milwaukee Social-Democratic Herald* 6 Feb 1909: 3.

"I.W.W. Gives Billy Sunday Pain." *Solidarity* 17 Apr. 1915: [1].

"The I.W.W. or the Socialist Party." *Milwaukee Social-Democratic Herald* 10 May 1912: 4.

"Industrial Relations." *Masses* 7 (Oct.–Nov. 1915): 21.

"In the Kaiser's Gallery." *Chicago Daily News* 6 Sept. 1917: 1.

Jacobs, Dan N. *Borodin: Stalin's Man in China.* Cambridge: Harvard UP, 1981.

Kammen, Michael. *Mystic Chords of Memory: The Transformation of Tradition in American Culture.* New York: Knopf, 1991.

Kennedy, John F. *To Turn the Tide.* Ed. John W. Gardner. Foreword Carl Sandburg. New York: Harper, 1962. ix–xiii.

Knightly, Philip. *The First Casualty from the Crimea to Vietnam: The War Correspondent as Hero, Propagandist, and Myth Maker.* 1 New York: Harcourt Brace Jovanovitch, 1975.

Kraditor, Aileen S. *The Radical Persuasion, 1890–1917: Aspects of the History and Historiography of Three American Radical Organizations.* Baton Rouge: Louisiana State UP, 1981.

Kreymborg, Alfred. "Carl Sandburg's New Book." *Poetry* 13 (1918): 155–61.

Lenin, N. "A Letter to American Workingmen." *Class Struggle* 2(1918): 521–33.

———. *A New Letter to the Workers of Europe and America.* New York: Socialist Publication Society of Brooklyn, 1919.

LePrade, Ruth, ed. *Debs and the Poets.* Intro. Upton Sinclair. Pasadena: Upton Sinclair, 1920.

"Like a True Artist." *Solidarity* 27 Nov. 1915: 2.

"Lincoln and Socialist Principles." *Milwaukee Social-Democratic Herald* 6 Feb. 1909: 2.

Lowell, Amy. "Carl Sandburg." *Poetry Review* 1 (July 1916): 46–47.

———. "Poetry and Propaganda." *New York Times Book Review and Magazine* 24 Oct. 1920: 7.

———. *Tendencies in Modern American Poetry.* New York: Macmillan, 1917.

Mackail, J. W. *The Life of William Morris.* 2 vols. 1899. New York: Haskell House, 1970.

Manly, Basil M. *Final Report and Testimony Submitted to Congress by the Commission on Industrial Relations.* Vols. 1, 4. Washington, D.C.: U.S. Government Printing Office, 1916.

Markham, Edwin. *The Man with the Hoe and Other Poems.* Garden City: Doubleday, Doran, 1935.

Mitgang, Herbert. *Dangerous Dossiers: Exposing the Secret War Against America's Greatest Authors.* New York: Fine, 1988.

Monroe, Harriet. "Chicago Granite." *Poetry* 11 (1916), 90–93.

"More on Direct Action." *Milwaukee Leader* 10 June 1912: 8.

"Mr. Sandburg's Poems of War and Nature." *New York Times Book Review* 12 Jan. 1919: 13.

Nash, N. Frederick and Gwenna Weshinsky. "Carl Sandburg and *The Day Book.*" *American Book Collector* 3 (Nov./Dec. 1982): 23–34.

Nelson, Carrie. *Repression and Recovery: Modern American Poetry and the Politics of Cultural Memory, 1910–1945.* Madison: U of Wisconsin P, 1989.

"News and Views." *International Socialist Review* 15 (June 1915): 764.

Nielsen, Aldon Lynn. *Reading Race: White American Poets and the Racial Discourse in the Twentieth Century.* Athens: U of Georgia P, 1988.

Niven, Penelope. *Carl Sandburg: A Biography.* New York: Knopf, 1991.

Paasivirta, Juhani. *The Victors in World War I and Finland: Finland's Relations with the British, French and United States Governments.* Trans. Paul Sjoblom. Helsinki: Finnish Historical Society, 1965.

"Paterson, N.J. Is on the Map." *Solidarity* 19 June 1915: [1].

"Politics: Dollarettes and Epithets." *Newsweek* 6 Nov. 1961: 24–25.

"Prosecution Stupid, Says Sandburg." *Labor Defender* 1 Apr. 1918: 1.

Radosh, Ronald. *American Labor and United States Foreign Policy.* New York: Random House, 1969.

Reedy, William Marion. "Carl Sandburg's 'Chicago Poems.'" *International Socialist Review* 17 (Aug. 1916): 122.

Reid, Robert L. "The *Day Book* Poems of Carl Sandburg." *Old Northwest* 9 (1983): 205–18.

"Revolt Develops Poet." *Western Comrade* 2 (July 1914): 23.

Robins, Natalie. *Alien Ink: The FBI's War on Freedom of Expression.* New York: Morrow, 1992.

"Sabotage 'Jackass Tactics' Indeed!" *Milwaukee Social-Democratic Herald* 17 Aug. 1912: 3.

Salerno, Salvatore. *Red November/Black November: Culture and Community in the Industrial Workers of the World.* Albany: State U of New York P, 1989.

"Sandburg's 75th Birthday Celebrated by the Nation." *Publishers Weekly* 17 Jan. 1953: 190–93.

Scripps, E.W. *I Protest: Selected Disquisitions of E. W. Scripps.* Ed. Oliver Knight. Madison: U of Wisconsin P, 1966.

Shore, Elliott. *Talkin' Socialism: J. A. Wayland and the Role of the Press in American Radicalism, 1890–1912.* Lawrence: U of Kansas P, 1988.

Sims, Norman, ed. *Literary Journalism in the Twentieth Century.* New York: Oxford UP, 1990.

Smith, C. Jay. *Finland and the Russian Revolution, 1917–1922.* Athens: U of Georgia P, 1958.

Smith, Gibbs M. *Joe Hill.* Salt Lake City: U of Utah P, 1969.

"Smoke and Steel." *Times Literary Supplement* 9 Dec. 1920: 816.

"Somersaults for God's Sake." *Nation* 1 Dec. 1920: 621.

Spargo, John. "How Karl Marx Helped Lincoln Preserve This Nation." *Milwaukee Social-Democratic Herald* 19 Mar. 1910: 2.

Spence, Jonathan. *To Change China: Western Advisors in China, 1620–1960.* Boston: Little, Brown, 1969.

Talbert, Roy, Jr. *Negative Intelligence: The Army and the American Left, 1917–1941.* Jackson: UP of Mississippi, 1991.

Travin, Pyotor. "How Lenin's Letter Was Delivered." *New World Review* 38 (1970): 118–20.

Untermeyer, Louis. "Carl Sandburg's Smoke and Steel." *New Republic* 15 Dec. 1920: 86.

———. "Cornhuskers." *Dial* 5 Oct. 1918: 263.

———. "Enter Sandburg." *Masses* 8 (July 1916): 30.

"Untitled." *Outlook* 18 Dec. 1918: 619.

*U.S. Military Intelligence Reports: Surveillance of Radicals in the United States, 1917–1941.* 34 reels. Frederick, MD: U Publications of America, 1984.

Vaughn, Stephen. *Holding Fast the Inner Lines: Democracy, Nationalism, and the Committee on Public Information.* Chapel Hill: U of North Carolina P, 1980.

"Violence Must Be Repudiated." *Milwaukee Leader* 3 July 1912: 8.

*War Poems from the Yale Review.* New Haven: Yale UP, 1918.

Weinstein, James. *The Decline of Socialism in America, 1912–1925.* New York: Vintage, 1969.

"What the New York Volks-Zeitung Thinks About Haywood." *Milwaukee Leader* 27 Dec. 1911: [9].

Wilshire, H. Gaylord. "Why a 'Workingman' Should Be a Socialist." *Challenge* 27 March 1901: 1–3.

Wilson, Arthur. "Sandburg: A Psychiatric Curiosity." *Dial* 70 (1921): 80.

Wilson, Edmund, Jr. "The Anarchists of Taste." *Vanity Fair* 15 (1920): 65+.

Winters, Donald E. *The Soul of the Wobblies: The I.W.W., Religion, and American Culture in the Progressive Era, 1905–1917*. Westport: Greenwood, 1985.

Work, John M. ed. *Proceedings of the National Convention of the Socialist Party*. Chicago: Socialist Party of America, 1908.

# INDEX